the
television
news handbook

VIN RAY

an insider's guide
to being a great
broadcast journalist

Foreword by
JOHN SIMPSON

Macmillan

First published 2003 by Macmillan
an imprint of Pan Macmillan Ltd
Pan Macmillan, 20 New Wharf Road, London N1 9RR
Basingstoke and Oxford
Associated companies throughout the world
www.panmacmillan.com

ISBN 1 4050 0120 8

While every effort has been made to ensure all of the information
contained in this publication is correct and accurate, the publisher
cannot accept any responsibility for any omissions or errors that
may occur or for any consequences that may arise therefrom.
The publishers would be grateful for any new or corrected information
and will make the appropriate change at the earliest opportunity.

9 8 7 6 5 4 3 2 1

A CIP catalogue record for this book is available from
the British Library.

Typeset by Set Systems Ltd, Saffron Walden, Essex
Printed and bound in Great Britain by
Mackays of Chatham plc, Chatham, Kent

For Peg and Vic Ray

contents

foreword

Television news is a young medium. You see that every time you walk into a newsroom or a studio, or switch a television set on and watch the reporters. The rate of promotion is remarkable, and most people have left the business by the time they reach their fifties. As a result, the collective memory of those who work in it tends to be pretty short. Most people assume that, technology apart, things must always have been pretty much as they have always been. It's hard to explain how greatly things have changed in television news over the past thirty years.

We have, for instance, come to regard Britain as being the centre of the industry, with the BBC, Sky and Independent Television dominating the international market, and the two big agencies, Reuters and APTN, supplying the world with pictures from their bases in London. APTN may be the television arm of a famous American text news agency, the Associated Press, based in New York, but when it decided to go into television it quickly became clear to the management of AP that it would be impossible to set up an effective news operation outside London. Even CNN had to open up its international main base in London, four thousand miles away from its home city, Atlanta.

If your operations are in Britain, the chances are that plenty of your staff will be from there too. As a result, the entire worldwide business has a markedly British accent. Nowadays this may seem a matter of course; yet it is only fifteen years or so since the Americans were the dominant force in world television news, throwing unthinkably large resources of people and equipment into every major event. Not any more.

I say this, not to boast, but to show how enormously influential Britain's involvement in international television news has become. It isn't just accidental, nor is it merely because English has emerged in the last twenty years as the global language. It is the result of several important factors, which are worth examining in some detail.

First and foremost, there is a powerful tradition of objectivity and lack of bias in British broadcasting, which goes back many decades. In 1977 I was sent to South Africa to be the BBC correspondent there. I was nervous, because the South African government regarded the BBC as an enemy and was always on the lookout for opportunities to attack us and if necessary throw us out. I was also a little vague about the attitude I was expected to take; should I, as a matter of course, condemn the apartheid regime, or was there some dubious understanding between the BBC and South Africa, whereby we closed our eyes to some things in order to keep on broadcasting? I wasn't just uncertain about the facts of the relationship, I was worried that my conscience wouldn't allow me to stick to any secret agreement which might have been reached.

In the end I went to see my ultimate boss, a crabby old Ulsterman called Waldo Maguire, who as the head of BBC news and current affairs had often seemed deplorably timid and safe to those of us who fancied ourselves as the Corporation's young Turks; especially over the issue of Northern Ireland. I sat down in his art deco office in Broadcasting House, with its light wood panelling and its engravings by Eric Gill, and asked him to tell me how I should do my new job.

He listened to me, then pushed his chair back and walked over to a safe in the corner of the room. From it he pulled out a file and handed it to me. As far as I remember, it only contained two rather fragile documents, smudgily typed on flimsy paper. They were records of meetings of the BBC board of governors, dated within days of the outbreak of the Second World War, and they were in effect staff instructions on how to report the war and in particular the tone they should adopt in broadcasting to the enemy in the German Service. As

I read them, I felt a weight lifting off me. They were all about being honest and open, and not keeping news back simply because it was bad. We had an absolute duty, the smudgy words said, to tell people what was happening as quickly and as fully as we could. As for the tone, we should address even individual Germans as though we were sitting talking with them in a neutral cafe somewhere. 'Above all,' said the flimsy piece of paper, 'there must be no room for ranting.'

The shrewd old man across the table – as I write this, it occurs to me that he must have been in his late fifties, as I am now – watched me as I read all this. 'You see, laddie, if you're a journalist ye've just to tell people what's going on. If ye want to influence them, to tell them what to think, then ye should be in politics instead.' That, at any rate, is how I remember the conversation. Waldo died of a heart attack not very long afterwards, as he sat fishing by an Ulster loch, and I've no idea what happened to the bits of flimsy paper he used to keep so carefully.

But the message was clear. The news was all that mattered, whether it was uncomfortable or not, whether it fitted into my own personal views of right or wrong or not. But it wasn't my function to rant about apartheid, or anything else. I had to present the facts as honestly and frankly and openly as I could, and leave it to the audience to decide what they felt about them. In fact, of course, when I reached South Africa I found it all remarkably easy: you had only to tell people what was going on, and how the apartheid system was structured, for them to realize what it was all about. There wasn't any need to rant: the facts spoke for themselves. Later, when I travelled to the Soviet Union, or to China, or to Saddam Hussein's Iraq, or to Slobodan Milosevic's Serbia, I found that the same principle applied. There was no need to preach, nor to twist the facts; I just had to do the job. It was a tremendous relief.

Not that broadcasters are required to be moral eunuchs, blandly laying out different views as though they have equal value. If several thousand Muslims have disappeared from the town of Srbrenica, we should not rate a denial by the Bosnian Serb leadership as being of equal value with the basic information. You must be fair, but you are not required to create some kind of equivalence between innocence and guilt. So a reputation for objectivity and balance has been one major part of the success of British television internationally.

But influential broadcasting isn't solely about the facts, essential though they are. It's also about good and effective communication: intelligent and intelligible writing, well-shot, well-edited and informative pictures. 'Television news,' said an old and experienced friend of mine, who used to produce many of my news reports, 'should please the mind and ravish the eye.' I don't suppose he often got what he was hoping for from me, but I learned slowly that there was more to making a television report than simply writing a script and finding pictures – any pictures – to illustrate it.

It's hard for journalists, who take their words seriously, to come to terms with a medium where the words should complement the pictures rather than dominate them. For several years, after I switched from radio to television, I regarded my script as the central point of the exercise; the pictures were there because – well, because it was television. So the long-suffering picture editor would have to paste any images he could find over the words I had written: the American president, the British prime minister, a naval ship, bombs falling, a factory assembly line, starving Africans. Each image would last at the most for ten seconds, to be succeeded by some other, unrelated set of images. It was a confusing muddle, which gave the viewers' eyes too much pointless, unrelated information and their ears too many words, and too many facts, packed in as tightly as a correspondent's suitcase.

It was only by working for programmes like *Newsnight* that I came at last to understand that television requires proper sequences, entire episodes that illustrate and illumine the subject. Slowly, I realized that words were not enough: that you had to allow the viewers to see things for themselves, and to draw the proper conclusions from what they saw. You aren't giving a university lecture, you're telling a story, leading people with you through the narrative – their companion, not their professor. It isn't at all easy: you have first to understand thoroughly what is going on yourself, then film the circumstances that best illustrate the story you are trying to tell.

No form of journalism is harder than good reporting for television: by contrast, newspaper journalists have it remarkably easy. In television, you should not only be on hand for the subject you describe, you have to make sure your cameraman gets the right pictures for it; and then you have to turn these pictures into a clear, comprehensible narrative: the hardest part of all.

In 1945 Raymond Chandler, as clever a film scriptwriter as he was a novelist, wrote: 'The challenge of screenwriting is to say much in little, and then take half of that little and still preserve an effect of leisure and natural movement.' That kind of writing, apparently relaxed and easy yet properly informative as well as fair and accurate, is one of the central arts of good television news, and it is one of the aims of this book to describe how it is done – by no means an easy task.

Vin Ray's book is important and timely, because television journalism plays such a key role nowadays that it has to be as good as we can make it. Vin, who has been a friend and colleague of mine for years, is precisely the kind of person a big organization needs if it is to perform properly.

He has perhaps the most influential role in BBC News, building the organization in the best and most effective way, by appointing new people and moulding the careers of those who are already working in it. He is responsible for developing on-air presenters, correspondents and reporters, from the household names to the latest arrival; and he has hired most of them.

There was a time when television news was regarded as a brutal, irreflective, hustling kind of affair. Brawn, appearance and ego were prized above other qualities. Years after I was appointed a BBC reporter in 1970, I found out the chairman of the appointments board had told the other members that day that the main criterion they should bear in mind as each candidate came in was: is this the kind of man – there were no women news reporters in television then – who would walk into a brothel? If the answer was yes, he said, the man should get the job. I suppose I should make it clear that I was rejected at first, and was only appointed most reluctantly afterwards in order to make up the required numbers.

Those days, thank God, have been over for more than a quarter of a century; but it was the arrival of more civilized people like Vin Ray in the rough neighbourhood of BBC television news that gradually affected the general ethos. It was Vin who spotted the potential and gave jobs as foreign correspondents to George Alagiah, Jeremy Bowen, Matt Frei, Orla Guerin, Allan Little, Justin Webb, David Shukman and dozens of others. Vin coached the BBC's political editor, Andrew Marr, when he arrived from newspapers, and helped him become the most effective communicator in front of camera in British television news. Nowadays only the oldest among us, the real antiques, predate his influence. If BBC News as it is today has been shaped in the likeness of any single individual, that individual is Vin Ray: calm, thoughtful, cultured, determined, with a clear awareness of the direction in which the BBC must travel.

No one is better suited to describe to television journalists – new and established – how the job should best be done. This book is, quite simply, a master-class; and it is taught by the person best equipped to do so.

John Simpson, 2003

introduction

Shortly after midnight on 31 August 1997, I stumbled sleepily downstairs in the pitch black to answer the phone. In that twilight zone between a drink and a hangover, I struggled manfully to comprehend what the man on the other end of the line was trying to tell me. That man was Richard Sambrook, now Director of News at the BBC, and what he was telling me was this: 'Diana has been in a car crash in Paris and it looks like it may be fatal.'

It may seem strange now – I was the BBC's World News Editor at the time – but the only Diana I knew was our then Moscow Correspondent, Diana Goodman, and I couldn't for the life of me work out what she was doing in Paris. Then, albeit slowly, the enormity of what he was saying began to sink in. We each agreed to call three key people and get them to phone in to a conference call that I would arrange for ten minutes' time; that way we could divide up the calls and deployments.

And so it was that an hour later, in the wee small hours of a Sunday morning, a phalanx of correspondents, camera crews, producers, fixers, picture editors, satellite trucks, engineers and radio studio managers were hurtling towards the cross-Channel ferry and on to the French capital. A satellite truck was found in Paris; the Brussels bureau was moving *en masse* across the border; space segment was booked on a satellite. The machine was in full swing.

We agreed to phone in to the conference call every hour through the night and, one by one, left for the newsroom at Television Centre. I arrived in west London at five in the morning and, walking through the double doors in to the newsroom, I wanted nothing more than to bottle the moment. A newsroom in full flow is a truly awesome sight. At the nine o'clock editorial meeting the following morning a senior editor was moved to ponder whether we would ever see such a big story again.

Almost exactly four years later, I was returning to my office from a rather dull meeting when my secretary called with what, at that moment, seemed a rather bizarre piece of news: a plane had crashed into one of the towers of the World Trade Center. I left my office and got the lift down to the newsroom wondering who was where in North America ('Who have we got there?' is always the first reaction). As I walked through the newsroom every screen flickered with the live pictures.

On the foreign desk each person was talking on at least two phones and standing up – the sure sign of a 'breaker'. And then it happened: a truly awful, yet seminal moment, both in world history and in 24-hour television news. A second plane had hit the other tower live on air; and we all knew immediately that we were working on the biggest story of our careers. It was just after two o'clock on Tuesday 11 September 2001. I did not get back to my office until the following Monday.

What both these stories had in common, besides their enormity, was the reaction they induced in journalists across the country – indeed, around the world. Wherever they were, whatever they were doing, they dropped everything and headed for their newsrooms. No persuasion needed, no phone calls made. All day and all night they toiled, doing just whatever it took to make it happen. To witness such professionalism, commitment, talent and sheer stamina is truly a privilege.

And this is my point: to be able to feel that you are part of such momentous events is one of the central reasons we went into this line of work. I have tried to be honest in this book about the downsides of working in broadcast news – because there are downsides – but I would challenge anyone to find a job that matched it for excitement, adrenalin and a sense of public service.

Journalism is a high pressure occupation at the best of times; on the big occasions the pressure is acute. Great broadcast journalists will always deliver, whether the story is big or small; but the mark of the really great journalist is his or her ability to rise to the occasion, and produce work that becomes part of the history of the events themselves.

There is a kind of alchemy which produces great broadcast journalists. A confluence of learned craft, natural talent and luck which delivers a fusion of truly memorable words and pictures or sounds. But the work of great journalists also brings about change and enhances people's lives by helping them understand the things they need to know about in order to function properly in a free society.

Let's face it, our society is not short of information. Through newspapers, radio, television, the internet and various mobile devices there is now more information available than ever before. A better informed world is a better world, but information alone doesn't necessarily make us wiser. However, great journalists do. Indeed, the central paradox of this explosion in news output is that there is now a greater need than ever before for trusted, good journalists to select the most significant stories and explain why they matter in a way our citizens enjoy and understand. Great journalists turn what audiences *need* to know into what they *want* to know.

But being a broadcast journalist is a privilege, and not one to be taken lightly. Your work can potentially touch the lives of millions of people – potentially *change* the lives of millions of people. That privilege is part of public service. Good broadcast journalists never forget why they exist: because of their viewers and listeners. They never forget that their first loyalty is always to their audience. Everything else – including seeking fame, fortune and profits – is secondary to that loyalty.

In short, for a society to function to its optimum capacity it needs good journalists. So the aim of this book is to motivate a broad range of the best and cleverest outsiders to become newcomers to the industry; to help new journalists become good; and to inspire the good to become the best. To explain what you need to get into the industry; what you need to do to get on once you are in; and what you need to operate at the highest level.

So it is directed at a very wide audience: school kids who may be thinking about a career in journalism; university or college students thinking likewise or actually studying journalism or the media; existing and established journalists who want to develop their careers; print journalists thinking about a switch to broadcasting; and even the household names or journalists nearing retirement who just want to stay involved in the debate about what makes good journalists and good journalism – and who still want to get better at their craft.

It is also for anyone interested in the way television news works. More people get their news from television than any other source, so given its importance in society it should be open to scrutiny and show more of its internal workings than it instinctively likes to.

The book is split into three sections. Part One looks at what it takes to operate at the very highest level. In the first chapter the biggest and best names in broadcast journalism set out what they believe are the mental and physical qualities and the craft skills needed to be the best.

Chapter Two is a masterclass, which sets out how to translate those qualities into practice. This chapter began life as a guide, written specifically for the BBC, called 'The Reporter's Friend'. Now updated and expanded, it is pitched at the very highest level and has been used to develop and train new and existing reporters in the BBC. It is an attempt to tackle my greatest passion and the biggest challenge facing television news: the need to pursue a serious news agenda for the widest possible audience. Its target audience was established correspondents in the BBC, but I wouldn't have written it any differently for any other audience, inside or outside the BBC, beginner or award-winner.

So, 'Storytelling' looks at the way to construct stories, the need to condense information and, crucially, the writing techniques required to make them flow from beginning to end.

'Writing and Language' uses some memorable scripts to demonstrate how to use narrative, opening sentences, phrase-making and many other linguistic tricks of the trade to lift your writing out of the ordinary. I have been asked in the past whether one can learn to be a great writer. I think you can, but there's only one person who can teach you: yourself. And you do it by reading. Great writers are great readers. I have tried throughout this book to look at what the best journalists have in common, and one thing they all share is this: a book tucked under their arm – constantly. Novels, poetry, biographies, anything really. I can't guarantee that reading will actually make you a great writer; but I know that a failure to read widely will stop you being the writer you could be.

'Context and understanding' is about how to give audiences the background and context they need to understand stories better; how to avoid assumptions about viewers' knowledge; making connections for them and really making sure they understand why stories matter. It is also about how to avoid boxing stories into the preconceived stereotypes we have of the world.

This section also looks at the use of focus groups and what has become known as 'dumbing down'. Journalism, like the societies it is serving, evolves all the time. But we must make sure it evolves and modernizes around certain core values and key principles – in the case of television news, this means reporting serious and significant issues in a truthful way to the widest possible audience.

The confusion over 'dumbing down' arises because critics of television news often fail to understand the nature of the audience for mainstream television news. A broadsheet newspaper will adapt its coverage for its own narrow audience. A tabloid will be equally attentive to its core readership. But responsible television news needs to appeal to the entire breadth of the society it serves. In essence, it should have a broadsheet agenda with the approach of an intelligent tabloid. Any rush to move from significant stories to an agenda based on celebrities and entertainment would constitute 'dumbing down'; but trying to make a serious agenda accessible to a wider audience does not.

Indeed, if we are attentive to the agenda but don't report it in a way that engages and enlightens all viewers, then this in turn will 'dumb down' our citizens by disengaging them from the issues that matter.

'Packaging' looks at scripting pictures, natural sound, using interview clips and many other aspects of putting a news package together. 'In vision' looks at pieces to camera and the increasingly required craft of 'going live': how to use locations, the language of live broadcasting and working live in the studio.

The section on 'Pictures' looks at the visual grammar of television news and how to use sequences of pictures to construct packages. It also considers the vexed question of when and how to use violent pictures. And the final part of the masterclass, 'You', looks at issues such as voice, appearance, style, attitude and assessing your own work.

The whole purpose of this masterclass is to help reporters, producers and editors to make the stories our audiences need to know about – no matter how foreign, or how political, or how difficult – engaging and interesting.

The second part of the book looks at getting jobs and developing your career. Chapter Three examines the benefits and drawbacks of working in broadcast journalism as well as how to survive and prosper in it. It also tackles the need for a more diverse workforce, looks at how to come from print to broadcast and how to put a good showreel together.

Chapter Four offers advice on getting from school, through university or college, into a first job, while Chapter Five relates the stories of existing journalists who have made that journey. Chapter Six, on interviews for jobs, is for everyone from complete newcomers to the most experienced journalists. I wrote it because of witnessing firsthand so many good people let themselves down in interviews. I am also shocked at how many people come for interview without really knowing what to expect. So I hope this chapter will help dispel some myths and level the playing field a little. It will also give some insight into what the industry deems important.

Part Three is a database of contacts that might help you along the way. Despite the fact that I am a BBC executive and the majority of contributions to this book are from BBC correspondents, this is not a BBC book nor is it simply a book about BBC journalism (though I hope there is very little my colleagues would disagree with). In writing it I consulted widely and there is a very strong consensus across the industry about what makes good broadcast journalism. So I have used examples of work – good and bad – that were most easily available to me to illustrate what constitutes best practice.

Neither, despite the title, is the book solely about television. The broad principles about making what is significant interesting apply to all forms of journalism. And all of the book applies directly to radio except the masterclass, and much of that is also relevant to the 'senior service'.

My job at the BBC is to recruit and develop good broadcast journalists. That might mean a relative newcomer with potential working over-nights on a twenty-four-hour network. It might be deciding the next move for an established foreign correspondent. Or it might mean recruiting a high-profile print journalist – like Andrew Marr or Jeff Randall – and training them to be a broadcaster.

Becoming a great broadcast journalist rarely happens overnight. Some are good journalists and perhaps need to develop their broadcasting skills. Some are great in front of a camera but less mature as journalists or writers. But broadcasters are always on the lookout for fresh talent or, equally often, raw talent, which can be forged into the great journalists of the future.

A study by the Journalism Training Forum estimated that there were 70,000 journalists working in the UK in 2002 and that an extra 20,000 would be needed by the year 2010. The expansion in news output currently knows no bounds. There are more programmes, more networks, more websites – and therefore more jobs – than ever before. Luckily, in schools and universities, the desire to work 'in the media' is enormous and expanding at least as fast as the opportunities available. In turn, universities and colleges are offering a dazzling and increasing array of courses related to journalism and the media.

The issue is quality. Quality requires news organizations which can provide years of tradition and the framework for good journalism; and it requires good journalists who will never let standards drop, never stop learning the craft (because you never do) and who will use their professionalism, intelligence and breadth for the greater good of their fellow citizens.

I hope this book can help existing and aspiring journalists along the way.

Vin Ray, 2003

acknowledgements

It is impossible to write a book of this nature without getting the help and advice of a huge number of people. But while I never spurned any help, I didn't always take the advice I was being offered, so it is important to point out that the responsibility for the content of this book is mine and mine alone.

That having been said, I owe a huge debt of gratitude to all the reporters, editors and executives who contributed to the first chapter, 'What makes a good broadcast journalist?'. They took to the task with relish and all displayed the kind of enthusiasm and writing skills which they believe a good broadcast journalist should have. My apologies to all those who contributed but didn't make the cut. Such was their enthusiasm, I was overwhelmed with offers – all of them fantastic. There just wasn't enough room.

Thanks, too, to all those who wrote down their experiences of getting into broadcast news for Chapter Five. They too went well beyond the call of duty and offered far more than they had been asked for.

Special mentions go to Duncan Herbert and Tira Shubart for their help in producing the masterclass section, and to Richard Sambrook and Adrian Van Klaveren for encouraging me to write it in the first place and allowing me to use examples of BBC work. In compiling the storytelling masterclass, I also sought the help, time, advice and thoughts of Richard Ayre, Malcolm Balen, Mark Damazer, Neil Everton, Tony Fallshaw, Julie Hadwin, Robert Hall, Carla Hargis, Brian Hanrahan, Phil Harding, Jay Hunt, Nigel Kay, Crichton Limbert, David Loyn, Charles Munro,

Tim Orchard, Mark Popescu, Ian Pritchard, Ned Warwick and Adrian Wells. I am also grateful to all the BBC's correspondents and reporters whose work, fantastic commitment and willingness to engage in debate provided the bulk of the material for the masterclass.

Rob Brown from Westminster University and Jan Howarth and Liz Howell from City University were fantastically helpful in offering me their expertise in journalism education and interviews, as were Jackie Owen and Ann McDonald from BBC Human Resources.

Special thanks to Jonathan Baker and John Owen who gave me additional insights and ideas and helped tone down some of my wilder assertions.

I am deeply indebted to Jessica Parfitt, who compiled the database with intelligence, enthusiasm and deep reserves of stamina. As a recent graduate, her thoughts and views about studying journalism were also invaluable. Mavis Lissenden, Claire Cornell and Tony Loughran also helped enormously with the database.

I'm also grateful to Julian Alexander, who had the idea for this book as it stands; to John Simpson, who wrote the foreword on planes somewhere between the Kalahari desert and Kabul; and to my editors at Macmillan, George Morley and Morven Knowles, who guided me through with plenty of patience and even more charm.

But my biggest thanks of all go to my partner, Sara, and my children Louis, Theo and Olivia, who coped with my physical absence a lot of the time and my mental absence most of the time. Living with a broadcast journalist is bad enough, let alone one who thinks he can write a book. Their patience – like that of others who live with broadcast journalists – knows no bounds.

part one: to be the best

The *sine qua non* of journalism is to be in a state of perpetual amazement and bewilderment, tinged with a touch of anger, at the way the world works. That needs to be coupled with an endless enthusiasm to challenge authority, find some answers and pass them on. Once you've lost that it's time to pack it in. Or so I keep telling myself.

John Humphrys, BBC *Today* programme presenter

1 what makes a good broadcast journalist?

What exactly does it take to be a good broadcast journalist? Well, it takes excellent craft skills such as writing and storytelling; traits like curiosity, passion and courage; and certain physical attributes such as a good voice and an ability to speak naturally into a microphone.

But don't take my word for it. I asked some friends and colleagues in the industry what they thought it took to be the best. What follows is what they told me.

THE MENTAL QUALITIES

What was it that killed the cat . . . ?

The absolutely essential prerequisite cannot either be taught, or even refined. It is a sense of curiosity. You've either got it or you haven't. If you don't, then no amount of teaching can give it to you. If you don't have an intrinsic inquisitiveness about how the world works – at every level from how you design a garden to how you bring peace to the Balkans – then go and do something else which will be more socially useful or make you some money. Jeremy Paxman, BBC *Newsnight* presenter

What makes a good broadcast journalist? The same things that make a good journalist in every other area. Curiosity and scepticism. If you're not consumed with curiosity and deeply sceptical about authority in all its manifestations, then don't do it. Broadcasting technique can be learned: how to write a workmanlike script and deliver it so that you don't sound like an automaton; how to construct an interview; how to write over pictures; how to do all the fiddly bits with electronic gadgetry. But you can't train somebody to want to know. John Humphrys, BBC *Today* programme presenter

It all boils down to curiosity. Are you interested in events? Do you want to find out more? Do you find it impossible to walk past a ringing phone without wanting to pick it up? If the answer to these questions is no, try a different career. Being curious, of course, doesn't guarantee success, but it is the sine qua non. Jeff Randall, BBC Business Editor

First and foremost it's about curiosity – not just an interest in knowing, but a need to know. Journalism is more a compulsion than a profession. It's a job you do because you cannot bear not to. A good journalist wants a ringside seat at events that the rest of the world would rather see from a distance, if at all. And a great journalist wants to make the world watch and care, even when it would rather look away. Orla Guerin, BBC Middle East Correspondent

Good broadcast journalists are insatiably curious, and interested in the truth of everything. Accomplished gossips, they should have visiting rights in many worlds but should not belong too exclusively to any. They should not accept honours nor be impressed by the trappings of power. They're practised observers, noting detail and nuance, with the memory of an elephant. They don't mind being unpopular. Anna Ford, BBC News presenter

Enthusiasm and passion

Good broadcast journalists are excited by news: instantly making connections, thinking what happens next . . . They like beating the competition, but the very best people want to combine the facts with analysis – sharing their passion for the broader story as well as the latest developments. I also believe these days that good broadcast journalists celebrate the 24-hour news culture and the power of technology. Sometimes on News 24 or BBC World we now have presenters in Kabul and Washington linking live to the streets of Delhi or

Johannesburg so we can bring in the latest pictures and the latest interviews in perfect quality – and it's impossible not to get a buzz out of such immediacy and such great technology. Roger Mosey, Head of BBC TV News

If you don't love the job of being a reporter, if you are not passionately interested in the world then go do something else. The editors and the audience can spot a timeserver very quickly; you may not ever be fired but you can look forward to a very dull career. The world's newsrooms are full of people whining about the breaks they never got. In this game you make your own breaks. Nothing is more calculated to alienate an editor than whining. If it isn't working for you then get out and do something else.
Fergal Keane, BBC Special Correspondent

Facts are sacred but attitude helps. Andrew Marr communicates not just because he knows his stuff inside out but because he puts it across with such evident relish, enthusiasm and excitement. Television exposes insincerity and boredom in journalists as much as in politicians – good ones stand out; they're excited by their assignment, they believe what they're saying, their passion communicates itself. Bill Neely, ITV News International Editor

Good reporters need to make it clear when they broadcast that they care and that they are engaged because if they're not, nobody watching or listening will be. Jay Hunt, Editor of the BBC *Six O'Clock News*

A good broadcast journalist must take the significant and turn it into the interesting for a frequently distracted audience. The journalist must understand that people not policies are news, that scepticism is part of the job but that cynicism has no place. Excellence in broadcast news comes from a passion for the world and sense of awe for what we do.
Chris Cramer, President, CNN International Networks

Courage

I think at times you need to be courageous. If you are confident of the facts, your sources and the way you have compiled the story, then be prepared to face

flak. Not just from those who may be shown in a bad light by your story, but you may also have to tell editors back at base that their perception of the story is wrong. It is all very well being given a brief by an editor to follow this or that angle, but if you get to wherever the story is and you find that the editor is 'off-beam', have the courage to say so. Don't always follow the herd.
Jon Sopel, BBC presenter and correspondent

There is more to courage than a narrow physical definition. Some of the toughest decisions have nothing to do with bravery under fire. Having the courage NOT to run with something you are unsure of is just as important as having the guts to go with a controversial story you truly believe in. Approach stories with an open mind: resist the pressures of editors or subs who have a very definite idea of what the story is or who have a headline they want you to justify. In that lonely land after the broadcast you will be the one left doing the explaining! Above all be true to the facts as you know them.
Fergal Keane, BBC Special Correspondent

Radicalism

What makes a good broadcast journalist? The capacity to keep your ego under control; to wake up in the morning with ideas burning holes in your brains; to get angry, laugh, cry at the news of at least something first thing in the morning. To be inquisitive, nosey and politically motivated. All the best hacks in history have been motivated by the desire to see change. There is no such thing as a neutral journalist. We are all shaped by who we are, but we should recognize who we are and counter it with a desire to reflect other views of events beyond our own. But we should never desert what we believe in and what drives us. If you meet a flaccid broadcast journalist, shoot him or her!
Jon Snow, Channel 4 News presenter

I'd like to describe the good qualities of Charles Wheeler, John Humphrys, Martin Bell and Brian Barron (not one of them younger than his late fifties, you notice, and most of them older). These would be: a restless and unceasing curiosity; an impatience and irritability with bullshit and self-importance, especially the official kind; an ability to dominate a story so that no one does anything without referring to you first; and a single-mindedness in tracking the story and nailing it down. And one last quality, which my friend Martha Gellhorn had, together with Jon Snow and many others: a pervasive radicalism, independent of party politics, and a permanent sympathy with underdogs and victims. John Simpson, BBC World Affairs Editor

Membership of the 'Awkward Squad'

The refusal to take no for an answer . . . An innate distrust of every public relations person, spokesman, politician or lobbyist.
Jeremy Paxman, BBC *Newsnight* presenter

A determination, even a passion, to cut through the crap and tell people what's really going on, using clear and often memorable language. Someone who always thinks about what they are writing and never uses bolt-together clichés. Someone who aims for clarity above all but never sacrifices truth on its altar. A bloody-minded persistence comes in handy, too.
Mark Mardell, BBC Political Correspondent

Good journalists should be watchdogs of government and those in authority, constantly questioning their actions and words. They should never take things for granted, or assume what was accurate once remains accurate.
Margaret Gilmore, BBC Home Affairs Correspondent

Teamwork

A vital element is listening to others – too many of us see asking for help as a sign of weakness – the people around you may have the word you're searching for. And studio managers, picture editors and camera crews are good at what they do too, so seek and take their advice. Teamworking is essential.
Denis Murray, BBC Ireland Correspondent

Good journalism is the art of hunting and chasing. It's about split-second decisions, about instincts, about extreme stress and extraordinary camaraderie. It is (on occasions) about trusting your colleagues with your life, and holding theirs in your hands. Orla Guerin, BBC Middle East Correspondent

*In TV you are not working alone. You are working with your crew, picture editor, the satellite truck engineer, the producer and so on. They are part of the journalistic process too. I have found the more you try to involve them in the process (*not *story-making by committee), the better the results. So, yes, being a team player is a help.* Jon Sopel, BBC presenter and correspondent

Resourcefulness – and 'a rat-like cunning'

A good journalist is someone who says in response to any question, 'I may not know the answer – but I know how to find out.'
Gavin Esler, BBC *Newsnight* presenter

There is, it seems to me, one absolute truth about journalism, which we all need. The big trick is not what you know, but how quickly you can find out. Denis Murray, BBC Ireland Correspondent

There is no way of improving upon Nicholas Tomalin's description thirty years ago of the three qualities necessary for real success: rat-like cunning, a plausible manner and a little literary ability.
Jeremy Paxman, BBC *Newsnight* presenter

Humility

For a sustainable career, you also need humility. It's a heady business. You meet the rich, famous and powerful. If you're not careful, you start to believe you are part of their world. Feet leave the ground and then, BANG! At all times, remember who you are, what you do and why you're there. Living life stylishly is fine; I strongly recommend it. Do the job with a swagger. Look the part. But remember this: when the chairman of ICI invites you to dinner, it is because you're the BBC's business editor. Far too many reporters go to swanky events without a thought in their heads about stories, information or insight. Jeff Randall, BBC Business Editor

Here you need to achieve the impossible! To match the ambition and toughness necessary to be a real operator with a humility that might allow you to remain a decent human being at the end of the day. The business has its share of ego-driven monsters. Most have one goal in life: their own greater glory. My plea is to have a life with other dimensions. The world of the broadcast journalist might not seem conducive to family life or to nurturing outside interests. But I would argue that the rounded human being, a person with a hinterland beyond the newsroom, is a more valuable asset than the worker drone.
Fergal Keane, BBC Special Correspondent

THE PHYSICAL QUALITIES

Take a look in the mirror . . .

The usual and proper answer, which I have given at various times to desperate politicians, sportsmen, even actors, is 'Be yourself!' The absurdity of that answer is that if you can do that, you are in no need of further instruction: you have already achieved the ultimate aim.

How so? Because, no matter how relaxed, how confident, how natural you are in life, the microphone is a sword of Damocles hanging over you, and the television camera is a basilisk eye. Nobody, but nobody in the world, when they start talking into a microphone sounds as they do talking to a friend in a room at home. And that is the goal. (Many famous broadcasters never made it.) At first, nerves evoke a vocal tune which is that of a public speaker, a high school reciter, an orator, a person addressing a parent-teachers' meeting – worst of all, somebody trying to be natural.

What is the secret of 'being yourself'? There is none. Listen to yourself on tape. Get your friends to tell you if it sounds like their friend or a broadcaster.

Don't try to imitate anybody. Don't learn to 'project' (as TV directors always instruct you). Tell them there's been no need to project since Thomas Edison.

It took me about twenty years to forget the radio microphone. My wife says it took me nine years to settle down into looking and sounding like myself on television. Lots of luck!
Alistair Cooke, Presenter of BBC Radio 4's *Letter from America*

Above all, the confidence to be yourself – that is not to act or fake a personality that is not your own. Next, good and direct language – the old Orwell and Daily Mirror injunctions against using Latinate words rather than shorter, pungent Anglo-Saxon ones. And putting in the brainwork that condenses a complicated story in such a way that the viewer gets a sense of it, vividly, without it being badly distorted. Finally, of course, an enjoyment of pictures and a readiness to put them first wherever and whenever you can.
Andrew Marr, BBC Political Editor

One of the best broadcasters I ever heard was a guy called Sean Duignan, who was RTE's Political Editor, and later Albert Reynolds' press secretary. And the trick that 'Diggy' pulled off was that he sounded exactly like himself at all times (on air and off). That may sound bonkers, but if you listen closely, even the most experienced broadcasters sound quite different delivering a script, and then doing a 'two-way'. So I would argue that this is one of the chief abilities any broadcaster should have – being as natural as possible, not just in delivery, but in use of language too. I always tell young journalists that they should try and imagine that they're telling the story to their mates, who aren't in the business, and who haven't heard anything about it.
Denis Murray, BBC Ireland Correspondent

They need to have the confidence to speak they way they really speak, write the way they really talk. The most convincing on-screen correspondents are those who look and sound the way they would if they were talking to you face to face. Jay Hunt, Editor of the BBC *Six O'Clock News*

The voice (of authority)

The really great broadcast voices – like Alistair Cooke's, for example – can make a mundane, humdrum script sing. Such voices should be warm enough to listen to by the fireside, like a friend you've invited home, but they must also ooze authority. Some of Radio 4's newsreaders could be reading out their shopping lists, but still manage to make them sound like important global events. And it's not only the timbre of a good broadcaster's voice, it's also the fact they read and talk for meaning. The worst broadcasters in the world are those who get into a sing-song, see-saw, up and down delivery where every sentence sounds the same, whether it's an 'and finally' or news of an African famine. Why should you believe what they say when everything they talk about sounds identical? Ben Brown, BBC Special Correspondent

Vocal delivery is too often a dreadful combination of the adenoidal whine, the staccato burst, the relentlessly sing-song or the ludicrously over-hyped. Yes, a sense of urgency is important when you are talking about events of great national or international importance, but authority comes from a calm and purposeful delivery. When confronted with stories of extraordinary drama, or appalling horror, watch how the emotion of the moment can affect your voice. You can end up sounding maudlin without even noticing it. Step back, compose yourself and track again. Fergal Keane, BBC Special Correspondent

The extra ingredients are an understanding of the rhythms and cadences of words as well as their meanings; a natural tact which will determine the right tone of voice for each story. Film star looks have (fortunately) nothing to do with it. Martin Bell, former BBC correspondent

The looks

In my view looks hardly enter into it. You can be ugly as sin and still a great TV broadcaster – and there are a few who have proved it!
Ben Brown, BBC Special Correspondent

They should have a clear and pleasant voice and an arresting personality. Their looks don't matter a lot. Anna Ford, BBC News presenter

They don't need to be good-looking – case in point yours truly! Denis Murray, BBC Ireland Correspondent

The stamina

Sheer physical stamina is more important than ever before. The new terrain of broadcasting – 24-hour rolling news and the advent of new technology – calls for deep reserves of energy. You will find yourself filing at all hours from all kinds of places. Even if your body copes well your mind can drift. The old days of hard partying are gone. Be prepared to encounter tough conditions as a matter of course. Fergal Keane, BBC Special Correspondent

Even the most gifted newshounds, analysts and writers can blow it through laziness, lack of effort or poor application. Fleet Street is full of the dead bodies of talented hacks whose lassitude ruined them. Jeff Randall, BBC Business Editor

The bladder

An ability to appear calm, collected and coherent when chaos is all around – including in your earpiece. A quick grasp of facts and an ability to distil them into reasonably simple, short thoughts. An attractive speaking voice and, if you are on the road, a strong bladder. Jennie Bond, former BBC Royal Correspondent

THE CRAFT SKILLS

A way with words

The difference between a good broadcast journalist and an excellent one is the writing. A superlative correspondent has the attitude, has the presence – but

he or she also has the intelligence and verbal dexterity to write in phrases you will always remember. Their scripts are defining moments in the stories themselves. You can go a very long way to being better than average if you have wit and enthusiasm, but you can't be brilliant if you can't write.
Jay Hunt, Editor of the BBC *Six O'Clock News*

A great broadcaster is someone whose words you remember forever after hearing them once – I still remember Martin Bell's opening line as a trainload of smiling, waving Soviet soldiers left Czechoslovakia for the last time: 'They overstayed a welcome they never had.' Or his opener over a panning shot of the Hiroshima-like ruins of Vukovar: 'To the victor the prize and the prize is a heap of rubble.' This is communication at its best – the fantastic fusion of memorable images and unforgettable words.
Bill Neely, ITV News International Editor

Good broadcast journalists never forget that first and foremost they are in journalism; and whether in radio or television, that the most important part of their work is the text. Sloppiness, ambiguity or inaccuracy is alien to their nature. Invariably, the best broadcast journalists also have a love of the language and a natural feel for when it is appropriate to understate or go in hard. They are economical with words and with clichés.
Peter Sissons, BBC News presenter

It's about the language you use, the sentences you construct, the words and phrases you select, the analogies you choose, the jokes you make. A great paragraph in a newspaper may well make a lousy one on radio or TV, especially if it's inverted, over-extended and bogged down in subsidiary clauses. What works for the eye more often than not won't work for the ear.
Ben Brown, BBC Special Correspondent

In radio you will need an ability to write descriptively. I am not talking about purple prose, but clear-eyed descriptions of places and people and events. Keep it simple. It is often said that radio is a writer's medium. Not entirely so. Radio is a listener's medium. Not everybody has the talent to produce the moving description, but any half decent reporter should be able to describe the events unfolding before them.

Good television writing is a rarity. There is too much of a tendency to settle for the average and mundane. Reports glutted with cliché are too common. This is partly the result of an explosion in the number of outlets but – and this is a controversial point – it is also a consequence of declining standards in education. Those who do not read generally make poor writers. In writing for television remember the maxim that less is more. Always look for a more economical way of stating something; beware the piece which has wall to wall commentary, no breaks for natural sound and no space for the viewer to absorb the images. Try to be bold in the way you write, without straying into bias or hype; the opening and closing lines in a television piece are key.
Fergal Keane, BBC Special Correspondent

It's about being a wordsmith. The most complex issues have to be distilled, explained and made accessible to the public. The best broadcast journalists weave stories which stay on in the audience's mind long after the news bulletin has ended. Shuilie Ghosh, ITV News Home Affairs Editor

Underwriting is an art; overwriting a crime. The best correspondents can write with such clarity that a viewer who sees their report just once can understand the story. Jonathan Munro, ITV News Head of Newsgathering

A flair for storytelling

A good journalist must be a good storyteller. Too many reporters make the mistake of thinking that their job is only about imparting information, but if you can't tell a good yarn no one will watch or listen or read your story and thus you will have failed to impart any information either. I always think, 'how would I tell this story to a mate in the pub, how would I get them interested, what would I tell them first?' Like a good movie there must be a beginning, a middle and an end. Kirsty Lang, BBC FOUR News presenter

The best television news journalists also have the ability to use the pictures available, which by necessity may be limited, to tell the broader story. Martin Bell was a master of this; John Simpson still is. A good television correspondent will have the ability to distil with clarity a complex story into two or three minutes. It is the skill of simplifying a story without making it simplistic. Mark Austin, ITV News presenter and correspondent

The most important and often the most neglected area of all is storytelling. It's all very well assembling the facts, but you have to make them interesting to the viewer or listener. When a newspaper article gets too demanding or too complex, you can always put the paper down and go back to it later. On radio or TV, if you lose the audience for a second it is normally too late. You do not get another chance. So be interesting; do not over-complicate; write in straightforward English, but engagingly. Equally, don't go so far that you have simplified everything to meaningless sound bites. One of the greatest challenges of broadcast journalism has always seemed to me to be able to present difficult issues in an accessible way. Jon Sopel, BBC presenter and correspondent

The most powerful stories are about those without power: a refugee in Bosnia, a helpless victim of a natural disaster, a child caught in violent circumstances he cannot understand. The best broadcast journalists have an ability to focus on this part of the story and have the confidence to take sides on behalf of the victims. It is not so much about objectivity or neutrality, but about a controlled passion. Martin Bell's coverage of Bosnia for the BBC is perhaps the best recent example. The ability to observe and highlight the unexpected is another talent shared by the best broadcast journalists. When tens of thousands of people were dying in Rwanda and Zaire of hunger and dehydration, the most harrowing sound was not the suffering but the silence, and the most distressing television image was the lack of visible grief. The dying had long ago accepted their dismal fate. Robert Moore, ITV News Washington Correspondent

Above all, the best broadcasters are good storytellers who bring alive, through words and pictures, not just dramatic events but feelings, concepts, and trends.

They are guides who help us understand the world by identifying what matters, explaining it with insight and placing it in context.
Niall Dickson, BBC Social Affairs Editor

If you don't grab your audience by the lapels in the first ten seconds you are already losing some. If you don't pepper your report with similar attention grabbers you'll lose more people. Bill Neely, ITV News International Editor

It doesn't matter whether you're a cub reporter on local radio or Alistair Cooke doing your billionth Letter From America, *you must talk to (not at) your audience with sufficient clarity, simplicity, quality and originality that they don't wander off to put on the kettle and never come back.*
Ben Brown, BBC Special Correspondent

A passion for the skills required to tell the story

Treat the pictures you have to write to like a good acquaintance: take notice but maintain a polite distance. The story is in the detail – the telling cutaway, the abandoned teddy bear, the half eaten ice cream – and the detail only works if you can relate it to the broader picture.

Sound bites are often overrated, especially in a foreign language with a dodgy voice-over. If you don't have a decent 'clip' I would rather hear lots of natural sound. A laugh or a belch will often say as much as fifteen seconds of hot air. If possible use immediate translation done by a good translator on the spot. Far more dramatic. When you have finished the edit – and assuming you have time – listen to it with your eyes shut, at least once. If there is enough sound to imagine the pictures, it's OK.

While the cameraperson gets the shots, spend time talking to the people involved. Everyone has a story to tell. It will make the all-important set up shots more interesting, more relevant, and might shed new light on the story. Look for 'real moments': the smile that gives the game away, the spokesman who loses his temper with a sidekick. Anything that chips away at the greatest danger to all broadcasting . . . FORMULA. Avoid it like the plague. Easier said than done!

Ask yourself with every story: why is this interesting? If it really isn't, then don't do it. Every story has a beginning, a middle and an end . . . even at one minute thirty seconds. Matt Frei, BBC Washington Correspondent

A willingness to step aside for pictures and sound

A willingness in a visual medium to give primacy to the pictures. It is a labour of love, to caress them rather than overwhelm them with commentary, and to know when to shut up completely and get off the screen. The most difficult art in TV news is the art of writing silence.
Martin Bell, former BBC correspondent

The tempting answer to the question 'What makes a good TV journalist?' is 'A good TV cameraman'! In my view the strongest television news stories are all about the power of the image. It is most often the image that remains in the memory and in war zones, at the scene of natural disasters or wherever news is breaking, great TV news cameramen will always capture the moment in a way others cannot. So to an extent a television reporter or correspondent is only as good as the pictures he has to work with.
Mark Austin, ITV News presenter and correspondent

Pictures and sound will often tell the story far more eloquently than a reporter's script. The skill is to know when to step back.
Robert Moore, ITV News Washington Correspondent

The right balance between engaging and informative

The best broadcast journalists have 'screen presence', a kind of energy which comes across. Increasingly I see broadcast journalists who have the fluency and some presence but no knowledge or real journalistic skills, so what they report has no meaning. If you've only got the journalistic skills, you'd do better to remain in print. If you've only got the presentation side, then go in for showbusiness. To be a good broadcast journalist you need both.
Lindsey Hilsum, Diplomatic Correspondent, Channel 4 News

A good broadcast journalist is also someone who appreciates that to be informative you don't need to be dull, to be interesting you shouldn't be gimmicky, and to be accessible you mustn't patronize. Above all, you need to know where to draw the line – and that tends to come with experience.

Nigel Dacre, former Editor of ITV News

Originality: a desire to be different

Try to find imaginative ways of telling the story. Get the attention of the audience. Just like the great newspaper correspondent, the television or radio reporter who gets noticed is the one who does what nobody else has thought of, like John Simpson donning a burka to enter Taliban-ruled Afghanistan or Jon Swain walking over the mountains into Kosovo. Television, though, has more room for big characters with whom the audience can develop a long-term relationship. You will be told relentlessly that the story is more important than the reporter. Of course it is, but if conveying the truth of the story means you need to involve yourself on screen, don't be afraid. It needn't always be an occasion of great derring-do; just try to use your imagination and move quietly. The brash and loudmouthed are numerous in our business; they may look like they are tough and effective but I've always favoured the route of quiet cunning myself!

Fergal Keane, BBC Special Correspondent

Television journalism is the art of eye-witness reporting. It uses pictures and sound to convey the beating heart of a story. It brings together the eye of the stills photographer and the headline writer. It is about finding the moment; the image; the clip; the close-up that captures the event. It relies on few facts, just essential detail and no more. At its best the image comes to life with a single telling phrase. Like all journalism, television reporting is about the struggle for authenticity; its enemy is the cliché, seeing an event not for what it is but through the coverage of the past. The best television reporting finds its own voice and dares to be different.

Gavin Hewitt, BBC Special Correspondent

The best have a unique style of their own which separates them from the rest — you can see this in the work of, say, John Simpson, John Cole and Jeremy Paxman to name three very different characters, each of whom has set new standards in broadcast journalism.
Niall Dickson, BBC Social Affairs Editor

A knowledge of your audience

A good broadcast journalist never forgets that he or she is the eyes and ears of his audience. He can give his viewers and listeners an idea of what it's like to witness a news event or, if the reportage is exceptional, give them an idea of what it is like to be one of the people caught up in what's happening.
Jeremy Bowen, BBC presenter and correspondent

They need to understand their audience acutely. That doesn't mean abstract demographics. It means simple facts about the way they live, the way they speak, what matters to them. They need to be able to communicate effectively with those watching or listening because they understand them.
Jay Hunt, Editor of the BBC *Six O'Clock News*

Knowing your audience helps too — knowing their prejudices, current or deep, so you know what you have to penetrate; getting your story into perspective so you're communicating the most information to the broadest number of people.
Bill Neely, ITV News International Editor

For my money, good broadcast journalists have an ability to see their own specialist subject from the point of view of someone who isn't interested in it, or knowledgeable about it. It follows from this they strike several difficult balancing acts:
a) To start the story from a point at which the average viewer might be able to pick it up, i.e. from some common conception about the theme at issue.
b) To pitch it at a level comprehensible to the average viewer — which means being simple, but also saying something the viewer doesn't already know.

(Some are often simple, but bland; others are interesting but complicated; the knack is to find a message that is both interesting and simple.)
c) *To convey enthusiasm about the subject, without hyping it.*
Evan Davis, BBC Economics Editor

Objectivity

What distinguishes excellent journalists is they have a healthy distaste for rules and bureaucracy, but they also have core journalistic values running through them like a stick of rock: they report with impeccable accuracy, they know instinctively there are two sides to every story, they discard the froth and head for the real substance. So viewers can both enjoy their thrill in chasing a story and trust their fairness: they know that when our top journalists say something matters – it really does, and they're not relying on one sectional view. That's what you get from Andy Marr on politics or John Simpson on foreign affairs.
Roger Mosey, Head of BBC TV News

Broadcast journalists must accept what print journalists don't have to – that there is a statutory obligation on them to be fair and impartial, and that their own opinions must remain hidden. Good broadcast journalists would behave in this way even if the law didn't demand it.
Peter Sissons, BBC News presenter

They should have authority and reliability and give an unbiased view which is as close to the truth as is possible that day. Anna Ford, BBC News presenter

Paranoia

I really do think insecurity is a common characteristic of those television reporters I have most admired. So much of television reporting is the effort that goes into it – getting up and out on site earlier than everybody else, making the extra call, seeing what's just over the hill. To keep doing that,

even when you have established a reputation, even something of a name, needs the extra spur of the nagging fear that whatever you did yesterday, you may not be able to do today. It's the fundamental truth of our business that each day is a completely clean sheet. It is its huge attraction and ultimate drawback.
Michael Buerk, BBC presenter

Something to say

I think a good broadcast journalist somehow manages to take control of what can be a lot of unwieldy material – whether it's a sound recording, or pictures, or a live situation that's about to get out of hand – and harnesses it to tell a story in a compelling, clear and novel way. And actually I think the best news broadcasting tends to be personal: viewers and listeners don't just want to see what you saw, they want to hear what you thought of it.
Jeremy Vine, BBC presenter

I've got an awful lot of mediocre stories to my name but my best despatches had, I think, one thing in common – they were more than just reports of what I saw, I had something to say about what I saw. Over the years I developed a discipline – even before I got to the particular feeding centre in Somalia, or the school protest in South Africa, or the border between Albania and Kosovo I would work out what that event meant, why it was important. Then I would write down the basis of a piece-to-camera which made that one central point. I would change and amend the actual words to suit the location but the central theme would remain. So even on a running story (when you go back to the same or similar locations day after day) my despatches tried to say something different. I always considered it a failure if all I did in a piece-to-camera was describe what the viewers could, in any case, see for themselves in the pictures we beamed back.

Some might argue that this is putting the cart before the horse, deciding what the story is before actually seeing it for myself. My reply is this: I worked as a specialist correspondent – there were very few occasions when I was arriving at a story entirely cold. I was paid to know what it was I was heading

into. Indeed, we are in a privileged position and I think we have an obligation to be prepared.
George Alagiah, BBC News presenter and former correspondent

Something not to have: preconceptions

Good journalists overturn stereotypes, while bad journalists reinforce them.
Gavin Esler, BBC *Newsnight* presenter

Too many journalists depart on a story with preconceived notions of what the story is and what people will say but some of the best of the stories I've got have just slipped out of my interviewees when they are relaxed and chatty because I've put them at their ease, their guard is down and they feel comfortable talking to me. Kirsty Lang, BBC FOUR News presenter

The good journalist is driven primarily by curiosity to uncover and explain, to open up hidden worlds or cultures to wider scrutiny and to embrace the struggle for something as elusive as 'nirvana': truth. The bad journalist puts themselves at the centre of the story, arrives with too many preconceptions and allows their own emotion to displace thought or explanation in their stories.
Mark Urban, BBC *Newsnight* correspondent

[A good journalist needs] *an appetite to ask questions, a determination not to answer the questions before gathering all available evidence and an ability to put across the conclusions effectively and in context.*
Steve Mitchell, BBC Head of Radio News

I'm often amazed at how many people pitch up in strange places with nothing to say apart from the most vacuous and inane of comments. Do not apply the same template to every story. Too often we get journalism which recognizes no difference between countries, regions and peoples.
Fergal Keane, BBC Special Correspondent

IN CONCLUSION

There is plenty of career advice to follow in this book. But here's an early tip to help further your career: say what you really think – but always let the bosses have the last word. And here are the bosses:

A good broadcast journalist is driven to discover, unearth, reveal more about the world; has a passion to communicate and explain, without using jargon or talking down to the audience; understands the chemistry of their medium be it sound or pictures; and knows that news is all about people and what affects their lives. Richard Sambrook, BBC Director of News

Enthusiasm: making yourself available particularly when others are not. Ideas: keep them coming even when your first ones are knocked back. Awareness: watching, listening and reading what's about, whether or not it's your side or the competition. Wordcraft: making it simpler often makes it sound better. Stewart Purvis, former ITN Chief Executive

You can't teach it. You can't define it. You can't fake it. You'll know it when you see it. That's about as near as I can get to answering the question. An ability to trot out facts isn't enough. Pick away at the seams of those facts to get at the things that really matter. Be genuinely interested in ordinary people – if you're too detached from their hopes and fears you're an academic not a journalist. If you're jaded by the work after thirty days or even thirty years, get out of the job. One golden rule? Have something to say. Nick Pollard, Head of Sky News

A superb broadcast journalist has a passion for our world and for helping people to understand it better. An honest broadcast journalist recognizes it is not always possible to be objective, while it is always both possible and essential to be accurate, fair and responsible in your reporting. A smart broadcast journalist has an insatiable curiosity and does not pretend to know it all. The

*best broadcast journalists are clear, concise and compassionate in their reporting
and in dealing with their colleagues.*
Eason Jordan, Chief News Executive and News gathering President,
CNN

Well, that's the theory. The next chapter will deal with what it all
means in practice.

Remember that, when it's all over, nothing else matters – not fancy titles and prizes and an ego-driven salary to go with them – but the good opinion of those who have worked with you and against you. Especially those who have worked against you. If you've got that you've got everything. If not, it isn't worth the hassle. Go and keep bees instead.

Martin Bell, former BBC correspondent

2 the tv news masterclass

This is a masterclass for journalists about the art and craft of storytelling in television news. About making serious news accessible and explaining why stories matter.

Good journalism helps people make sense of the world and gives them the information they need to live their lives. The first challenge is finding the right information – selecting the right stories. The second is to make those stories meaningful, relevant and engaging.

There are many different ways of telling stories, yet much TV news remains formulaic. This masterclass has compiled some of the best examples of reporters' work with the aim of improving storytelling and making everyone involved in TV news think more about the fundamental principle of how we make what is significant interesting.

The examples used here are from BBC programmes and correspondents.

When he was US President, Woodrow Wilson was once asked how long it took him to write a speech. 'That depends,' he replied. 'If I'm to speak for ten minutes, I need a week for preparation. If fifteen minutes, three days. If half an hour, two days. If an hour, I'm ready now.'

He might have had trouble crafting a two-minute television package against the kind of deadlines we work to these days. But the thinking behind what he said rings true: the more clearly and succinctly a story needs to be told, the more work needs to go into it and the more difficult it is.

And therein lies the challenge of this imperfect yet immensely powerful medium of television news: telling difficult and often complicated stories to a universal audience in a clear and engaging way in absurdly short periods of time.

So this masterclass aims to help broadcast journalists meet that challenge, using pictures, sounds and words to translate their expertise or presence on the ground into effective storytelling. To preserve and report a serious news agenda in a way that engages, includes and, ultimately, enlightens the audience.

Good television news should deliver the answers to three questions any viewer is entitled to ask: What's happened – what are the latest developments? What are the issues I need to understand in order to make sense of those developments? Tell me why it matters – why should I care?

The very best correspondents can do just that: bridge that often huge gap between their own very detailed understanding of an area or story and explain simply and engagingly how it will affect the daily lives of their viewers. The more serious and difficult the agenda we pursue the more important it becomes that we have the skills to portray stories in a clear and accessible way.

Yet there is sometimes a tendency for news organizations, which are intellectual by nature, instinctively to shy away from this kind of clarity, confusing a call to be clear with being patronizing and confusing a call for simplicity with being simplistic. But stories need to be told simply in order that they are clear and easy to understand. The more simply a story can be told the more powerful it will be.

But finding the right balance between being informative and being engaging is not always easy. Try too hard to be engaging and your journalism or programme can become more style than substance. Too far the other way and your reporting will be so dense and full of detail that the bored viewer will neither understand nor watch.

Authority comes mostly from a deep understanding of your subject. It is not enough merely to be able to 'perform' in front of a camera. The two go hand in hand. This book has many examples and tips which will hopefully improve your storytelling and your performance, but it doesn't replace a fundamental truth: you must have something to say. The ability to walk and talk in front of a camera may be a valuable thing – but it is worth very little unless you have something worth saying.

Research shows that viewers are reassuringly savvy when it comes to what they regard as gimmicks or tricks of the trade: they can recognize when style is triumphing over substance. And when it does we are held in lower esteem and our authority is diminished. Yet without the ability to engage and entertain our audiences, authority and expertise are worth nothing.

The audience often sees things very differently from journalists, who tend to interpret coverage according to the internal structure of their company – dividing stories into political, foreign, business or social policy. But audiences have a habit of dividing coverage into just two categories: interesting and dull. So this masterclass has no separate sections on politics, social affairs, business and economics or regional reporting. But there is a section on context and understanding which applies some universal truths to all areas of reporting.

And none of this has anything to do with being young, glamorous or good-looking – the qualities possessed by top correspondents are laid out in the previous chapter and go hand-in-hand with two other key characteristics: perseverance and a healthy level of paranoia. The latter because it prevents complacency; and perseverance because acquiring these skills can be a long haul.

But above and beyond any guidelines, the best correspondents have a sense of confidence. Confidence to lift their writing above the ordinary and the safe; to inject a 'lightness of touch'; confidence to do less, say less – and communicate more; and the confidence to be themselves – and not just 'play the part' of a television correspondent.

So, much of this guide emphasizes the need for you to be yourself. Correspondents watch and learn from each other's work – they must. But a style of reporting which works for another correspondent may not work for you. It's crucial to view other people's work, but be careful. Some aspects of top correspondents' work will be worthy of emulation, but you must find the qualities that make you and your own work interesting and unique. And we should always remember that the best journalism often surprises and challenges – and in doing so goes well beyond simple guidelines.

The best broadcast journalists should be seeking to maintain an unbeatable combination of authority, expertise, passion, originality and great storytelling. You may feel your work has achieved this already. If so, congratulations. But I will leave you with the words of the critic Robert Hughes: 'The greater the artist the greater the doubt; perfect confidence is granted to the less talented as a consolation prize.'

And so to storytelling.

2.1 **storytelling**

Only great minds can afford a simple style.

Stendhal

Obscurity of expression generally springs from confusion of ideas.

Macaulay

Everything should be made as simple as possible, but not one bit simpler.

Albert Einstein

Style is what gets left out.

Bertold Brecht

What's the story?

Before you start, stop. And ask yourself: what's the story? There are only so many elements a viewer can take in through one television package and it is crucial that you select the elements which most clearly explain the story. This also forces you into the harder decision of which elements to leave out.

This is the essential starting point. Before you start writing, you must be crystal clear what the one or two key points of the story are. Otherwise you risk competing with yourself and the pictures to cram your piece and your writing with too much information: keep it simple. As Andrew Marr says in Chapter One, you need to put in 'the brainwork that condenses a complicated story in such a way that the viewer gets a sense of it, vividly, without it being badly distorted.'

On a running or fast-breaking story it's easy to get trapped into dealing with pictures and facts in the order in which you get them. Similarly, when you have shot a lot of material yourself, you naturally want to include as much of your own material as possible. Don't. Your job – on behalf of the viewer – is to sit back, consider, and decide upon the crux of the story. Then choose which pictures and elements are crucial to telling it, and, most importantly, which can be ignored. Focus on the story with a sniper's rifle, not a scatter gun. Think how you would tell a friend what the story is in one sentence and bear that in mind as you put the piece together. Too much information will make your writing style tortuous and cramped, reduce the possibilities for natural sound and confuse the viewer.

You must strike a balance between giving the viewer the benefit of your expertise and that same viewer clearly and completely understanding what you're trying to get across. Unfortunately, when in doubt, less experienced correspondents err on the side of including that extra fact or sequence which makes the story more difficult to understand. Bear in mind the difference between the *subject* of the story and your *treatment* of it. The British film-maker John Grierson wrote, 'You can write an article about the postal service, but you must make a film about one single letter.' Don't try to 'write a whole article' in a television news piece.

Your job is to take an often confusing or complicated situation or series of events and make sense of it for the viewer, and in doing so it's most often what you leave out that really matters. So keep it simple – go back and talk it through with the programme editor or producer if you feel you are being asked to turn too many corners and include too many elements.

A longer piece is not automatically a better piece. In fact, the reverse is almost invariably true. Despite the habit many correspondents have of asking for more time, there are too many pieces which have plenty to say, but which don't have the pictures to sustain a lengthy script. A three-minute piece can often be 30 per cent *less* effective than a two-minute piece – not the other way round.

The best television news pieces try to convey no more than one or two basic thoughts and often those thoughts will need to be repeated within the piece. If your story needs to be seen more than once before it can be understood (and too many do), then it will have totally failed. In broadcasting, there is only one chance for viewers to understand. You are distilling information, not packing it in. Get to the point, stick to it, know when it's finished and then end it.

STRUCTURE AND FLOW

When you're sitting in a room telling someone a story you can usually tell by their expression whether they care or understand. You're getting feedback while you tell them. They may even ask questions as you go along. But you don't have that luxury when you're putting a television package together.

The order in which you tell the story and put the pictures together – the structure – is crucial in helping the viewer understand your report. Imagine telling a friend what the story is and bear that in mind as you put the piece together. Newspaper reporters use the 'inverted pyramid', with key information at the front of the article and the less important elements at the back as the story peters out. But if you're telling a story in conversation you have to maintain interest all the way through – and in some cases build up to a climax.

A television story is most easily understood if it is told chronologically, with the elements arranged in the sequence in which they happened. But this isn't always possible. Much specialist journalism is about exploring policies and arguments which have no strict chronology to them. Whatever the structure, a television news report should *flow* from the first sentence to the last. Each sentence should flow easily into the next; each sequence into the following one. Joining ideas and thoughts together with no jagged edges and in the clearest possible way is essential.

The most effective and powerful pieces are those with elements arranged in the best logical order for understanding and told in a way that holds the viewer's attention from beginning to end. But sometimes a lack of pictures means there is a trade-off, or tension, between the best order for understanding and putting the sequences together in a way which keeps the audience watching.

So it is by no means always easy or obvious. But the ability subtly and seamlessly to turn corners from one sequence to another is often what marks out the really good news writer – pulling the best of the sound, the pictures and the story together to maximum effect.

The key to structure and flow lies in two things: firstly, fitting sequences together into an order which best uses their logical and natural connections; and secondly, moving from one sequence to another by relating thoughts and sentences to each other with 'transition' words or phrases. You must use the skill and power of your writing to make each new sequence of pictures or interview clip 'hold hands' with the next one. And always remember that every story has a beginning, a middle and an end.

Transitions between sequences

The most obvious transition words or phrases are those like *and, so, but, with that, even so, and so*. These connect one sequence of pictures or interview to the next and achieve a sense of flow through the piece.

At its very simplest:

script: . . . worried that school exclusions have now reached record levels.

new sequence – teacher

script: <u>So</u> teachers like Sue Bloggs have decided . . .

Adding 'so' makes the transition from one sequence of pictures to the next. Similarly:

script: . . . by rationing the number of students from private schools.

new sequence – university

script: <u>But</u> this new university in east London has chosen a different method. It . . .

Or this could have been:

script: But that's not what this new university in east London is doing. It . . .

Crucially, that little 'but' gives a sense of continuity – it flows from the previous sentence and takes you seamlessly from one set of pictures to the next. Referencing back to the previous sentence has the same effect:

script: . . . will stop at nothing less than independence.

new sequence – troops

script: But however hard they fight for that independence, these troops . . .

or into a graphic:

script: . . . are worried that the measures go too far.

new sequence – graphic

script: So, what exactly would the measures mean to someone earning £30,000 a year?

Some other transitions:

nearby,

two miles away,

within hours,

two hours later,

and this is why,

and here's the reason.

These are all phrases which help to 'hold hands' with the previous sequence or sentence. But try to avoid the over-used *meanwhile* and *in a separate development*.

Too often, correspondents start a new sequence of pictures almost as though they were starting a new piece. Consider these sentences – each beginning a new sequence of pictures in the same piece:

sequence 1: 'It's the first religious festival they've been able to have . . .'

sequence 2: 'These survivors may be celebrating today, but the reality . . .'

sequence 3: 'These three sisters are cyclone orphans . . .'

sequence 4: 'This place is between relief and reconstruction . . .'

sequence 5: 'Yet another legacy of the cyclone . . .'

The beginning of each sequence could be the beginning of an entirely new piece. There are no transitions from sequence to sequence. No connections. No flow.

Sometimes a transition can be more sophisticated. In a report from Kosovo, for example, one correspondent moved from a sequence of a funeral to one of a soldier returning home with the words: 'The funeral was over by the time this man returned home from the fighting at the front.' Again, this took the viewer seamlessly from one sequence to the next. As does this:

script: . . . the UN is investigating 606 individual cases of murder. We knew some of the victims.

new sequence – prison

script: Now it's time to meet some of the murderers.

This example references ahead and cleverly sets up the move to the next sequence of pictures: 'We knew some of the victims,' over the end of one sequence, 'Now it's time to meet,' over the start of the new sequence.

Transitions in and out of interview clips are just as important.

clip: . . . depends on what happens.

new sequence

script: And what happens depends on this man . . .

Or into an interview clip:

script: . . . but locals feel resentful. The question they want answered?

new sequence – interview clip

clip: Why should these outsiders get special treatment when . . .

Consider the correspondent's script in the following example about suicides in prisons.

clip (union officer): It's something that unfortunately we experience a lot at Brixton. It's quite stressful, and to be honest with you, the staff really are totally and utterly demoralized.

script: Last month, twenty-one prisoners tried to kill or seriously harm themselves in Brixton. The Government says it wants inmates who need help to get the same treatment as on the NHS, but that's far from the case currently. The minister promised extra staff . . .

The script does not naturally flow on from the sound bite. The union officer is one 'block'; the script is treated like the next 'block'. And the language is stiff – 'that's far from the case currently' is not a phrase you would be likely to use in conversation. The script could have been:

clip: . . . the staff really are totally and utterly demoralized.

script: . . . and that's not surprising – twenty-one prisoners tried to kill or seriously harm themselves in Brixton last month alone. The Government says inmates should get the same treatment they would get on the NHS – but that seems a long way off . . .

This achieves a sense of flow and a conversational delivery. Don't think of a package as a series of blocks or elements – it should be one continuous flow.

If a transition from one sequence to another doesn't seem possible through language, then use natural sound from the start of the next sequence to indicate a change.

STRUCTURE AND CHRONOLOGY

Two notions which seem to have entered the mental guidebook of some reporters are that you must always include the latest pictures and that you must always start on the strongest pictures. Neither is true. That doesn't mean to say you shouldn't – often you will want to. Just that you should judge for yourself – it's not set in stone.

For example, on Budget day, pictures of the Chancellor arriving back in Downing Street may be the latest available, but viewers coming to your story for the first time (and you should always assume they are) may be confused if you invert the chronology of your story by putting those pictures at the top of the piece or including them where they disrupt the flow.

The best correspondents can build up a sense of tension around the strongest pictures and put them in their right chronological place allowing a proper narrative around them.

For instance, using the strongest rioting pictures at the start of a piece rather than taking the viewer through the events and tension leading up to the riot may be powerful but can destroy the chronology and make for a complicated narrative which is harder to write – and to follow.

Here's an example from Matt Frei in Indonesia:

script: The port of Ambon in one of Indonesia's spice islands. Five thousand people trying to get on to a ferry made for 500. This is a desperate exodus. No one wants to be left behind. No one and nothing. What makes people take a journey like this with all their belongings?

new sequence – police shooting into a crowd [strongest pictures]

script: This does . . . Bedlam.

This David Shukman script on Tornado missions over Serbia also draws the viewer in:

script: This is where the air war starts. A 2,000 pound bomb – the largest the RAF has – is loaded into an RAF Tornado in Germany. These weapons are meant to break the Serbian military and force Mr Milosevic to the peace table. The planes begin their mission, two men in each, six bombers in all, many other aircraft in support. The sight is formidable, but so are the complications.

The information and ideas are layered, with sentences and sequences following on from each other, flowing, building and unfolding. Information is much more easily absorbed this way. The converse, and poorly constructed piece, has one fact after another, one sequence after another, with no connections.

In the end, one can only generalize about how to structure TV pieces – they are all different and there are many different ways of structuring the same piece. But first and foremost, be clear what the story is, then try to tell it with the pictures and sound first. Remember, the story starts from the first words of the intro – not the first words of your piece. And remember that, however short the piece, every story has a beginning, a middle and an end.

But above all, *let it flow*.

Get involved in the cue

As far as it's possible – and it isn't always – the cue, or intro, should 'sell' your story rather than 'tell' it. Nothing will kill your piece quite like a cue that says it all and leaves you to repeat what's already been said. A good cue will leave the viewer ready and anxious to hear more. Yet very few correspondents get involved in writing the intro. The easiest way to help a cue sell your piece is to suggest a cue yourself – you may not always have time to write one but you'll almost always have time to talk to the producer who's writing it. The cue is part of *your* story, so always try to be involved in writing it.

For the viewer, the cue is the first 'sequence' of your piece. So you should take some ownership of it – it needs to set up your piece, leave the viewer wanting to see and hear more and move seamlessly into your opening sounds, pictures and words.

Often a cue will be the top line of a story – or the subject of the story – while your report explains the impact of it. The cue may say that the US Fed or the central bank has cut interest rates; your report may look at the impact on US firms in Scotland. The cue must get from one to the other in a seamless way. So if you're not writing the cue yourself, let whoever is know how your piece starts so they can bridge the gap. If you don't bridge that gap the viewers are forced to do it themselves with the result that they miss the beginning of the piece while they try to make the connection. Confusion (and viewers lost) will be the only result.

Sometimes a cue will also lay out some of the context or background to a particular story to enable you to tell a story in a certain way. Again, you must be certain what has or has not been said. Consider the following cue, broadcast by the BBC, to introduce a report on the European Champions' League Final – a football match decided by what many fans agreed was the goal of the season, scored by the French player, Zidane.

cue: Hampden Park in Glasgow played host to the biggest game in European club football this evening, as Spanish and German fans flocked to the city for the UEFA Champions' League final. The match was won by strong favourites Real Madrid of Spain. They defeated Bayern Leverkusen of Germany by two goals to one.

This cue leaves nothing else to say. And most viewers in Britain would not be very interested in a match between two foreign teams, important though it was. It could have been this:

cue: Thousands of Spanish and German fans descended on Glasgow tonight to watch the most important game in European club football. They saw a match decided by a spectacular goal – and what's more, it was scored by the most expensive player in the world.

This cue teases the viewer into watching more – it is storytelling, rather than just the provision of information. Many viewers may wonder who the most expensive player in the world is; others will want to see the goal. The cue leaves them wanting to see more. The reporter's piece could then have built up to the goal which settled the game, with the chance for some clever script lines like:

script: So, what do you get for 45.5 million pounds?

picture and natural sound: Zidane goal

script: This.

A story does not always have to be told in a 'linear' way. You can keep an element of surprise and use the cue as a 'tease' which *hints* at what the viewer might be about to see without telling the whole story. This is called a 'drop cue'. For instance, the following cue set up a piece from Libya about a car which had been designed by Colonel Gaddafi:

cue: The roads of Libya could soon become the safest in the world – if a new car designed by Colonel Gaddafi himself lives up to its reputation. 'The Libyan Rocket', as it's been named, was unveiled today. It's said to be the product of many hours' work by the Libyan leader, and is purported to have high-tech safety features which make it 'a vehicle like no other'. John Simpson is in Tripoli, and was one of the first to see it.

This cue *should* have been a 'tease' which 'sold' the story, but at twenty-eight seconds it's far too long and it didn't leave the correspondent with much else to say. It could have been:

cue: They call it the Libyan Rocket – and they say it will make the world a safer place. It was even designed by Colonel Gaddafi himself. But what exactly is it? John Simpson, in Libya, was one of the first to see it.

At fourteen seconds, this cue is shorter and 'teases' the viewer into the piece, leaving the correspondent to tell the story.

And whatever you do, NEVER let the first line of your piece repeat a line that has appeared in the cue.

Don't raise questions you don't answer

It' s not that you are literally raising questions in your script, but as a viewer watches your report – logical questions come up in his or her mind. It's crucial that each succeeding sentence or sequence in your piece answers these questions. This can take the form of the viewer wondering, 'Why?' 'So what happened?'

One recent report explained how US marines had flown over the Antarctic and dropped ultrasound scanning equipment down to a doctor who had found a lump in her own breast. The report did not say why she couldn't return home for the treatment (one could *assume* it was because the weather prevented her from leaving) and neither did it say whether the drop was successful. If the reporter didn't know he should have said so. The viewer was just left wondering.

If a correspondent builds a story around a lost or orphaned child in a conflict, viewers want to know what became of the child. Again, if the correspondent doesn't know, he or she should say so.

Charles Wheeler in Kuwait in 1991, for example:

script: We don't know how widespread this is, but in four days in Howallah we were constantly asked to meet Palestinian victims of beating and worse.

Here's Hilary Andersson in Nigeria – the last sentence is important:

script: The people here are hiding many of the most severely burnt survivors afraid they'll be blamed for starting the fire. Victoria Orisha Mugu has been hidden behind her hut in the suffocating heat of the day. Fifty per cent of her body is covered in burns, her wounds are too distressing to show. She's been left untreated in a breeding ground of infection. The Red Cross finally convinces her to go to hospital but there's no ambulance and the family can't afford any other means of transport.

man asking to camera: 'I humbly beg you people to assist us'
The villagers ask to borrow our car . . . Back at Sapala hospital the latest victim to die was removed to make way for Victoria. Infection had set in to her wounds in her village. The doctor said she had no hope of survival. She was given a blessing. We later found out she died.

The key thing is to be able to recognize the questions you raise and acknowledge when you can't answer them.

Charles Wheeler, again:

script: Our report I'm afraid has more questions than answers but perhaps that is the nature of post-war Kuwait where nobody is really in charge. One more unanswered question is this: could these things really be happening without the involvement of the government in Kuwait? I put that to a neutral who has access to senior ministers which we don't. 'Some of them,' he said, 'are closing one eye to what's happening to Palestinians, and others are closing both eyes.'

It may be that you've tackled one aspect of a story and left the viewer to wonder about another or that something you've said raises an obvious question for the viewer. Don't raise questions you don't answer. If you don't know the answer then say so – then the audience knows what you know. But don't ignore it.

2.2 writing and language

The indispensable characteristic of a good writer
is a style marked by lucidity.

Ernest Hemingway

There is no such thing as good writing, only good
rewriting.

Mark Twain

Given the choice between a trivial story brilliantly told
versus a profound story badly told, an audience will
always choose the trivial told brilliantly.

David McKee, *Story*

Dawn – and as the sun breaks through the piercing chill of night on the plain outside Korem it lights up a biblical famine, now, in the twentieth century.
Michael Buerk in Ethiopia

If there is one area which really separates the best correspondents from the rest it is good writing. The script is the very heart of the reporter's contribution. Some of the most effective scripts are often quite 'spare' in their style – short, simple and clear sentences, memorable for a combination of clarity, directness and then the injection of a telling phrase or twist of words. And often delivered with the timing of an actor.

Good writing often involves taking risks with words (not the facts!) and sentences. The issue for many broadcast journalists is not that their work is poor, but that it is pedestrian or ordinary. This is because they write in a kind of 'comfort zone'. The 'safety' of their scripts means their work is rarely lifted out of the ordinary. The very best television news writing manages to combine some sentences which are out of that comfort zone without becoming flowery or cliché-ridden, while at the same time maintaining the short sentences and simplicity that makes television work. The best scripts can be defining moments in themselves; and the very best are once heard, never forgotten.

The examples of writing used in this section have a number of crucial things in common – they are all bold and confident; they have mostly short, simple sentences; they all complemented the pictures; and all the writers have discovered a way of writing that suits their particular voice and delivery. It is vital to understand the importance of delivery because what might appear to be brilliant writing for one correspondent can appear hackneyed when read by someone else. You must find your own style.

Ultimately it is far easier to write memorable scripts about matters of life and death and far harder to write them about, say, pension reform or interest rates. But good writing and delivery and a lightness of touch will lift and illuminate the driest and most difficult subjects.

The beginning

Always put a lot of work into crafting the opening sentence. It often has the most impact and getting it right will help you enormously through the rest of the story. Before you can enlighten your viewers, you will have to engage them. Less experienced correspondents will play safe with an opening sentence: 'The Chief Inspector arrived . . .' More confident correspondents will use an opening sentence to set the tone for the rest of the piece: 'He might have been excused for thinking his day could not get any worse . . .' But beware the brilliant prose which has nothing to do with the pictures. Unfortunately, those pictures still need scripting (see the section on scripting pictures, page 83).

A well-crafted opening can set the tone of a piece and give a sense of narrative – the sense of a story or drama about to unfold:

An afternoon in Dili. Time for war. A dirty war. Matt Frei in East Timor

A quiet rural corner of the United Kingdom at the end of the twentieth century. Denis Murray over pictures of riot squads in helmets pouring out of helicopters in a field in Northern Ireland

Through country green and quiet, through towns grey and sad, the coffins moved today. Carrying young and old, Catholic and Protestant, nationalist and unionist, a baby and a grandmother. Coming together in mourning, the like of which has never been seen on one day in the Troubles.
Kate Adie starting a piece on the Omagh funerals, using the tolling of church bells to punctuate each sentence

In the back row of a school photograph stands Harold Frederick Shipman, aged five. A confident boy in a bow tie, Fred – as everyone called him – was clever. Gavin Hewitt

Down a leafy lane, where quiet people lived quiet lives, war has left waste, death and hate. Jeremy Bowen in Kosovo

For these survivors, life itself has become an aftershock.
Matt Frei returning to the Bhuj earthquake

With the panache of a General Patton, the first North Vietnamese tank swept into Saigon. The men from the jungle had arrived. Brian Barron

Earlier than expected. Bigger than expected. The attack was prepared at sunset from the ships of the US Sixth fleet in the Adriatic. We could just make out the Yugoslav coast as the unseen electronic countdown began.
Kate Adie on the USS *Gonzalez*

Good writers can make a virtue out of a lack of pictures to start pieces. For instance, these opening words from Justin Webb over the German Chancellor entering a lift: 'Gerhard Schroeder at his new party head-quarters this morning. He was going up, but not very far. His party and Government are going nowhere.'

These words *complement* the pictures but tell you far more than the pictures on their own and they help to draw the viewer in. This piece from Brian Hanrahan in Belgrade started over pictures of a door closing and a canteen: 'Most politics in Yugoslavia goes on behind closed doors. It takes crises to force them ajar and give the public a glimpse of what the politicians are doing. And with more parties in parliament than tables in the dining room, it's an opportunity for endless intrigue.'

This opening sentence from Gavin Hewitt, on General Augusto Pinochet returning to Chile, was written entirely over one shot of a plane taking off: 'At just after one o'clock this afternoon a Chilean Air Force plane climbed into the sky above Lincolnshire – and General Augusto Pinochet was free. The man who described himself as Eng-land's only political prisoner had been hurried onto the plane without formality. The end of an extraordinary legal battle.'

This opening sentence from Jenny Scott uses irony and a lightness of touch to illuminate a dry subject (on mortgage lenders calling, unusually, for higher interest rates): 'So, let's get this straight. Lenders who make their profits out of selling us mortgages want to discourage us from taking out big mortgages?'

A good writer can make even the dullest pictures work for them.

The telling phrase

A well-written, well-delivered turn of phrase can surprise, delight, challenge, move or enlighten a viewer, all the time engaging and drawing the audience into the story.

Life here has come down to scavenging, mourning, burying, burning, remembering and regretting. Jeremy Bowen in Kosovo

Another reminder that it was Indonesia that coined the phrase 'to run amok'. And Ambon is just one of a score of places where they are doing just that. Matt Frei

They outstayed a welcome they never had. Martin Bell on Russian troops leaving Czechoslovakia

It was a soundtrack for a troubled city. Brian Hanrahan on the violinist Nigel Kennedy playing in Belgrade

Words with a twist:

I counted them all out and I counted them all back. Brian Hanrahan on the number of British aeroplanes – which he was not allowed to disclose – joining the raid on Port Stanley in the Falklands

Their chances of survival are like the weather – below zero. Martin Bell at the Potomac air crash

While East Timor has abandoned all hope, the UN has decided to abandon East Timor. Matt Frei in Indonesia

The leaders of East Germany are passing not just into history but into prison.
Martin Bell

These are phrases you hear – and remember – and which can make
even the dullest stories come alive. Here's Andrew Marr on Ian Duncan
Smith restructuring his Conservative Party leadership: 'But will it be
restructured with nail clippers or a chainsaw?'

Atmosphere

A good writer can help the viewer almost taste and smell the atmosphere – the drama, the elation, the fear. This is how John Simpson
described the city of Belgrade and its people moving from daytime to
a night that would inevitably bring more bombing:

The all-clear siren sounds, for the time being. By now, it's after five,
the time when Belgrade starts to change. The cafe culture is over for
the day. Now people make tracks for home and the illusion that life is
normal begins to fade. The trams stop running at eight o'clock. This
is the last one. As the evening wears on, Belgrade becomes a different,
more frightening place. The uncertainties and fears grow stronger. No
one knows what the night will bring. And no one here believes any
longer that, just because they are civilians, they will be safe.

Here's Matt Frei opening a piece on the new – and unwanted –
phenomenon of down-and-outs in Japan:

It's 11.15am. The queue is getting longer – and more nervous. Some
people have been here since dawn. Expectations are rising. They're
afraid that the free bowls of soup will run out. For many, this could be
the only hot meal of the week. Listen to the sound of hunger.

natural sound

No, this is not North Korea. Nor a slum in China. But Japan – and these are the homeless of Osaka.

'Listen to the sound of hunger' is a bold – but very effective – script line. Notice how short the sentences are.

Allan Little at the funeral of Laurent Kabila:

Laurent Kabila bequeaths this continent a legacy of chaos and fear. Fury, not grief, is the public sentiment here. The pent-up rage of years of state brutality. The sins of the father are suddenly, and in a literal sense, visited upon the son. At thirty-one, Joseph Kabila inherits his father's civil war. He finds himself at the heart of a conflict involving at least seven African nations.

Narrative

Sometimes a narrative can give a sense of 'roundness' to a piece – ending it, in a sense, back at the beginning and giving a piece a sense of completeness and closure. Here, John Simpson goes with a Yugoslav family into an air-raid shelter for the night, but starts and ends with a script – and very ordinary pictures – which give a much broader sense of what's going on:

This is a city Tito built. New Belgrade. A dormitory suburb for the post-communist middle class. On a day like this everybody likes to get out into the sun. It's only at night that clear skies mean heavy bombing. Each part of New Belgrade has its air-raid shelter. Tito thought they might be needed against attacks from Russia. Never conceivably from NATO. It's 7.15 and the Glogovats family are getting ready to go to the shelter for the night.

The piece goes on to outline the family's night in the shelter, concluding:

Outside, the bombing was just starting. As has happened for almost every night for nearly four weeks now, the city was hit several times. Emerging this morning, after yet another night of destruction, the Glogovats family had not the slightest idea of what it had all been about. Over New Belgrade, the smoke was billowing up from one of the targets. Tito's vision of a wealthy, pro-Western, non-nationalistic Yugoslavia has gone up with it.

Both the following clips used a strong but simple narrative style to set up the story they were about to tell. John Simpson, again, in Baghdad on 15 January 1991:

Early morning on the day which will one way or another decide the future of Iraq. The boats moved across the Tigris river as usual but there were few passengers. Five shops out of six were shut. Challenge Day, as it was called, was declared a holiday.

Stephen Cape on the Shipman case:

Eighteen months ago in this incident room up to fifty detectives started an inquiry which became Britain's biggest murder investigation. They looked at over 100 suspicious deaths and in this file they amassed evidence against one man – a family GP.

Here's an extract from Nick Witchell's broadcast on an historic day in Northern Ireland:

There have been so many mornings when the news in Belfast has been bleak . . . Northern Ireland has seen false dawns before, so nobody is expecting too much. But down on the peace lines where the wall that divides some Republican and Loyalist areas in Belfast, people were daring to hope that one day their lives and their surroundings might return to normal.

And later:

The fear and distrust is understandable. The roll of horror is long;
Bloody Friday, Bloody Sunday, McGurk's bar, the Abercorn,
Warrenpoint, Ballykelly, Enniskillen, Greysteel, Omagh and so many
more. The agonies of a community which for so many years has been
at war with itself.

**Stephen Sackur on a death by radiation in Kentucky. The report starts
with a crackly tape recording spoken in a southern American accent:**

clip: My name is Joe Harding and I have a story that I think everyone
in America should know about.

script: Joe Harding died nineteen years ago, but his tape-recorded
voice still haunts the Paduka nuclear plant.

**Make a virtue of the chronology of a story. This segment from a Nick
Witchell report uses detailed time references to describe the eclipse
over the English west country:**

Just before ten o'clock, from the airborne camera, first contact, when
the edge of the moon, just visible in the top right-hand corner here,
starts its progress across the face of the sun. Under leaden skies the
watchers are ready. 11.06 the sun is a crescent band of light. The
spectacle is about to begin. 11.07 the Isle of Scilly, the moon is racing
over the Atlantic at high-speed. The light is fading fast. Automatic
lights come on and seabirds make roosting calls. 11.09 St Michael's
Mount off the Cornish coast is in silhouette. At 11.11 on the eleventh
day of the month over Falmouth, the airborne cameras show the last
rays of light as the moon covers the face of the sun.

And so on, concluding:

It had been a day when the heavens had promised much but delivered rather less thanks to the weather. A day when people in Britain had a once in a lifetime encounter with the star which gives this planet life. And its people a sense of their place in the universe.

Here's Fergal Keane, ending a piece about an old lady in a refugee camp in Kosovo:

This camp already has a high proportion of old people. Those who must wonder if they'll ever see home again. For the family of Hanusha Marina it's a very pressing question. She is more than 100 years old. These eyes have seen empires come and go, have seen two world wars. 'I lived through the Nazis,' she told me, 'but I've never known anything as bad at this.' And so remember the name of Hanusha Marina. Record that for a 100 years she lived in her father's land and that she is spending the last days of her life in a refugee camp.

Carolyn Quinn on the demise of Peter Mandelson:

opens: Most ministers hope they'll never be forced to resign. Peter Mandelson's now done it twice.

closes: This morning Peter Mandelson left his home here a minister with all the trappings of office. Tonight his political career is in tatters. The fixer supreme brought down by this latest and most devastating fix of his own making.

And John Simpson again, closing his award-winning piece on the liberation of Kabul from the Taliban. Simpson chose to end his piece on pictures of a little boy flying a home-made kite: 'And there's one thing more – children can fly kites again. Freedom is in the air here. John Simpson, BBC News, Kabul.'

Some tricks of the trade

In his book *Our Masters' Voices*, Max Atkinson looks at the language and body language of the most successful political orators. And two of the most successful techniques – 'lists of three' and 'contrastive pairs' – can be put to very effective use in broadcast news, whether live or packaged.

Contrastive pairs is a simple device most useful, as the name suggests, when there are two sides to contrast: '. . . but while today's developments mark the *beginning* of an era for some staff here, they mark the *end* of the road for those . . .'

Or: 'Nine-Eleven: we all know how it began – but no one knows how it will end.'

Or: 'As the Stock Market closed, the heavens opened.' (Over pictures of pouring rain in the City.)

Three-part lists take advantage of the fact that a list of three has a sense of completeness to the ear: '. . . the intention is to offer teachers more support in the classroom, improve their morale and draw more new recruits into the profession.'

Or: 'After the silence, in St Paul's, 3,000 white rose petals were dropped from the Whispering Gallery, perhaps the most poignant part of today's service. Petals to represent 3,000 lives lost on 11 September. 3,000 human beings murdered. 3,000 families destroyed.'

Or: 'How many tankers out of how many depots into how many petrol stations?'

In another context: '. . . he seemed calm and controlled but not contrite. He clearly doesn't see the need to say sorry.'

This 'list of three' – calm, controlled, contrite – uses another device which can work well: alliteration. You should not overuse any of these devices, but they can all make your scripts and your live broadcasting more effective.

Keep it tight and concise

Vigorous writing is concise. A sentence should contain no unnecessary words, a paragraph no unnecessary sentences, for the same reason that a drawing should have no unnecessary lines and a machine no unnecessary parts. This requires not that the writer makes all his sentences short, or that he avoid all detail and treat his subjects only in outline, but that every word tell.
William Strunk and E B White, *The Elements of Style*

The fewer the words that can be made to convey an idea, the clearer and more forceful the idea. David Lambuth, *The Golden Book on Writing*

Can you defend every word in your script? You should be able to. You must make every sentence count and every word count. You should understand the power of short sentences. Some of the most effective scripts are those with least words – short sentences and a very high proportion of natural sound.

Look back through the examples of scripts used above and you will see they all have at least one thing in common: very short sentences. Here, Jeremy Bowen begins a piece about a visit to an elderly Serb in Kosovo – notice the length of the sentences:

natural sound – knock on door

The flat stank of urine and decay. Something was very badly wrong. She said her name.

natural sound – she says her name

She is seventy years old and a Serb in a place where Serbs are no longer welcome. She was weak and confused. Her front door had been kicked in, the neighbours said by Albanian fighters from the KLA. Her photo album was open. The family in better times. A young Serb paramilitary, perhaps a grandson with a machine gun. Her husband in the Yugoslav army in the Second World War. She kept looking back.

Then we realized the decomposing body of her husband was in there with her. He'd been dead for six days.

Here's Brian Barron in the Philippines at the fall of Marcos:

As revolutions go this had its fair share of bullets. A climax in the night outside Mr Marcos' sanctuary – Malacanang. The name itself symbolizing one of the cruellest, most corrupt regimes of modern Asia. Tonight the citadel fell. His opponents scrambled over the gates. Were the bullets aimed at people or into the air? Nobody knew.

But being concise doesn't mean to say you should leave out all detail. Nor should you assume you can only say something once and hope the viewer understands. A small amount of deliberate redundancy in ideas is sometimes helpful. In other words, repeating a certain key detail or fact in a slightly different way can help the viewer absorb the information.

But if you're trying to include too much information you won't be able to write short, declarative sentences, which are essential in television news. Always try to avoid subordinate clauses and overlong sentences. Try not to go over twenty words. Long sentences are not only harder to understand, they're harder for you to deliver.

At the same time you should vary sentence length and structure – if all your sentences are the same length and of a similar structure the story will sound boring. But never write sentences that are too long. The viewer must find each sentence clear and interesting. The longer the sentence, the less likely it is that you'll achieve either. Consider this opening sentence to a piece broadcast by the BBC, built around a speech by the Prime Minister:

script: Determined to re-brand New Labour as the party of business and enterprise, the Prime Minister today chose an audience of venture capitalists to describe the Tory right and the Labour left as the jealous snobs who resented new people turning ideas into big money.

clip (Prime Minister): I want this Government therefore to be the champion of entrepreneurs . . .

Just one sentence, containing forty-four words, starting on a subordinate clause – and assuming the audience knows what venture capitalists are. There are many ways of rephrasing it, but it could have been this:

script: Another re-branding for New Labour. This time as the party of business and enterprise. These businessmen heard the Prime Minister lay into both Tory right and Labour left. Jealous snobs, he called them, who resented new people turning ideas into big money. His vision?

clip (Prime Minister): I want this Government . . .

Same number of words, five sentences, flow and a more dynamic narrative.

When Strunk and White wrote their seminal *Elements of Style*, advising writers that 'a sentence should contain no unnecessary words,' they probably did not envisage the emergence of what the BBC presenter Michael Buerk calls 'verb murder'.

Today in Washington. Around the country. Television reporters. Talking like this. Short staccato bursts. Fragments not sentences. Dropping most verbs. Everything present tense.

So began a special report by the American NewsHour Media Unit looking at what it called the vanishing verb. Verb-less sentences elicit strong emotions. Some of the most experienced correspondents use some sentences without verbs, partly in trying to make great phrases, sometimes to avoid smothering the pictures and often because it's conversational. Sometimes it helps the storytelling: 'Then the Irishman . . . brooding . . . brilliant . . . back to form.'

But beware. Television uses the spoken word, not the written one, so it's fine to vary the rules occasionally, but don't drift into the habit of using verb-less sentences just for the sake of it. Do it only in moderation, not just because it's grammatically incorrect, but because it becomes over-stylized if used too often. Make sure you know when you're doing it and why you're doing it.

Telling details

Good storytelling often requires some small details to be picked up and pointed out: a smile, a couple holding hands, a half eaten meal, a gun in a handbag, a briefcase on a railway line after a train crash. With good writing – storytelling – small details can paint a big picture.

For instance, instead of beginning with 'The president arrived in Cardiff', you might say 'At twenty-three minutes past three a train left Paddington bound for Cardiff. On board was . . .' This heightens the sense of a story about to unfold. Here's John Simpson on the day Kabul was liberated from the Taliban: 'It was 7.53 local time. Kabul was a free city after five years of perhaps the most extreme regime anywhere on earth.'

Here, Charles Wheeler uses a small detail to explain an abduction in post-war Kuwait when none of the witnesses will appear on camera: 'Jihad's story begins with a car. A light blue Toyota registration number 3902. He set off with three friends in search of petrol when the car was stopped by armed men and, according to neighbours who watched from the balcony, all four were taken away.'

John Simpson in Zimbabwe points out what farmers were eating: 'The Mvurwi club, the centre of the white community's social life, was almost empty. Even the bar was deserted, although it was lunchtime. In the dining room, three members were eating their beef curry.'

Gavin Hewitt, on the life of Dr Harold Shipman, picks out a detail from the marriage certificate: 'An ambitious Shipman went on to study medicine, but there was a complication. A seventeen-year-old girl called Primrose, whom he had recently met, was pregnant. They married quietly, out of town. The certificate describes her as a window dresser.'

Matt Frei, on suicides induced by the failing economy in South Korea, spots something written on the pavement of a bridge in Seoul: 'The police have tried to prevent people scaling the metal arches for extra height and a more certain death, with grease. Etched in the grease is the determination of the desperate. The message on the pavement below simply reads "JUMP".'

These are all examples of using small details to 'tell a story'.

Write the way you talk (or should talk)

'Needing some shopping, I'm going to the supermarket. Bye.' If you speak like that you have a problem. So why do correspondents write clauses like that in their scripts? Write the way you talk in polite conversation – and if it doesn't sound like the way you'd say it, rewrite it.

A common fault among correspondents is starting pieces with long subordinate clauses. This sentence started a piece about the Rapid Reaction Force: 'With plans agreed for a new European rapid reaction force, which can now call on 12,500 British troops and half the Royal Navy for operations alongside European armies, Britain's political leaders have gone into battle.'

Sentences like this are unnatural, hard to deliver and leave the correspondent out of breath by the time they come to the active part of the sentence. Write as if you were telling a friend or just one viewer. When you try telling the same story to one person you become more conversational and your language becomes simpler and more direct.

The key, of course, is to read your script aloud and if it sounds like writing, rewrite it. When laying your script on tape try not to read it direct from the screen or page. Try memorizing your script, then standing up and delivering it. This will help your delivery sound more natural. You must be happy with how it *sounds*, not how it looks on the page or screen (see the section on vocal delivery on page 143).

Use clear, direct language

Talk to be understood by the truck driver while not insulting the professor's intelligence. Ed Murrow

Obscurity in writing is commonly a proof of darkness in the mind.
John Wilkins

It's crucial to develop the confidence, competence – and occasionally courage – to write simply. And bear in mind that simple means easy to understand, not simplistic. Contorted sentences are impossible to follow – and difficult to deliver. Use the fewest words possible and the simplest constructions. And keep rewriting. Reread, rethink, rewrite. And then rewrite again. And each time *read your script out loud*. When you think it's finished try to get a second opinion on your script – preferably from a programme editor but, ultimately, from anybody. A second pair of eyes will help determine whether the audience at home will understand what you're trying to say.

Avoid sesquipedalianism (that's using big words to you and me). Always remember that you're writing for a diverse audience from across the whole social spectrum. By all means use words that are not universally known, but make sure the context is clear. Do not allow the viewer's ability to make sense of what you're saying depend on understanding the definition of an obscure word.

'The Japanese economy is *moribund*.' As a journalist, you should know what that means. But many viewers do not. 'Most schools in the borough are in a *parlous* state.' 'The Chancellor, accused of *profligacy*.' Again, there are many simpler – and better – alternatives.

Here's a sentence from a piece previewing the Conservative Party leader's conference speech: 'The Tory leader will talk about decentralizing decisions away from Whitehall and encouraging diversity to allow local solutions to different problems.' Ugh. Here's another from the Westminster village: 'The Government is hypersensitive to accusations that it tries to discredit those who dare disagree with it.' This is 'insider' language and leaves the viewers on the outside, excluded. In a live two-way, one correspondent gave this answer: 'His aides say the President is going to adopt a *contrition strategy*.' A *what*? Far better to say: 'He's going to say sorry and he's going to say sorry again and he's going to keep saying sorry.'

Listeners who are baffled by a word in a news bulletin are unlikely to reach for a dictionary. And if they do they won't be listening to anything you're reporting. If *you* have to look it up in a dictionary you definitely shouldn't use it. Keep to one important thought or idea per sentence and use everyday, simple and informal language. A word you're unlikely to hear in spoken English is rarely appropriate for broadcast.

What does that mean? Jargon and all that

Think straight and then you can write straight. William Safire

Remember Churchill's reply to an Admiralty request about building the floating piers for the invasion of Normandy:
Q: *'Permission is hereby urgently requested for immediate implementation of your directive.'*
A: *'Implement me no directives – ever! If you mean should you build the piers, build them! Carry on!'*
Alistair Cooke, Presenter of Radio 4's *Letter from America*

In as long as it takes to say or wonder, 'What does that mean?' you've lost your viewer – or the viewer's lost your story. One and half seconds to lose a viewer.

Always avoid jargon. Or if you absolutely have to use it – translate it. Jargon may provide the ideal short cut you need: qualifying the figures you've just quoted with the term *per capita* may be what you needed. But it will never be what your viewer needs. An Asian culture may be

Confucian to a correspondent standing in the middle of it – but it'll be *confusing* to viewers sitting in their living rooms at home if it's not set in context. You may be an expert on *venture capitalists* but your viewers are not, so don't assume they know what they are – they may never have heard of them before.

DROVUA

Have you heard about the dispute between MAFF and the NFU over the DTI licences? It happened on the same day CPS officials met ACPO leaders. The morning after the JLA, the HVO and the KLA all got together in Pristina.

DROVUA. You know what that means, don't you? Sorry, I *assumed* you did. It means: Don't Rely On Viewers Understanding Acronyms.

Dawn revealed the full extent of the cliché . . .

Some expressions become so overused and so worn that they lose all the power and meaning they might once have had – they become clichés. Clichés do not make dull writing any better and they often devalue the significance of important stories by making them sound trite.

Miracle cures are rarely miraculous – they are the result of years of research. To say a group of council residents has *declared war* on the council devalues the notion of a real war being declared. A *brutal murder* implies that murders might sometimes be kind or considerate.

Some stories can practically write themselves in clichés. But clichés are for writers who are not creative enough to avoid them. Use your own words and keep those words simple and direct. You don't have to litter your writing with expressions. The most direct writing can often be the most powerful. The most powerful pictures require the fewest words. There is sometimes a fine line between powerful writing and clichés (indeed some of your best writing may yet become clichés!). But

reporters must get beyond reporting people 'trying to rebuild the fragments of their shattered lives'.

And 'puns' too often sound like trainee school clichés. A duck in the
picture doesn't give you licence to start talking about people *ducking
issues* any more than a minister in a classroom makes it inevitable you
should say, 'It was back to school today for . . .' They work far better
on paper than on air. If in doubt, don't.

There are many style guides with exhaustive lists of clichés, but
really a cliché is any expression or combination of words that have been
used too much. So can you avoid them? *That remains to be seen.* You
should make a *last ditch effort* to avoid saying the *writing's on the wall.*
But *in the final analysis, one thing's for sure – only time will tell.* So be
careful, or your viewers will leave in an *exodus of biblical proportions.*

'You', 'us' and 'we'

If you were to mention a viewer by name, that viewer would swing
round and pay attention at once. Well, you can't do that, so another
useful tool is to personalize the way you write to the point where that
viewer thinks you're talking to them anyway.

Compare this: 'The Bank of England today cut interest rates by half
of 1 per cent to 7.5 per cent' with this: 'Good news if you have a
mortgage – bad news if you rely on savings for your income. The Bank
of . . .' It's pretty obvious which of these scripts talks to the viewer and
which talks about a remote process in the City of London.

Obviously, it is not our job to portray everything in terms of good
news and bad news. If you use 'you' or 'we', it has to apply to the
majority of the audience and you have to be confident that viewers will
feel you're talking to them. You mustn't force it – it must sound natural
– but it is a way of involving the audience and making them feel an
issue has a direct bearing on them and is not just a remote political
issue or process.

So think about whether it may be appropriate to personalize your script to help include the viewer. If you're using the phrase 'ordinary people' maybe 'you' or 'you and I' would be better. Here's Mark Mardell, in a piece to camera, on the proposed introduction of ID cards:

If you're anything like me, you'll carry around a wallet that's already stuffed with ID cards. Here we go [takes a batch of cards from his wallet] – library card, rather tatty driving licence, one to get me into work, press card . . . And now the government's suggesting we need a new, official card that'll carry lots of information. And there are a number of ideas about how it would look.

Jenny Scott, on a government report into savings plans:

We're not saving enough for a rainy day. We're not even saving enough for a sunny day. Partly because there never seems to be enough money left over at the end of the month and partly because of the dazzling array of savings products on offer. Today's report is designed to simplify things. And, boy, does the system need it.

And use your script to ask questions on the viewers' behalf: 'So exactly how important is this?', 'What does it mean to someone waiting for an operation?', 'So, should anyone in Britain be worried about this?' Use words like 'imagine' to draw the viewer in and help you write a more conversational script, which in turn will make it more accessible.

Humour

Is there ever a role for humour in television news? Well, yes, up to a point. But for humour think 'lightness of touch', think 'wit', think 'irony' – but don't think 'jokes' and don't think 'puns'. Lightness of touch is apparent in all the best scriptwriters – it's crucial. It can enliven difficult subjects or pieces with few engaging pictures.

Humour can occasionally help to avoid taking something absolutely at face value – but even then it works through lightness of touch, not by cracking jokes or being frivolous. And don't allow lightness of touch to be mistaken for cynicism. Here's Andrew Marr following Liberal leader Charles Kennedy – with a lightness of touch – at his party conference:

script: Charles Kennedy defies the ordinary rules of leadership. He moves sedately and he doesn't take himself too seriously. In the entrails of the conference centre, as the scrum moves towards the hall, a bemused cameraman cries out:

sound – cameraman: Where are we going?

clip (Charles Kennedy): This is a very good question. It's when people say that at the end of the leader's speech that I get really worried.

script: No chance of that.

It might be wrong to say *never* use puns or jokes, but beware – a news bulletin is rarely the best place to demonstrate your wit. Much of what's meant to be funny turns out to be cumbersome, clunky and hard work for the viewer. Only use humour when the material or story is absolutely appropriate. And always make sure the programme editor knows what you're doing. Too much humour in a programme can hit the wrong tone and make the bulletin feel lightweight and lacking in authority.

If in doubt, don't try to be funny. If you're really good at humour, you should probably be on the stage.

Numbers

When you consider that tripling something is an increase of 200 per cent not 300 per cent and that 'three times greater than' is the same as 'four times as great as' it's easy to see that numbers can catch you out.

And if you're struggling to work it through, imagine what it will be like for the viewer who'll have just one chance to hear it.

So keep the use of numbers to a minimum. They're easy for a reporter to get wrong and hard for a viewer to take in. The audience cannot memorize or process figures they only hear once. They can go back over them in a newspaper, but not in a broadcast. And many numbers, while interesting, are not always necessary or essential.

Where you can, try to use words instead of numbers. Try to make the numbers real – last year, next year or ten years ago instead of the date. Sometimes it will be better to say the equivalent of so many pounds for every person in the UK instead of so many billion pounds.

Fractions are easier to understand than decimals and percentages, so where you don't have to be exact, phrases like two out of three are better than 65 per cent, and around a third is better than 35 per cent.

And try to round numbers off. Quoting exact numbers isn't much use if the viewer can't take them in. 'Less than half' is easier than thirty-six first time, sixteen the second. Almost five hundred is easier than 497.

If the exact numbers are crucial to the story then use them. But make sure your figures add up. Don't ask the viewers to do any calculations – they can't do that and watch your report. Get someone else to check your numbers. And mistrust any calculation involving percentages.

Television news is not about providing all the facts – or numbers. It provides a sketch or an impression. So it is better to give one illustrative fact or number than a lot, no matter how interesting they may seem at the time.

Writing to graphics

If you want to set the context for a story or you have a particularly complex issue to explain, you may want to use graphics. But you should only use graphics when you are sure they will demonstrate what you want to say better than moving pictures would. The audience is not interested in wading through a sea of charts and graphs unless they are clear and relevant. Graphics are not an excuse for conveying countless numbers and facts.

The key to making any graphic work is for the graphic to be clear and for you to co-ordinate your script with the graphic – either in the timing of any moves if it involves movement or graphs or, if you are using numbers or quoting someone directly, using the same words or numbers in your script as appear on the screen. Not vaguely the same. Not almost the same. *Exactly the same*.

Although you're unlikely to be designing the graphic yourself, try to make sure the screen is not crammed full with too much information. Be careful with graphs – trying to absorb a combination of background image, graph indices and movements with additional numbers in a short space of time can be very difficult. If a graphic changes or moves you should try to keep the movements evenly spaced. If there's a choice, go for more pages with less information on each page, again, evenly paced.

You must try to find a balance between giving the viewer time to absorb complex information and not leaving the screen still for so long that the viewer loses interest. The graphic and the script have to be clear and comprehensible there and then – the viewer cannot go back and read it again.

Any graphic should be a seamless part of the story and not an 'interruption'. You should pause briefly at the end of the graphic to let the viewer take in information before making the transition to the next sequence, making sure your writing allows the graphic to 'hold hands' with the new sequence of pictures.

Keep your delivery conversational. Keep your language clear. Keep your script tight. Bear in mind the points in the section above about numbers. Don't let your script stray from the graphic. Try to 'pace' changes in the graphic at even spaces.

2.3 **context and understanding**

One should not aim at being possible to understand,
but at being impossible to misunderstand.

Quintillian

What would be nice is if after one of those financial guys,
someone turned round and said, 'What he actually meant
was' . . .

BBC viewer in focus group

The whole problem with news on television comes down
to this: all the words uttered in an hour of news coverage
could be printed on one page of a newspaper. And the
world cannot be understood in one page.

Neil Postman

The problem for television news is that it is at once both an immensely powerful medium and yet an inadequate way of explaining complicated issues in a comprehensive way. Academics, sociologists and newspaper columnists the world over have criticized the shortcomings of television news for years, but they have rarely – if ever – come up with realistic, practical alternatives.

If you want to pursue a serious news agenda then you will be reporting plenty of stories which will be complicated, difficult to explain and very often from faraway lands. But remember why you exist: to help your audience understand. Your audience – not yourself, not your colleagues, not your contacts, but your viewers and listeners. So approach it from their point of view. Be on their side.

A word about the audience . . .

Much of radio and pretty much all newspapers have a target audience, and one which they know well. The *Sun*, the *Daily Mail* and the *Financial Times* for instance will each have a clear idea of who their audience is and how much they can or cannot take for granted about what their audience knows.

But most television news is broadcast to a universal audience. This means you are reporting the world's events to people who read the *Sun*, to people who read the *Financial Times* and to everyone in between and either side. The trick, as one of America's greatest broadcast journalists, Ed Murrow, said, is to 'talk to be understood by the truck driver while not insulting the professor's intelligence.' But this is easier said than done.

Because of their background, the natural tendency of most correspondents is to err on the side of the professor. Too far that way and the audience will tell you they just don't understand. Too far the other way and you will be accused of being simplistic and 'dumbing down'. The truth is that broadcasters know far more than they have ever done about what audiences think of their news coverage. And what audiences think is not what broadcasters always want to hear.

Most broadcast journalists don't get to go to focus groups – and that's a shame. To watch and hear real, ordinary people looking at news programmes is a salutary experience, and one which more journalists should witness. The interesting – and often depressing – thing about these encounters with the real world is that no matter what the subject and no matter what the demographic make-up of the group, the results are always broadly the same: 'make it easier to understand, make it simpler, break it down, give us some more history and background'. And, contradicting this last request, 'don't put so much in each report'.

Should we base everything we do on focus groups? Absolutely not. Should we ignore them altogether? Absolutely not. The danger of relying too heavily on focus groups is that you will slowly be dragged down the hill to the lowest common denominator in your story selection, your language and every other aspect of your reporting. Your audience will not respect you for that. There is a difference between what an audience wants to know and what it needs to know.

But having said that, every journalist should go to at least one focus group in their career. For one thing, it is encouraging to see that, by and large, people really *want* to understand. But it's also good to be reminded not just that 'real' people don't follow news the way you do – you shouldn't need reminding of that – but the *extent* to which your audience doesn't follow news the way you do. Seeing this first hand will make you go back and work that bit harder to engage your viewers and really help them understand.

New readers start here . . .

These two quotes, both from focus groups about television news, perfectly reflect one of the central themes which always emerge:

'I am almost embarrassed to say it sometimes, but there are things in the news that I don't understand and I think these news reports assume that you have all this background knowledge and historical knowledge of what went on before.'

'You would understand that report more if you had watched a documentary for an hour on it beforehand.'

The dilemma is one which journalists grapple with every day: how much background, how much history, how much context does a viewer need to make sense of the events you are trying to tell them about? And how much can you *assume* the viewer knows?

On a conventional news bulletin, the most precious commodity is time. But let's imagine there's a story about the Kashmir conflict between Pakistan and India and you have two minutes and fifteen seconds to tell it – 135 seconds in total. What proportion of that 135 seconds should be used to give the viewer some historical perspective, some background knowledge and some context to help them 'ground' the story? The more of that time that's taken up with the history and context, the less time there is for the story of the day. Yet unless we provide a substantial amount of that background, viewers say they don't have enough context to understand the story in the first place.

And many stories, like Kashmir, the Middle East conflict and Northern Ireland, run on over many years. So should we repeat the same background information every time we do a story? Or once a week? Or once a month?

We should ask ourselves frequently how we arrived at this particular juncture in a story. On long-running stories we sometimes make the mistake of covering the latest twist when the viewer hasn't reached first base. Viewers may not have enough context or background to understand the latest twist, like going to see a play and arriving during the last act. Audience research shows a significant desire for pieces which 'pause up' and provide a sense of 'new readers start here'.

Never assume anything

The single most common theme in every bit of audience research done for television news is that journalists assume viewers know far more about stories than they actually do. They make assumptions, they use jargon – they assume the viewer has read and seen as much about the story as they have. And in doing so they disengage the viewer.

It would be wrong to underestimate the intelligence of your viewers, but equally you shouldn't overestimate what any viewer knows about the background to a story. News is your life and work – most people don't follow it the way you do. It is crucial to ask yourself constantly how much you are assuming the viewer already knows about what you are telling them.

Remember that, particularly if you are a specialist, you are intimately involved in your area on a daily basis. Sometimes correspondents have a tendency, especially in complicated stories, to fill in story gaps in their minds with the information they know – clearly something the audience can't do. If you are a specialist, it's important you understand the assumptions you are most likely to make in your area and that you work on ways of clearly and simply explaining the more complicated themes and issues that come up regularly in your brief. Talk them through with non-specialists (and preferably non-journalists) to see what works best.

Are you *assuming* the viewer understands what economic growth is or what the relationship between the pound and the balance of payments is? Are you starting from the point of *assuming* the viewer understands why Malaysia is important to Britain? Do you *assume* that because you explained what the Public Private Partnership is last night you can call it the PPP for ever more? If you are making these kind of assumptions, the chances are you are confusing the viewer. How you get round these assumptions depends on the type of story you are doing, how the editor sees the piece, the cue or the role of any graphics.

One piece about some diplomatic progress in the Middle East conflict contained, without any context or explanation, these phrases: 'pre-1948', 'the Oslo agreement', 'the settlements', 'pre-67 borders' and 'unrest in the refugee camps'. A better informed world is a better world. But don't confuse information with understanding. On a running story which you're reporting night after night it's easy to begin to assume that the audience has a certain amount of background on a story. But research shows that viewers don't have as much loyalty to news programmes as we think, so they're not watching night after night.

If you find explaining a reference time-consuming and tedious, you should ask yourself if you really need the reference in the first place. Often you will, but some technical terms and names do nothing to help the viewer understand the essence of your story.

And having achieved clarity in your own script, don't fall into the trap of choosing interview clips which you understand because of your own specialist knowledge but that will leave the audience wondering what your interviewee was talking about. This clip was used in a piece about the Euro without any context whatsoever: 'The principles that were set out in October 1997 seemed to the investors I talked to to be sensible. Of course there are advantages in denominating your costs and revenues in the same currency across a vast market.'

What 'principles'?

Remember: a television package is not a vehicle for you to unload all your specialist knowledge, but rather a way of using your specialist knowledge to explain something complicated with clarity and simplicity.

The simple rule is: never assume anything.

Making connections: 'What does this mean to me?'

Ask yourself this: why should viewers care about this story? Much of the work a journalist does involves interpreting public policy or big business developments in one form or another. Yet too often we report these developments as though they were remote from people's daily lives and concerns.

Any specialist will be able to tell you what has happened and why it happened. But the key thing is understanding the impact of what's happened and being able to communicate it clearly to the audience. The question most often asked by the audience is: 'Tell me why it matters – how will it affect me?'

For example: the government has announced the largest review of state pensions since they were established. Why? Essentially, because people are living longer and the state can no longer afford it. The natural question for the viewer to ask is: 'What does this mean to me?'

It may not be possible to tell every single viewer what it means to them, so give some examples. And if the impact is unclear then say so, and then the viewer knows what you know. Where there is a connection we absolutely should make it. If you are reporting economic turmoil in Russia or South America, the logical question which flows for the audience is 'will this affect me?' and you should always attempt to answer that. That's your job – making sense of it for the viewer; making connections.

Are viewers interested in the developing world? If you ask them as baldly as that the vast majority will say no. But consider this: Europe is building walls (literally) along its borders to keep out the ever increasing number of illegal immigrants and asylum seekers trying to enter from developing countries. And UN forecasts about population growth predict that by the year 2050, 90 per cent of the world's people will live in the developing world. These people will continue to leave their home countries in ever increasing numbers – with less and less regard for the consequences and their own lives – unless conditions in their own countries improve. So the plight of developing countries has a direct impact on our own. There: connection made.

Try to make your stories relevant to the viewers. Tell them why they should care. It's hard work, but it's what the best journalists do.

'Tell me why it matters'

If you can't tell the viewers why it has a direct impact on them then tell them why it matters. Not everything can, or should, be made directly relevant to our specific audience. It would be patronizing, and audiences can understand that some stories or issues can be hugely important without having a direct bearing on them. This is particularly true of some foreign coverage. But even when it has no direct bearing we should still make every effort to explain why we are covering a story and why we think it is important. Otherwise we risk confusing the audience about why we cover certain stories over others.

For example, when reporting from Indonesia, if we say it has more than 13,000 islands, the fourth largest population in the world and it's wider than the Atlantic ocean, the sheer scale gives you a sense of why it's important. Add to that the UK's economic and trading relationship and the viewer becomes clearer about why it matters. Here's Matt Frei, for example, in a piece about tension between Taiwan and China, explaining 'why it matters':

One reason why Taiwan can afford to be so confident are these – silicon wafers. No computer can function without them. Taiwan produces over two-thirds of the world's entire supply and if these factories had to stop working, the global computer industry would grind to a halt. What happens here matters to the rest of the world.

Here's Emily Buchanan on the growth of Buddhism in the UK and 'why it matters':

It's difficult to count the exact number of Buddhists in the UK. Some estimate there are tens of thousands, but what is certain is that Buddhist influence is growing, reaching places like this – a maximum security prison holding some of the country's most dangerous criminals.

Too many stories – small changes in policy or a dispute between two foreign countries, for example – appear to be of little significance. So always ask yourself whether the viewers will be clear about why your story matters. It will make a huge difference to their understanding. If you can't answer it you might begin to wonder why you are doing the story in the first place.

Demystifying

Correspondents must demystify subjects which may appear complicated or dense. And they must provide a background to explain subjects not widely understood because of their technical content or cultural context. Good writing will shine a light on difficult issues and help the viewer to understand them. Here's Denis Murray on the Drumcree parade in Northern Ireland, over pictures of Orange marchers:

The issue in some ways is about nothing. Men in seventeenth century regalia and a meaningless stretch of road. And yet it's about everything. To Orangemen, the right to celebrate their Protestant culture and heritage in their own country. And to Catholic residents the right to say no to sectarian triumphalism. In short, it's about which community is winning.

Here Andrew Marr sparsely and simply sets out the context of a committee meeting at a Labour Party Conference. He explains the players and the story of what could be a dry, in-house political battle:

An old-style Labour conference battle. The government wants to push its surplus national insurance billions to poor and middle income pensioners. But pension campaigners, led by the unions, want to restore the link with earnings giving the pensioners the increase as a right. All day the minister pleaded, 'Wait to see the rises we'll announce in just a few weeks' time. Trust us.' All day long the unions said, 'We don't.'

Here is David Shukman explaining what the updated Star Wars defence programme is meant to do and why it has become an issue once again; a brief but succinct lesson in military technology and geo-politics:

The Pentagon has long dreamt of deploying a missile shield. Ronald Reagan first conjured up the vision of a Star Wars defence. In this scheme the interceptor manoeuvres itself into the path of the enemy missile. Just colliding with it is enough to destroy it . . .

new sequence: US missile centre

Intelligence indicates that North Korea will have long-range missiles in five years' time, so the military feel deeply vulnerable and both major parties in America agree that a defence shield is now needed. When this place was built, the threat was from the old Soviet Union, which was hostile but at least predictable. Now the threat is from so-called rogue nations which, by definition, are completely unpredictable.

Stereotypes

One of the worst sins in journalism is to report to a preconceived formula with a preconceived notion of the story you are covering. Regardless of what you see before your eyes, you make the story fit your – or your editor's – ready-made narrative. Don't. These quotes from Chapter One about what makes a good journalist are worth repeating here:

Good journalists overturn stereotypes; bad ones reinforce them.

They should never take things for granted, or assume that what was accurate once remains accurate.

Approach stories with an open mind.

Too often we get journalism which recognizes no difference between countries, regions and peoples.

The BBC correspondent Allan Little tells the story of following a man in Rwanda who had lost his family and all his belongings and was trying to start life anew. Little said that many people had remembered and remarked on the story when he returned to London. The reason? Little had made the point that the man was an accountant and this had somehow surprised people. The audience's stereotypical view of a Rwandan was not that of a person with a normal job. A stereotype had been overturned, and the viewers were more engaged because of it.

Similarly, a recent report from the Gaza Strip showed a Palestinian girl at home having her piano lesson. The stereotypical view of a Palestinian is of a teenage boy throwing stones. Again, viewers were more engaged because this was something nearer their own reality. Again, a stereotype was overturned.

When viewers are asked what they think of when asked about the developing world, they say, 'Famine, starving babies, earthquakes, wars, victims'. Here's George Alagiah – overturning stereotypes – in Mali:

Every day the Sahara creeps further south, devouring as much as a mile in the space of a year. For those who live here in one of the harshest environments anywhere, mere survival takes ingenuity and commitment – qualities all too often forgotten in our tendency to portray Africa in its worst moments.

Avoiding stereotypes is sometimes made harder because of working with pictures, and writing against the expected narrative can make storytelling more difficult. But you must not apply the same template to every story. And remember this: if you are surprised by something you see – despite the indifference of hardened hacks who feel they've seen it all before – the chances are the audience will be surprised as well. Don't follow the formula – trust your instincts.

'It's all so depressing'

Try not to present every issue as an insoluble problem. Where there are solutions we should allude to them more often. And you should use your specialist expertise occasionally to look abroad or elsewhere to see how others have tackled a similar problem.

This is not a call for more good news and it doesn't mean you should be advocating solutions. But nor should you encourage feelings of helplessness and apathy by leaving the viewer feeling that nothing can ever be done to resolve an issue. One of the most common questions asked by audiences is 'How can I help? What can I do to make a difference?'

'Whatever happened to . . . ?'

Television news is like a lightning flash. It makes a loud noise, lights up everything around it, leaves everything else in darkness and then suddenly is gone. Hodding Carter, former US State Department spokeman

The quote above perfectly reflects a common criticism of television news – that broadcasters descend on a story, lead their bulletins for a week with dramatic coverage, then pull out lock, stock and barrel leaving the viewer wondering what happened. Everything then nothing. The circus moves on. There is a solution: to make sure we revisit those stories which hit the headlines and find out what happened. There is a huge demand from viewers to do this. So think about the stories in your patch that you have covered – some of them will deserve another visit, to find out what happened and whether and how the situation was resolved or moved on.

Specialist reporting

Specialist reporting is not aimed at – and almost never reaches – specialist audiences. Its purpose should be to engage the general audience with specialist insight. BBC Programme Strategy Review

Simplicity and clarity are nowhere more appropriate than with specialist reporting. Specialists are ten a penny. Good broadcasters are a rarer breed. To be a specialist *and* a good broadcaster is altogether more challenging. But at his or her best, a specialist correspondent is like a trusted guide taking viewers through a maze of complications and telling them 'what it means' in clear and simple terms.

It is only through having such depth of understanding that we can bring such clarity to making sense of it. The very best specialist correspondents can bridge that often huge gap between their own very detailed understanding of an area and explaining simply how it will affect the daily lives of their viewers – why it matters. Yet too often viewers can end up feeling like an elderly patient emerging from the doctor – they get the gist, but ask them what the doctor said and they're not quite sure.

Why? Television can be a very frustrating experience for specialist correspondents. There is sometimes a tension between the medium's need for simplicity and what is often a desire on the part of the specialist to unburden all that expertise. The task for a specialist can be difficult. He or she must work to all the basic guidelines set out in this book about television journalism and yet still bring an insight to stories that would not be available were a general reporter to do them.

Whose agenda? Interpreting your specialist brief

We must never shy away from covering certain stories because they are complicated, seemingly remote and hard to explain with clarity. It's crucial that any serious journalistic organization properly reflects the processes that drive the society and the world it operates in. That's part of what public service broadcasting – and serious journalism – is all about.

But never lose sight of what your specialist area means to your audience. If you only reflect stories through government policy or big business developments you risk being seen as remote and elitist. Take health, for instance. What does 'health' mean? If you consult a dictionary you're likely to find words such as well-being, physical condition, fitness, healthiness, vigour, strength. And it's likely that your audience will interpret health in this way as well. So bear this in mind – offer a broad range of stories. And always try to relate policies and processes to real people.

Beware thinking (or worse, telling a programme editor), 'It was in the *Lancet* last month so it's not a story.' The public at large do not read many specialist journals and don't follow the nuances of particular issues very closely. Don't get so specialist that you can't see what is of general interest.

Don't automatically opt for the 'see-saw' package – a sound bite in favour, a sound bite against and a piece to camera. You are obliged to be impartial in your approach, but a simplistic balance is not always good television journalism.

2.4 packaging

Always script the pictures

One simple rule will dramatically improve your television packaging: never use a shot – any shot – as 'wallpaper'. Never just write across pictures as though they weren't there, leaving the viewer wondering what they are looking at. Never, ever.

The words covering any new sequence of pictures must relate to or complement the pictures the viewer is seeing. Don't assume the viewers will understand what they're seeing. Relate the words to the pictures at or very near the beginning of every new sequence, preferably in the first sentence. If you don't, the viewer will begin to lose the thread.

There are occasions when you can use the first few words to make a point. For instance, over a sequence of pictures of a bread queue: 'NATO now controls the basics of life here. Bread queues are commonplace because the baking depends on electricity.' But if you do this, keep it concise and relate the words explicitly to the pictures as soon as possible.

Having scripted the start of the sequence, you can't move the script so far away that the words and pictures fight each other – but if you start each sequence together and return at the beginning of each new sequence you'll have plenty of room to develop your script. Here's a very simple example from Ben Brown who, with no new pictures to work with, used some library footage from the Gulf War. The second sentence scripts the pictures:

Every single member of the British armed forces must be fit enough to fight on the front line, according to Sir Charles Guthrie. *As fit as these soldiers in the Gulf, for example.* Sir Charles believes that allowing the disabled to join up could threaten Britain's very ability to wage war.

Your words should complement the pictures. Your script shouldn't work against them and clash with what the viewers can see, but then again neither should you tell the viewers what they can clearly see for themselves. In other words, you must develop the knack – as the best correspondents do – of saying what you want to say, and scripting the pictures at the same time. Always start from the point of scripting the beginning of each sequence of pictures.

This applies to library pictures too. Too often correspondents script library material as though it were less important (and therefore ideal 'wallpaper') than their precious on-the-day pictures. To the viewer they are all just pictures, and they all need proper scripting.

Don't always describe what you can see. Phrases like 'one of these', 'and this is the reason' or 'and here's why' will draw viewers in more than simply naming what they can see for themselves. Even if the only pictures you have are the exteriors of a building, you must still script the pictures, and you can still draw the viewer in: 'It was here, last Christmas, that first meeting took place . . .'

Give the viewer time to absorb very powerful images – don't just write across them. But at the same time never leave strong or powerful images unexplained, or viewers will lose the plot wondering what it was they were looking at (while you talk about something else). Always remember, in the right circumstances, what can really move your viewer most is not your script, but strong natural sound or – most powerful of all – total silence.

Natural sound

We don't live in a silent world, yet you wouldn't know it to see some television packages. Use as much natural sound as you can. Natural sound really helps the pace of a television package and helps viewers assimilate the pictures and the words they are looking at and listening to. They allow the viewer to 'take it in'. Put bluntly, a piece which is end-to-end script will sound boring and difficult to understand while a piece with plenty of natural sound will be better paced, more interesting and easier to understand. Every time you stop talking you give the viewer a chance to absorb the story.

And when you're out in the field, remember to shoot natural sound – don't just assume there will be some there when you get into the cutting room – you will need good sound as well as good pictures. And remember, natural sound is as important with library material as it is with on-the-day footage. Always look for it, always use it, and always write to it. If you're tight for time or have been asked to shorten your piece, always try to cut down on script, not natural sound. Hardly anything heightens the sense of 'being there' more than natural sound. So let it breathe.

Correspondents, whether old hands or newcomers, seem to find the proper use of natural sound one of the hardest lessons to learn. But, invariably, the best pieces have the most natural sound. And there's an old saying about broadcast news pieces: 'It can be as long as you like as long as it's quick.' Well, the best pieces seem quick because they flash by – regardless of how long they are – and leave you wanting more. The trick to achieving this is to use lots of natural sound and less script. A five-minute piece with lots of natural sound can seem quicker (and less turgid) than a two-minute piece which is wall-to-wall words.

This section on natural sound is very short. But it is among the most important in this book. Believe me.

Use library material like any other

When you are using library material, select it, edit it, script it and use the natural sound from it as lovingly as you would any other material. Do not rely heavily on date astons (putting the date on screen) – all pictures need proper scripting.

Sound bites

Many conventions have built up around the use of sound bites – some sensible, some less so and some plain lazy. The use of sound bites is one of the most formulaic parts of television news. They are often used when they needn't be; they are often not used to help tell the story; and they are too often used out of a sense of formula or duty.

In setting up a sound bite your script should not repeat what the viewer is about to hear in the clip, but neither should it leave all the work to the aston (putting the name on screen), unless the interviewee is so famous as to need no introduction. The interview clip is part of the story and should work seamlessly with your script, without the viewer noticing.

Your interview will normally be anything from three minutes to twenty minutes long. What you are trying to do is choose the best clip from the interview. The mistake that some correspondents make is to choose the clip that, on its own, best illustrates what you want it to say. The mistake is to have not thought about how you are going to write into and out of the clip. The 'in' point and the 'out' point should allow maximum flow from the previous and following sentences. It shouldn't seem like just a separate block of the story. So in choosing the clip, consider how it will flow into your script and help carry the story along.

Occasionally, the right interviewee with the right answer can allow you (in small doses) to ask a question which the clip answers:

script: So what was it that upset him so much?

clip: The fact that . . .

Another example:

script: One crucial question remains unanswered – where would they enter from?

clip: The easiest way in is through Macedonia, though that may not be acceptable.

There are many different ways to use sound creatively. Start the interview clip, then introduce the person talking, then finish the clip. Use a short clip to help move your own narrative along – start your narrative sentence, break into your own script with a clip, then conclude your sentence. All of these techniques can be used to break the formula of the way we put pieces together and add an element of surprise. Even a refusal to say anything can be scripted surprisingly. Here's Mark Mardell during the 2000 fuel crisis:

natural sound – shouts, off camera

reporter: Petrol tax down before the election, Prime Minister? Yes?

prime minister ignores and walks on

script: No answer came the firm reply from the Prime Minister.

If scripting into sound bites is difficult, finding the right sequence of pictures to draw the viewer in can be even more taxing. The key here is to try to avoid the obvious conventions. The most obvious – and contrived – is the walking shot. Always try and avoid them. Consider them an admission of defeat (not to mention lack of imagination). Your audience is far more sophisticated than you might think, and they take the view that these 'walkies' and some of the other set-ups we use are contrived gimmicks.

Similarly, avoid 'goldfishing' – interviewees speaking underneath your script until the point at which you want to hear them. The viewer's natural reaction is to try to hear what your interviewee is saying and not listen to you. Aside from obligations you may have towards fairness or right-of-reply, if an interview doesn't add anything, don't use it. If it's good – let it run. Don't feel you have to use fifteen seconds every time. And think about using interview clips over pictures of the interviewee doing something else – sometimes more interesting than a straight talking head.

If you're using a clip of someone for whom English is not the first language, beware – you may understand what the person is saying because you've heard the clip several times, but the viewer has just one chance to understand it. It might be easier to ask the interviewee to speak in their own language and then translate it. And if you are using a voice-over, make sure it's done with a proper delivery. A flat voice-over, just thrown on in the edit room, will sound out of place. A viewer should never be surprised by an interview clip. Your script should write into the clip to set it up and then out of the clip to flow in to the rest of the story. Too many scripts stop in mid-air and let the clip start without flowing into the sound bite.

And remember, just as your script can assume too much knowledge, sound bites can too. Check yourself – it may work for you, but does it work for the viewer? Jargon is jargon, regardless of whether it's in a script or an interview clip.

Me, me, me – reporter involvement

Let's never forget,' a reporter says sarcastically in the film *Broadcast News*, 'we're the real story.'

There is a vogue among television bosses at present for employing presenters and reporters who are little more than an ego with a suit and an ability to walk around while spouting at the camera. As a viewer, one sits there, shouting at the screen 'Get out of the way, man.' It is a fashion which will pass. I hope. Jeremy Paxman, BBC *Newsnight* presenter

As a correspondent you are not – and never should be – the story. You are the messenger. As one editor put it, you should make your story stand out, rather than make yourself stand out in the story. So to what extent should you appear in a television package in order to convey the message?

Richard Bilton asking the
Agriculture Minister a question at a
press conference during the 2001
foot and mouth outbreak.

Reporter involvement, as it
has become known, can reinforce
the sense of your 'being there'
on the ground – a competitive advantage to some broadcasters, who
may be on the ground more than others. The viewer is more likely to
trust a correspondent who's there and can see the story at first hand. It
can also reinforce audience recognition of certain correspondents and
networks. Sometimes there are good narrative reasons for a correspondent to act as a vehicle, holding the viewer by the hand and 'taking
them on a journey'. Hearing your network's reporter ask questions can
help show you're there, 'on the ground'.

But be careful. What is merely reporter presence to some is author
intrusion to others. There is a fine balance to be struck between
audience recognition and the trust and authority that comes as a result,
and the story becoming as much about the correspondent as anything
else. And it's not just seeing yourself appear in the picture. Pieces full
of 'I asked', 'he told me', 'I went with' may be acceptable in small doses
but become self-parodying if used too frequently. There is a time and
place for reporter involvement but, like everything else, you must vary
your approach.

Some broadcasters will want to find ways of showcasing the fact that
their correspondents are 'on the ground' as much as they are. And to
point out when their material – pictures or stories – are exclusive to
them. These may be qualities which make you distinct from your
competition, but you must do it with subtlety and not too often. It's
just one tool in your armoury, and all the more effective for being used
sparingly.

Stay in touch with your editor

A reporter or correspondent should always try to talk through their piece with the programme editor at the beginning of the day. And then again once they start editing. One senior programme editor said, 'In the age of the mobile phone, this should not be difficult, but it never ceases to amaze me how many reporters make no proper contact, and that inevitably leads to problems.'

The reporter needs to talk through the contents of the piece, where it is likely to run in the programme and what length is required. A good editor will always have some room for manoeuvre if you have particularly good pictures or sound. But if you don't talk it through with them, they won't know. Remember they are dealing with many other demands, and many other correspondents, each day.

'Fitting in' to a programme

The tone and style a reporter adopts in a piece is obviously partly dependent on the nature of the programme they are working for. But it also depends on where their piece is placed in the running order. You might be close to the top of the running order, where the approach needs to be 'harder', with shorter, tighter interview clips and perhaps a sense of the wider perspective of the story. Or you may be lower down, where the editor wants either a local angle as an example of how the story is playing on the ground, or a more reflective piece, where the reporter might be asked for a more personal take.

Some stories are big enough to warrant several pieces. In this situation, your position in the running order can also dramatically alter what information needs to be in your package. This will depend on what's gone before your piece and what will follow it. But editors get very frustrated with correspondents who become inflexible or possessive over which pictures they 'must have' in their piece. One senior programme editor said, 'There's nothing worse than having a sequence of packages with the same shot appearing, even when it is the key image of the day.'

Leading with a feature-style item or having a hard news item at the bottom of the programme can give a programme completely the wrong tone and feel. Correspondents should be flexible and responsible – but above all they should keep talking to the programme editor.

Every editor's nightmare

Aside from technical problems, there is never – ever – an excuse for missing your slot or, if you are away from base, missing your feed. Late feeds are every editor's nightmare. Programme editors would rather have a marginally less polished piece there in time than one which risks missing its slot. And even if your piece does make it at the last second it will have caused chaos in the gallery, turned the running order into a jumble and destabilized the presenter and the programme.

Each correspondent always has his or her own very good reasons for editing up to the wire. But imagine the impact of six people all trying to feed at once, and at air time. The record suites become overloaded, the pieces cannot be checked, and if there's a fault on the feed there may not be time to re-feed and remedy it.

Missing your slot is thoroughly unprofessional and can destroy a lot of other people's planning and effort. Late feeds make for poor programmes. Always feed with time in hand.

'Preshooting'

For many news organizations, an expansion of output has meant correspondents serving more than one programme or network. This has added to the need to prepare material in advance: preshooting. It's sensible and efficient, but beware of the dangers.

Preshot material can sometimes soften a hard news story, forcing a correspondent into 'feature mode' rather than tackling a story head-on.

Correspondents can easily get trapped trying to work a script around some preshooting that either hasn't worked as well as it might, or was done at a point when it was assumed the story would be slightly different.

Your sense of ownership of the preshot pictures means you tend to want to use them come what may – and often more of them than would be the case if they were someone else's. Don't hem yourself in. Preshooting is often crucial and, more often than not, works extremely well, but be prepared to throw it away. Stay flexible.

2.5 in vision: pieces to camera and live reporting

It's an acting job . . . acting natural.

Alistair Cooke

PIECES TO CAMERA

Bridget Kendall in Macedonia explains
where troops and rebels are positioned
around the surrounding hills.

Pieces to camera, or stand-ups, can be
a crucial part of any television package.
They can help to establish the
reporter's authority and credibility.
The reporter in the field is the network's representative, and most
broadcasters want their reporters to build a relationship with their
audience and give the viewers a sense of 'being there'. But pieces to
camera can also damage your network – and your career – if you don't
make them count. Too many stand-ups are of the 'and if the killing
continues someone will die' variety. Whether you're in a lion's cage,
outside a school, or in a war zone, a stand-up can't say much – but if it
doesn't say something it's wasting the viewer's time.

A piece to camera must contain important information or, even
better, genuine insight to help make sense of what you're reporting. If
you're a specialist or in a bureau, build up a mental library of telling
comments and good phrases culled from what contacts or local people
have told you which might provide insight.

While completely 'ad libbing' pieces to camera can cause problems,
so can overwriting them and making them look and sound as though
you are memorizing a script. Naturally, in certain circumstances 'ad

libbing' is the only thing you can do and it can capture the mood in a dramatic situation. Use key words to prompt yourself, be as clear as possible and follow a logical order. Keep it simple. A contorted piece to camera with too much information will confuse the viewer and can prove difficult when you come to edit.

Keep stand-ups conversational – again, 'talk to a friend'. And remember, conversational levels are low levels, so don't shout. This can be a particular problem with stand-ups some distance from the camera. You lose any intimacy if you start yelling. Keep talking to the viewer and let the mic do the work. Choose a setting for your piece to camera which is interesting and relevant. A stand-up that could have been shot anywhere usually shouldn't have been shot at all. Ideally, find some meaningful activity relevant to the story rather than a bland setting in front of a building or beside a sign.

Where appropriate, seize the moment, as these pictures to camera demonstrate. Orla Guerin used timing and location to do a piece to camera as casualties were removed from their homes in Jenin. This is a good example of seizing the moment. And if the stand-up did not work, a 'safety' stand-up could have simply been filmed in the same location. Carole Walker did a piece to camera as Tony Blair enjoyed audience applause at a Brighton venue. Again, if it had not worked, she could have done an effective, if less atmospheric, stand-up later or even outside the venue.

But you should also beware of the 'pantomime stand-up' which leaves the viewer wanting to shout, 'There's something behind you!' These are stand-ups where the background is *so* distracting the viewer ignores the correspondent and just watches what's going on around them.

There are many types of piece to camera: the opening stand-up ahead of the story, a 'bridge' to move between one element of a story and another, or an end thought.

George Alagiah used this piece to camera in Zimbabwe to move from a farm invasion by so-called war veterans to another location:

[pointing towards squatters
from his Land Rover]
Anyone who was involved in the war
would have to be in their thirties or
forties now.

Most of these youths are much, much
younger. There is a war veterans' farm
nearby, it's just down the road.
[gets in car]

Here Niall Dickson demonstrates the
use of a piece of equipment in a hospital
operating theatre.

Pieces to camera can also be used to get around a lack of pictures, or to demonstrate a piece of machinery or a process or highlight a particular location.

Andrew Marr chose the podium at the Conservative Party Conference as the best place to round off a report on a speech by Michael Portillo.

Marr was able to emphasize the atmosphere of the speech in a very conversational tone. 'It takes quite a bit of guts to come and stand on a stage like this and speak without any notes or autocue for the best part of an hour. But the studied informality of today's conference had a message: "We are kinder, gentler Conservatives." Maybe, but they're still committed to spending plans which involve substantial cuts on Labour's programme and when we ask where those cuts will fall, the message comes back, "That's for another day." That day will come.'

When reporting live or doing pieces to camera, a certain amount of movement, body language or gesticulation can help make reporters look less 'stiff' and more natural. Giving yourself something to do can help you look more relaxed, but there has to be a purpose. So take these approaches in small doses and vary your style. Most people naturally use their hands in conversation – that's fine. Try talking naturally while you're sitting on your hands. It's quite hard. You must talk to the camera in the way you, not anyone else, would talk to anyone you were trying to interest in your story. The crucial thing is that your hands do not become a distraction. In an attempt to show their enthusiasm, some correspondents become very conscious of their hands and start waving them around, almost unnaturally. Don't. Unless you're holding something up or demonstrating something, always keep your hands below your chest.

Jeremy Bowen used a photo album and simple camera
movements in this piece to camera in Kosovo:

They left this flat so quickly they didn't take their
photo album, which is something refugees being
kicked out of their homes tend to grab.

They show really very ordinary lives: playing the
accordion at a party with friends and family; Mr
Alexevic on the telephone years ago when he was
quite a young man.

These are fragments of one couple's existence in a
community that has probably gone forever.

In recent years, many correspondents have taken to doing walking
pieces to camera. Okay, so you can walk and talk, but ask yourself why
you are doing it – what does it add to the story? If you can't answer
that, don't do it. There has to be meaning in the start point and the
end point or in what you see along the walk. Walking from one
place to another for no apparent reason can look and feel gratuitous. If
in doubt, don't. If you do decide to do a walking piece to camera, make

sure you are walking well before the camera starts rolling and you start talking. A piece to camera which begins with the reporter acknowledging the camera operator's cue to walk is always excruciating to watch.

Whatever the type of piece to camera, try to avoid always using a closing stand-up in your stories. Vary the formula and break the pattern. David Shukman used a walking piece to camera (PTC) to show the viewer a jet engine the day after the Concorde crash. If you are in an interesting environment or have an interesting prop to work with, then go with the idea. But if you are going to try it don't be half-hearted. PTCs are great explaining tools, so use them to their full effect.

[David Shukman walks along the length of the engine] This Olympus engine is like those fitted to Concorde. It's generally been very reliable and we can only guess at how the accident was triggered.

Conceivably, it was a bird strike, a bird getting sucked into the intake of the engine here [points].

Or possibly something went wrong with the turbine [points].

A fan blade perhaps breaking off and puncturing the casing of the engine here entering the fuel tank and causing that fire. Or the problem lay with the afterburners – the system which sprays fuel into the exhaust to give Concorde more thrust and power as it tries to take off.

During the Zimbabwe elections, John Simpson delivered a piece to camera while walking towards the camera alongside a queue of people waiting to vote.

The camera movements were simple and effective. Less is more – as long as it is thoughtful and meaningful.

And remember – take plenty of time to shoot your pieces to camera. It is a very important part of your package. Your piece to camera will probably be the longest single shot in the story, so it is essential to look and sound interested and engaged with the story.

One of the most common faults with stand-ups is poor lighting, particularly in the winter months. Make sure that you are lit properly and, where appropriate, the backdrop too. Take the time to do it properly. Appearance matters. Tone and body language are crucial (see the section on appearance, page 145). Check with the camera operator that you look OK. Understand which stance or camera shot suits you best – particularly if you're especially tall or round. Look at your pieces to camera and decide which position suits you best so you can advise the cameraman you're working with.

Record more than one stand-up if you have time. It will give you more options when you come to edit the piece and may enable you to freshen up a report which might otherwise run unaltered in consecutive programmes. Spend as much time filming your PTC as you would a sequence. Think about it. For some court cases, for example, think about recording – or pre-shooting – a stand-up at the scene rather than outside the court. Never 'knock off' the piece to camera as a last thought at the end of the day.

Use camera movement, but like everything, in moderation. If you must cut from an interview clip to a stand-up, use a camera pan or zoom (moving from the scene around you or near you to yourself) to avoid going from one talking head to another.

Don't be afraid of breaking eye contact with the camera during a piece to camera – after all this is how we act in conversation with real people. But it doesn't work all the time and you need to be very confident on camera to pull it off. Experiment. The head turn – facing away from the camera and then turning towards it at the start of the stand-up – is fine. But only in small doses, and only if you were looking at something to do with the story. See how it feels and make the decision in the edit suite – give yourself options.

Be sensitive when you are doing stand-ups in front of people in difficult situations, in a hospital for instance. There is a fine line between the background being relevant to the story and using people as 'props'. Sensitivity is required. It may be worth referring to your surroundings, especially if it's not clear where you are. It helps draw the viewer in. Put thought into your stand-up on location – you can't change a stand-up in the edit suite. So if you are experimenting with something different, shoot a standard piece to camera as a safety net.

It's worth repeating the golden rule: have something to say. There's nothing worse than a vacuous comment or cliché in a piece to camera.

And God forbid that the viewer should ever be denied the pleasure of seeing you at every opportunity, but you don't have to do a piece to camera at all . . . Much, indeed most, of this section on pieces to camera applies equally to the other key aspect of being on camera: live reporting.

LIVE REPORTING

Live reporting skills are an absolute prerequisite for any serious correspondent these days. With the growth of twenty-four-hour networks and the move away from every story being told as a conventional film package, live reporting has become increasingly important – and yet it is potentially very hazardous.

Live reporting needs to look and feel like the most spontaneous and natural thing you do before the camera, yet the circumstances in which you are performing are among the most planned and unnatural you will experience. It may seem a paradox, but the key to most live reporting is good forward planning, along with discipline in the length of your answers and, yet again, 'talking to a friend'.

Rule number one: keep to time

The most common fault in live broadcasting is over-long answers. If you have a lot to say, break your answers up into more easily digestible parts – four shorter questions and answers will be more effective than two longer ones. Don't get locked into getting it all out in the first answer. Try to keep your sentences short and tight, and try not to go over forty seconds in your answers. Any more and you will begin to lose your place, and the viewer will lose it before you do. Have the confidence to keep your answers short.

In the stresses and strains of live reporting, one of the first things to disappear is discipline and control over the length of answers. You must learn what a forty-second answer feels like, what a twenty-second answer feels like, and how to wrap up on time when a director gives you ten seconds to finish. Learn to speak in short sentences and use a stopwatch to get a sense of how many sentences you can use in thirty to forty seconds.

The very worst live reporting – for you and the viewer – involves long tortuous answers, in which you have long ago forgotten what the question was and how your answer began, and you haven't a clue how you are going to bring it to a close. A long, dull answer is never what any programme wants. But, as with the rest of your journalism, tailor your product to the output. A lengthy answer that may be more acceptable on a twenty-four-hour channel may give a thirty-minute bulletin editor an ulcer. Never be windy and always keep your answers tight on a short programme.

Your words – the language of live broadcasting

Beware completely ad-libbing. Correspondents rarely sound as articulate when they're reporting on the hoof as when they have planned what they're going to say. But beware memorizing full scripts – it's hard to think quickly at the same time as dragging a speech from your memory. Think through what you want to say and use key words to prompt you. You must find the balance between planning what you are going to say and sounding as natural as you can. A live two-way should be a natural conversation rather than a staged and pre-scripted one. It should have a sense of flow in the way a package does.

Try to hook the presenter's question into your answers. This is most easily done by repeating the end of the question: Presenter: 'So how will they take it forward?' Reporter: 'They'll take it forward firstly by . . .' Similarly, hook your own sentences together with transition words – *and*, *but* etc. Look for nice turns of phrase or groups of words, which eloquently, and memorably, describe what you're trying to say.

At the end of the two-way, if there's time, wrap it up by briefly repeating the key points. This is a device which the conventional package doesn't allow you to do, but which really helps the viewer grasp the relevant points. Here is Andrew Marr in Downing Street during the fuel crisis:

presenter: . . . but the twenty-four hour promise is a real hostage to fortune. How much is riding for Tony Blair on that?

Marr: Well, you can bet your bottom dollar that he is watching television news very carefully to assess the reports of tankers moving out of depots. How many tankers out of how many depots into how many petrol stations? That's the real question for the Prime Minister tonight.

One of the most effective techniques is to use your own personal experiences to help describe what's happening: 'I walked past a long row of shops this morning that had been looted,' or 'I was trying get some money out of the bank when' or 'Well, as I was driving into the city this morning.' Describing your own experience helps to paint a picture that the viewer can relate to and will help to draw the audience in. This was a technique used by Ben Brown at the scene of a volcano in Goma:

Q: Ben, we're told that aid is on its way. But where is it?

A: That's a very good question. All the time when I walk around Goma I'm stopped by people pointing at their stomachs as if to say, 'Look, we're hungry, we're desperate for food. Where is it?' Exactly that question.

Alluding to your experience in covering a story over a long period can also enhance your authority. Here's Rageh Omaar as the main statue of Saddam Hussein was pulled down in central Baghdad in April 2003:

'I've been reporting from Iraq for six years and throughout that time, I've tried to summon in my mind's eye what my reaction would be when I saw an American soldier in the heart of Baghdad. But nothing could have prepared me for this moment. It's utterly overwhelming watching the reaction of these ordinary Iraqis as they take part in crashing down that statue.'

Remember to use language that makes it feel live: not 'The Chief Inspector has said' but rather 'A few moments ago, the Chief Inspector told us here.' Phrases like 'I've just come from' or 'I've just spoken to' give live broadcasting a sense of timeliness and immediacy.

And don't forget that 'lightness of touch'. Andrew Marr in Downing Street again, this time on Peter Mandelson:

Now Mandelson is saying he's going to fight to clear his name – but who is he going to fight against? Some of his closest political friends. If I were a copper I would be standing here saying this is the scene of the crime behind me. And this is a 'domestic'.

Live broadcasting is an area in which specialist journalism can really come into its own. Only those with an intimate knowledge of a subject (and hopefully the memory of an elephant) can be put on camera at short notice and talk live about what a particular development means. But as with packaging, beware jargon, and if you use it, then explain it.

Analogies, metaphors and quotes

One very effective way of explaining or reinforcing a point is to compare it with something else – to use an analogy or a comparison. Here's Andrew Marr using analogies to explain Westminster politics:

On Margaret Thatcher and the Tory Party: 'She is a little bit like the revered but now intensely embarrassing older relative.'

On the effect of Alistair Campbell on Tony Blair and Number 10: 'It's a little like as if you are putting on a fantastic play while on the side you've got the lighting man fiddling around with the lighting switches. Then halfway through the play you peer out and you notice that the entire audience is sitting there absolutely transfixed by the lighting man. The messenger has become bigger than the message.'

On the likelihood of Peter Mandelson giving up politics: 'Peter Mandelson is not an obscurity kind of guy, is he? He is not somebody who is naturally going to take a back seat, and walk away from public life. It's a bit like suddenly hearing that Victoria Beckham is going to devote the next ten years to the ironing.'

On the Hammond report on Peter Mandelson: 'The overall effect is a little bit odd. There's all this mayhem, yet in the end, nobody has done anything wrong, and everybody is honest and decent. It is a bit like one of those implausible old romantic plays, where in acts one to four they are all trying to murder each other, and in act five they end up getting married.'

Used properly, analogies can help the viewer better absorb and understand the story you are reporting. Using quotes can be effective too. Here's Nick Robinson on an outbreak of hostilities between the Government and the media: 'As Enoch Powell said, "Complaining about the press is like complaining about the weather if you're a sailor."'

Your 'performance'

Reporting live involves a larger element of 'showbiz' than some correspondents feel comfortable with. But you are in the business of communication, and sometimes you may need to push your presentation and delivery a little harder than normal. It's what actors sometimes call 'being in the moment' or 'capturing the moment'.

Your interest and enthusiasm will overcome many difficulties. But if you don't care about the story, neither will the audience. Correspondents often fail to understand that the audience will pay as much attention to their facial expressions and gestures as to their words.

Relax. Try to enjoy what you're doing. If your muscles are tense, your performance will be too. Don't shout. Let the mic do the work. This whole book has emphasized the importance of a conversational delivery. Nowhere is it more important than with live reporting. Always bear in mind that it is *one* friend you are talking to. Watch yourself on tape and ask yourself, 'Is this how I would talk to someone if I were in a room with them, trying to get them interested in something?'

Avoid holding visible reams of paper, big notebooks or, even worse, clipboards. Key words from your script or the names of interviewees should be put on a small reporter's pad that can be easily hidden. Glance down occasionally, by all means, but try not to read from your notes unless it's relevant to the story or unless you want to emphasize that you are quoting directly from what someone else has said. On the other hand, you can make a virtue of any props related to the story: the resignation letter, the leaked report and so on.

If a story is breaking around you, don't try and pretend it isn't. If you're being given pieces of paper bearing new information, don't try to disguise it. Make a virtue of it. The viewers will feel the sense of urgency. If something is going on behind you or around you, don't hesitate to direct the camera operator live on air – it will add to the sense of being live.

You and the presenter

Whenever you can, discuss the questions beforehand with the presenter. In the studio, give them your suggested questions on paper. But be prepared. Expect presenters to wrongfoot you. Remember, they're dealing with many other things at the same time.

Try not to leave pauses which might make the presenter believe you've finished your answer. If you both start talking at the same time, you should stop immediately and let the presenter continue.

Don't fall into the trap of becoming a substitute guest in a live two-way. If a programme could not get the guest they wanted they might choose to interview a correspondent. But it is not your job to justify other people's positions, particularly if they are contentious. You can explain: 'The bank's Chief Executive may feel,' but don't let the presenter make you defend the Chief Executive's position.

And it may seem rude, but don't say hello and don't say goodbye. 'Good mornings' and 'Goodbyes' tend to get tangled up with what the presenter then goes on to say. It's up to you whether you use the presenter's name once, but don't keep on using it – it sounds contrived and has the effect of excluding the viewer. Also, it may prevent your contribution being clipped for use later in the day on different outlets.

What reporters say about presenters . . .

For reporters who have been out all day, dodging bullets or standing in the pouring rain since before breakfast or painstakingly gathering information about the story they're working on, the culmination of their day may be a live, location interview with a presenter. Now, being a presenter is a high-pressure occupation at the best of times, and one that requires a particular set of skills, but this is a fact not always appreciated by reporters in the field, who feel that – just occasionally – they are dumped right in the sticky stuff by their colleagues sitting in their safe, warm studio. You see, presenters have a lot going on around them (and in their ear), which can mean that they are not always in complete grasp of the facts when they launch into a live interview with a reporter. This in turn can lead to some tricky moments that require, from the reporter, some verbal dexterity and, because losing your temper on air is most unprofessional, a substantial dollop of lip-biting and patience.

So, just for fun, here are the top ten complaints, in order of frequency, that reporters make about presenters.

1 They ask about what you cannot see, where you are not located and where you have not been.
2 They do not appear to listen to the answer given.
3 They steal the first thing you told them you were going to say and use it in their introduction.
4 They ask questions that include the answer.
5 They repeat the same question in a different form.
6 They introduce you in the wrong location.
7 They include inaccurate statements in the question.
8 They ask long, mumbled questions down a distant line.
9 Is that a question? Or a statement?
10 They get your name wrong.

So be prepared. Apart from these complaints, reporters love presenters.

Location

So how can the location help you to tell your story? You must look for the locations which best explain it. Do it as a team – you have to take full account of what's feasible for the crew and engineer. Of course, any location has to be sufficiently interesting and meaningful for you to be there in the first place, but be careful of the backdrop being so interesting that it dominates what you are saying.

Even the most boring locations can be used effectively. But always ask yourself, 'Why am I here? What will the viewer gain from my being here?' The answer will help you judge what the best backdrop should be and arrange any movement. Always be clear that there's a reason why you're doing it. If you're not careful, being live for the sake of it can look self-parodying and gratuitous.

Using camera movement can sometimes be very effective in giving the viewer a much better sense of what's going on and the points you are trying to make. However, if you decide to do this, you must rehearse the moves first with the cameraman, and you must script the movement slowly enough to allow the camera to move without 'hose-piping' (a roller coaster of constantly moving pictures).

Here's Jeremy Bowen live in Jerusalem a few weeks after the new Intifada began. Bowen was on a rooftop overlooking the Old City and as he turns from the camera towards the panorama behind him, he points and the camera follows as he speaks:

'We're live in Jerusalem on a very important day indeed for the Middle East, on the edge of the Old City – the Holy City and the centre of the conflict between the Israelis and the Palestinians. You're seeing now West Jerusalem, the area which is over-whelmingly Jewish. And in that direction over there is East Jerusalem – the place the Palestinians want as their capital. The Old City is the heart of the conflict and I've been walking around the streets and the markets to get a sense of mood . . .'

[into a package]

Don't waste opportunities – if the Prime Minister appears behind you in Downing Street don't just ignore it, get out of the way of the camera and talk about what's happening. And don't be afraid to ask the cameraman live on air. That's what live broadcasting is – live.

Always be aware that a camera lens may see things very differently from your own eye. Always ask the crew if their lens can 'see' what you can see. If you want to know if the shot is OK, ask the cameraman and the gallery how you look and how the shot looks.

To move or not to move

Your movement is not compulsory, and should be used only to enhance your report. But a sequence of movements can help take your audience through different elements of your report, and help bring the story to life through a 'hands on' approach. Going through doors or round corners can help give a sense of scale or perspective.

Your audience is seeing the location for the first time, so some movement can give them a sense of where you are. But walking from one place to another for no apparent reason can also look and feel gratuitous. And moving from one seemingly frozen interviewee to another can feel very laboured and unnatural. Use movement when it feels natural and enhances the story. But if in doubt, don't.

The live two-way on the next double-page spread used movement to good effect: showing and describing the flooded region; the chaos wrought on one particular house; and interviewing the owner of the house and a man from the local authority.

If you do decide that your moving around will enhance your report, there are three things you must do: rehearse, rehearse and rehearse. The key to making any live sequence with movement flow seamlessly is rehearsing, and your ambitions should be proportionate to the amount of time you have to rehearse. Walk through the moves matching what you want to say with where you want to say it. Let the crew anticipate any difficulties.

Using a location

1 – Jane O'Brien begins a 2-way during the floods of 2000

2 – turns to first interviewee

3 – describes the surrounding area

4 – enters house

5 – cameraman backs through the house to illustrate damage

6 – into living room

7 – turns to second interviewee

8 – interview

9 – concluding thought

10 – back to studio

Allow the movement to develop slowly – don't feel you must move off immediately. Make one or two initial points before moving. And once you decide to move, don't rush. Allow time for the camera and, through it, the audience to take in what you're talking about.

Don't worry about teasing where you're going, or explaining what you're passing on the way. Start to introduce guests as you approach them to maintain a sense of pace. Make sure your guests, crew and anyone else involved with the site know exactly what you're trying to do. Never ad-lib camera movements live on air, unless something dramatic is unfolding that you need to illustrate.

Different types of live broadcasting

with an interviewee

Many of the people you'll interview will be professionals used to handling the media, but many others will be members of the public, and they can range from painfully shy to scared stiff. So try to keep them relaxed.

Always bear in mind that guests often can't hear anything, so tell them what's happening all the time – which story is running, or anything that's being said that you expect them to react to. Always give the interviewee a countdown. When interviewing a guest make sure the camera –

the viewer – can see both of the interviewee's eyes. Don't stand side by side looking at the camera. The camera should look over your shoulder at the guest.

Although it's more difficult, the same applies when you have more than one guest: have a straight line of guests angled away from the camera; have the camera shoot over your shoulder with the viewer able to see both eyes of all guests. Don't stand in a circle.

talking live around interview clips

Sometimes when a story is particularly starved of pictures or is late-breaking you may be asked to talk live around a series of recorded interview clips. A good performer can make a story come to life like this in a way that would be impossible in a conventional package, and tell the viewer far more.

In addition to all the skills mentioned above, you must try to make your words flow seamlessly into and out of any sound bites you are talking around. It's better to talk into them rather than just stopping talking and waiting for the clip. For example:

correspondent: If you think Fred Bloggs is going to let this pass without a fuss, just listen to what he told me this morning.

clip: I will not . . .

Again, keeping it conversational is the key.

Always make sure the director and/or producer are crystal clear about what you plan to do and what your 'out words' are – your last words before the clip should run. In the example above, it's 'listen to what he told me this morning'. And always treble-check whether you or the presenter is expected to speak off the back of a clip.

with vt 'floated in'

When there are pictures available but there is no time or desire to package them they can be 'floated in' live during a two-way. Using the latest pictures in this way can give urgency to a story. Floating pictures across two-ways can also be a good way of explaining difficult stories or stories with very few new or interesting pictures. When it works it can be extremely effective, but beware. It needs very careful co-ordination.

For a correspondent without a monitor this can be particularly difficult because they cannot see which pictures they are meant to talk over – and talking over the wrong pictures is worse than not having the pictures at all. You must be clear which pictures will be used, and in what order.

big screens, videowalls and live in the studio

Being live in the studio is easier to control in some ways, but is by no means without hazards. It is important to understand the difference between being live talking to a presenter and being live using autocue. The latter requires exceptional skill and not all correspondents will be able to master this effectively without constant practice and feedback.

Using a big screen (or videowall) is a good illustration of the difficulty that can be involved. This technique can be enormously effective in using a range of pictures, interviews and graphics to explain complicated issues. But the correspondent must come across in delivery and body language as though he or she were quite naturally talking to someone, and yet all the time reading from an autocue and all the time aware of when they should look or motion towards the graphics and the video next to them.

Often, the correspondent must also move seamlessly from talking to the presenter to talking to the viewer. This form of presentation is almost a specialism in itself. It is obviously safer and easier to master if it is pre-recorded, though that in turn eliminates the presenter-correspondent dialogue which the editor may deem crucial. Your writing needs to reflect the tone the format is trying to capture. Your style must be conversational.

Working closely with your producer is more important with the big screen than many other types of television news. Simple production points can make the difference between you looking polished or floundering. For example, you should always make sure that the interviewee in freestanding clips is looking towards you from the screen. Talking in and out of clips when the interviewee is looking away from you simply does not work. Make sure that the graphics help you. Screens that are too busy and video that serves no purpose do not help you – they make your job harder. Rehearse with the graphics. Your body language will be a lot more natural if you are clear where the words appear on the screen and can gesture accordingly. Be familiar enough with the script that you can turn to the screen without losing your place. Once again, the skill is not to *look* scripted.

If you are prone to wave your arms in a distracting way or let your hands hang limp at your sides, learn to control this. You may look more comfortable if you lean on something or hold a piece of paper in your hand. Experiment and take advice on what makes you look best. Feedback is crucial. Finally, if you're doing a one-plus-one sitting in the studio then always look at the presenter and not at the camera.

other things to remember about live broadcasting

Avoid bad weather, big crowds and people with alcohol. You'll lose out to all three. If it's pouring with rain, try to stay dry until the last moment. Always carry an umbrella with the name of your organization written on it (and certainly nothing else).

If you're working in very sunny conditions and forced to squint into the camera, turn your face up to the sun with your eyes closed for a few seconds then turn back to the camera. This will adjust your pupils and help remove the need to squint. You can buy tinted contact lenses for working in the sun.

Always carry an earpiece. If your clean feed (the sound in your ear) goes dead, shout – it's your lifeline.

Remember, your reputation for accuracy is paramount. Don't risk being 'never wrong for long'. It helps to get it first, but not at the risk of getting it wrong. Get it right. Never pretend you know something that you don't. Resist pressure to go with something you can't support. Attribute stories to their source. Be as frank and honest on air about what you don't know as you are about what you do.

2.6 pictures

Pictures, pictures, pictures

Many reporters now shoot their own pictures – some even edit their own packages. But whether you shoot your own material or not, it is important that you know which pictures work best and how to acquire them. It is crucial to understand that camerawork is a *journalistic* activity, not some remote technical process. Great camera operators are great storytellers. If you treat a camera operator or a picture editor as a mere technician, they will behave like a mere technician.

Here's one of the BBC's award-winning camera operators on working with less experienced correspondents: 'There are two things that really annoy me. First and foremost is correspondents who don't tell me what the story is about, in detail, and what we want out of it. The second is not being given enough time to do a good job.'

When the story becomes clear in your own mind, make sure it's clear in the mind of the camera operator. Explain, if relevant, what mood or feeling you want from the shots. Communication – discussing the story – is the key. Just as reporters want to know what is being shot, camera operators have to know how a reporter sees a story. It will affect and improve what they shoot. Expect the best from the crew. If you only ask for GVs (general views) that is what you will get. 'Knock off some GVs' is lazy journalism.

The key elements for the best storytelling are: sequences, close-ups, faces, detail, reaction as well as action, and lots of good natural sound.

Pictures of people

Never forget: it's about pictures, and it's about people. Viewers relate
most to people. So wherever you can (and provided it's not intrusive),
film real people with whom your audience can identify. And always try
to find strong characters.

A great deal of the news we cover examines things – issues, policies,
conflicts and tragedies – which affect people's lives. So focusing on
people gives a story an added meaning and makes it more accessible.
Research shows that viewers absorb more through personal examples.
So where appropriate, try to humanize your stories and scripts. Don't
just shoot the crowd. Pick an individual or a small family in the crowd
and build a sequence around them. We don't always need to know their
names (we may want to), but use them as a vehicle to tell this part of
the story.

Don't just shoot pictures of refugees: shoot what it's like to be a
refugee. And not simply pictures of people in a factory, but pictures
which show you what it feels like to work in a factory. You want to
capture the mood. The best camera operators can take an issue or a
fact and give it flesh and blood. They can turn it into a shared
experience for the viewer, and that is invariably achieved by using
people to illustrate the larger meaning.

Sequences

Sequences are the heart of good television. Good TV news packages
are made up of sequences which heighten the viewers' sense of involvement and show the event much as they would see it if they were there.
A sequence is a series of shots that breaks down what's happening into
its constituent parts and gives the impression of continuous action. This
will do two things: it will bring the action to life and make it interesting;
and, crucially, it will give you flexibility in the edit suite.

Good snooker players are always thinking several shots ahead and having to consider how the shots relate to each other. Good camera operators are the same. If you think about the shot you're taking, the shot you just took and the shot you will take next, you'll instinctively shoot more sequences and maintain continuity from one shot to the next.

In very basic filming terms, there are three types of shot that make up a sequence:

The long shot or wide shot places things – or the subject – in perspective.

The medium shot shows the subject and some of the immediate area.

The close-up of faces, hands, details. These can build up a sequence and also be used as cutaways.

There are many variants – just shooting eyes would be an extreme close-up; a 'point of view' (POV) shows what something looks like from the point of view of an observer you have filmed. Here's an example of shooting a sequence of a lumberjack chopping down a tree:

close-up: chainsaw starts

close-up: lumberjack's face

close-up: saw cutting into wood

medium shot: lumberjack and saw and tree

medium shot: same as previous but from behind

very wide shot: shows action and location

close-up: lumberjack's face looking up at tree

pov [i.e. what the lumberjack would see]: looking up at tree

wide shot: tree falling

The sequence above produces a 'kit of shots' which allows a huge amount of flexibility in the edit suite. It could be used for a short sequence or a long sequence, as required.

For any action sequence, don't just vary the *size* of the shot – vary the *angle* as well. Shooting from the front, back, side, on high or down low can make the sequence more interesting. Don't view everything from eye level. Again, it can also help in the edit by masking difficulties you might have in matching the continuity of a sequence.

Ideally, you should shoot matching close-ups, medium and long shots to give you choice in the edit room and a sequence. It is perfectly possible to shoot hours of material and not have a full sequence. Aim for fewer subjects, better covered through sequences rather than many bits and different subjects. Good sequences allow good storytelling and good scripting opportunities.

A man getting a shoeshine. This sequence starts with an angled tilt up revealing the man reading a paper while the shoeshiner looks down – into camera – to work on the shoes.

The second shot is a tight close-up of one shoe being polished.

The third element is a medium wide shot placing the whole action into perspective; the shoeshiner on a park bench while the customer leans on his workbench. It is simple, stylish and highly effective.

Here is a sequence of a woman shopping in Cuba. We follow her along the street using a variety of low wide shots, close-ups from foot to eye level, a medium close-up as she looks towards us through a shop window and finally a reverse wide shot as she looks through the same window. The variety of shots allow the reporter plenty of time to talk about the woman and her mission that day while giving the viewer a clear sense of her environment.

Here's a simple
sequence of someone
putting up a sign on a
farm gate during the
2001 foot and mouth
outbreak.

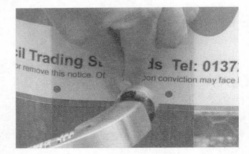

Close-ups

Try to get more close-ups than you think you need, though not if unduly intrusive. Viewers want a sense of involvement and first person experience, and this is most often achieved through detail and close-ups of faces. Close-ups of faces derive much of their impact from the emphasis on eyes. Eyes reveal what someone is feeling and, sometimes, thinking.

In some situations you will want to move the camera close to the subject rather than use the telephoto lens, which can produce a less intimate (and sometimes far more wobbly) effect. However, this only works when the subject is happy for you to film at such short range, and you must also be clear about how you may change their behaviour by filming so closely.

It is sometimes said you can tell a good camera operator from a less good one when you ask for a close-up. The more experienced ones will move the camera – the others simply their telephoto lens. But there is a balance to be struck. For instance, moving the camera a little closer and to the side and then using the telephoto lens can also be highly effective, with the subject unaware you are filming them so closely. The illustrations on the following pages show how a variety of shots can be used to create opening sequences.

In the sequence below, a Nick Witchell package from Belfast the morning that the new power sharing executive took control, creates a perfect opportunity for a sparse but effective script about new beginnings, using a lot of natural sound:

very wide top shot:
Belfast at dawn

wide shot:
over the dockyards

medium shot:
a delivery of fresh bread into a shop

medium close-up:
a bus driver through
the windscreen

wide matching shot:
bus driver and bus

close-up:
a newspaper headline being
read on the bus

[early morning, misty] wide shot:
the Tigris river with a small boat crossing

matching medium shot:
the boat, revealing three passengers

tilting close-up:
a padlocked shop as pedestrians walk past

medium-wide low shot:
a cat crossing a deserted market street

John Simpson reported from Baghdad on the day that bombing – and the Desert Storm campaign – was expected to begin. This opening sequence illustrated the atmosphere of the quiet worry of a semi-deserted city without explicitly referring to people's fears, which the Iraqi censors would have prevented.

A Daniel Lak story on old people in India
which ends in a piece to camera:

eye-level close-up:
an old man smoking and looking down

close tilt down:
another old man
checking his hand
of cards

wide shot:
two groups of old men playing cards
in the street

medium close-up:
face on, of two men with hands
of cards

tight close-up:
the cards on the
ground

medium shot:
Daniel Lak doing his piece-to-camera
with the old men behind

Details

Skill in storytelling involves great attention to detail. And attention to detail is often what marks out the best camera operators from the rest. Small details make a big difference. Nervous hands; pictures on a mantelpiece; someone whispering into an ear; a hand clutching a toy; details of a life. Be on the lookout for little vignettes around the edges which tell a story – particularly in stories which can otherwise be difficult to illustrate. These small details can say more in a few seconds than you can write. And they can create script opportunities for you that less detailed pictures would not.

This illustrated sequence built up a picture of the flat of a woman who was under siege:

the broken lock on the door;

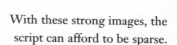

With these strong images, the script can afford to be sparse.

Conversely, try to avoid using shots of press conferences unless exceptional things have happened and they give meaning to the story. You will often need the interview clips, obviously, but the pictures can be deadening.

And remember to shoot reaction as well as action; those waiting for the boat as well as those getting off it; the children as well as the teacher; the excitement, fear, anger, awe of those watching or waiting – those reacting.

Violent pictures

There is an internal BBC video which was made to illustrate the issues surrounding the use of violent pictures. One of the sequences lasts about a minute, and once seen it is unforgettable. It was filmed in a South African township and shows a group of men pulling a man from his home, a wooden shack, and surrounding him. Trapped against the hut, the man, screaming frantically, is first beaten then cut, manages to stagger a short distance where he is beaten again and, finally, dismembered by machete. The film stops occasionally throughout the sequence as Peter Sissons, who did the voice-over, says, 'Should we have stopped here? Or here? Or even here? Or should we have just shown it all?' It is a chilling but brilliant example of one of the most difficult and contentious issues in television news: how much violent imagery should be included – or excluded – in news programmes? How much do audiences need to see to understand the horror and significance of what's happening?

Some of the most savage violence ever recorded was filmed in Sierra Leone by cameraman Sorious Samura. Samura filmed as rebels entered the capital city, Freetown. He filmed the destruction of his own home and went on to film teenage soldiers being almost casually shot at close range in the chest and head. He also filmed the brutal beating of a ten-year-old boy by soldiers. The footage was first seen on BBC News in a film by Fergal Keane who, along with his picture editor, used some of the pictures of the boy being beaten up and some of one of the soldiers being chased and shot, up to the point of the trigger being pulled – at which point he froze the picture. The brutality of grown men attacking a ten-year-old boy was what shocked me (and doubtless many others) the most. I had no idea what *hadn't* been shown or, in fact, whether there was any more to show. But there was. A lot more. And later that year I saw it all.

Samura's footage was entered for the Rory Peck Trust Awards, the industry's main award for freelance cameramen and women. Quite rightly, his bravery and ingenuity in such extreme circumstances was rewarded with the top prize. The Trust decided to show Samura's footage in its entirety at the end of the ceremony. The audience was warned that it was hard to watch and told there would be a five-minute interval while people could leave the audito rium if they wanted to. Many did. But many, myself included, stayed to watch. It seemed wrong somehow to reward it with the top prize and then be unwilling to watch it.

And there we sat, in stunned silence, as it quickly became clear that the scale of the savagery was far in excess of anything that BBC News had shown. The extent to which Samura had put his life on the line became clear too. The seconds that followed the point where Fergal Keane had frozen the frame showed a man falling to the floor and landing on his back. A huge spurt of blood shot two or three feet into the air for several seconds before it subsided. Other, similar killings

were filmed. Vultures were filmed picking over entrails. The room remained totally silent as we filed out. Hardened journalists and executives had sat, some covering their eyes, some turning away, trying their hardest to keep watching.

Keane's piece for BBC News had been a model, both of restraint and powerful writing – it was hard to better it (it was a genuine exclusive too – Keane had met Samura in a Freetown bar). Yet I couldn't help feeling, walking out of the auditorium that evening, that it was wrong for those pictures not be shown somewhere, somehow and Samura certainly agreed. Channel 4 felt the same way and showed them shortly afterwards. But the dilemma is clear. How should such footage be used? Should broadcasters show more? Do they *need* to show more to get the point across, or can the point be made without the need to resort to showing such distressing images? Are we changing the reality by not showing it 'the way it is'? How do we put such violent images in context?

These are really difficult issues for TV news editors and journalists in the field, and they evoke strong feelings. Those out on location will tend to feel that we should 'show it the way it is'; that a sanitized version of what's happened fails to reflect the reality on the ground. When he was still a correspondent, Martin Bell himself made the point that we are perfectly happy to show the 'bang-bang' – the tanks and mortars firing from the hillsides – and yet unwilling to show the results of the shells and mortars landing. Bell argued that we were glamorizing war in the process.

But there is another side to the argument. Many of the violent images which pass through newsrooms would do nothing but distress viewers and cause them to turn off (and let's be honest here – one fear among broadcasters is that they will alienate viewers). In the past, BBC News has received more complaints about violence in the news than any other subject. Some in TV news argue that effective script-writing and use of sound and picture has more impact than showing such 'bare' images. Some editors argue that the effect of showing these images diminishes over time as people fail to be shocked. Clearly, children are likely to be watching during the daytime and early evening. Should children be exposed to such violent images? And while the victims of violence need their story told we must also be sensitive to the way we portray them.

Most judgements in the newsroom are made on the basis of taste and decency rather than any measurable reality, because causal connections between violence in the news and the effects on society remain difficult to establish in a concrete way. In practical terms, no two cases are the same. Different pictures require different handling at different times of day.

This script by Hilary Andersson in Nigeria also makes the point without showing all of the pictures: 'Victoria Orisha Mugu has been hidden behind her hut in the suffocating heat of the day. Fifty per cent of her body is covered in burns. *Her wounds are too distressing to show.*'

There is no avoiding using some distressing images in television news. While some images will remain untransmittable, we still have a

Here, Martin Bell describes a room full of burnt bodies at the scene of a horrific massacre in Bosnia: 'What happened here can frankly not be shown in any detail, but the room is full of the charred remains of bodies and they died in the greatest agony. It's hard to imagine, in our continent and in our time, what kind of people could do this.' His moving script gives a sense of the horror without showing close-ups to prove the point, but using selected images like this shot of a burned hand.

duty to give viewers an unsanitized version of events provided that, when we do so, we explain to viewers *why* we are doing it. In an ideal world, decisions about disturbing images should not be the reporter's alone. Make sure someone views them with you. This is not a sign of weakness on your part. It is essential that you forewarn and involve your editor. It should be as routine as consulting a lawyer about your script.

If your piece comes in five minutes before transmission with unexpected unpleasant images in it, one of two things might happen. Either it won't be spotted in the frantic run-up to the programme and will be put straight to air; or an editor will look at the piece, deem the images unacceptable and remove it from the running order. Either way you will have made yourself very unpopular. Especially if it was the lead.

When considering which images you can and can't use, go with your first instinct. By the time you have watched them several times, their power to shock and surprise you will have diminished. The viewers will see them only once, and their first reaction will probably be similar to your own. So put yourself in the audience's position when you are viewing the rushes. Don't automatically put these images at the start of your piece. You will often be better advised to build up to these pictures as part of a narrative sequence that gives them a framework and context and helps prepare the viewer for what's coming. You won't sacrifice the picture power, but you will produce a better proportioned piece – and avoid accusations of sensationalism.

Some things to remember:
- Always signpost the fact that some viewers may be upset by a report. The audience should not be taken by surprise.
- Remember and use 'the watershed'.
- If you are going to use violent images, make sure the story really warrants their inclusion.
- Put the pictures in proper context. Never let distressing images appear 'from nowhere'.
- Don't linger unnecessarily long on any distressing images. If there

are pictures you are not using because they are too distressing then say so.
- Make sure that the presence of your camera was not the reason for any violence happening in the first place.

Let the subject leave the frame

If you are following someone or something that is moving, let them leave the frame of the shot before you stop the camera. It could be someone running or walking, or a plane taking off. Whether you pan the camera with them or simply leave the camera still, let the subject leave the frame. This will provide a natural end to the shot – and a natural editing point.

Pans and zooms

Pans and zooms are both overused by beginners. Excessive panning – 'hosepiping' or 'spraying the garden' – and over-zealous use of the zoom – 'playing the trombone' – leave the viewer with the visual equivalent of sea-sickness. Too much camera movement is simply distracting and makes concentration difficult. Of course, this doesn't mean movement should not be used. It is fine in moderation but there must be a purpose – to reveal something new in a scene for example.

A pan moves on a broadly horizontal plane, either following the movement of an object or moving the shot from one subject to another. Pan in both directions if you can. If you want to show how close the electricity pylon is to the school through a pan, first pan from the school to the pylon and then shoot it again from the pylon to the school. This will give you flexibility in the edit suite. And always remember to hold a static shot for at least five seconds at either end of the pan (or zoom). If there is a possibility that you will want to use a mix, hold the shot even longer.

Pans and zooms can be used very creatively: panning from the crowd to the organizer to set up an interview clip; zooming from a wide shot of a market to a correspondent on a radio mic for a piece to camera. But beware – done properly they can take a long time from the start point to the end point. If in doubt, don't. Or at least shoot a more conventional (or static) 'safety' take of the shot you want.

Most of the time you should let your subject do the moving, not the camera. Ideally, the viewer won't notice the zoom: possibly by using the zoom as the subject moves – for instance, in a shot of a plane taking off. Where you do move the camera, move with the subject, not in the opposite direction.

Think about the edit

Keep a mental checklist, or even written notes, of pictures you have shot for a story and make sure you have enough variety and content to work with in the edit room. Don't feel you can rely on using 'wallpaper' or GVs if you haven't bothered to shoot enough material or haven't thought about the edit. If you are trying to 'pad out' using indifferent pictures in the edit room, you will have an indifferent report.

If you begin to shoot before your subject enters the frame or continue to shoot after your subject has left the frame, you will give yourself a lot of flexibility in the edit room.

Interviews

In an interview, the camera should be placed behind and over the reporter's shoulder. This means the subject is looking at both the reporter and the camera. Then the camera can pull back, ideally physically moving back, for a two-shot of the reporter talking to the subject.

Put a lot of thought into the background. So many interviews are visually flat because there is no relevance, and therefore no interest, in the background. An interview clip may often be the longest single shot in the package – so make it visually as well as editorially interesting, don't just 'knock it off' (see illustrations below).

Try to allow enough time to shoot reverses, a wide set-up and even cutaways. All of these shots will give you much more flexibility in the edit room. Some interview set-ups and backgrounds are clichés in just the same way that some writing is. Try to avoid the obvious ones.

Anonymous interviews

There are times when it is necessary to disguise someone's identity. Try not to rely on 'pixillating' the face; shoot instead in silhouette, semi-darkness or simply show the interviewee's back while shooting the reporter reacting to their words. One of the most effective methods is to 'side-light' the subject and film the shadow on a wall. Sometimes traditional clothes, such as kafiyas in the Middle East, can cover the face.

Often you can shoot the hands of a person as a cutaway in this situation – usually a cliché in other circumstances – as they may have a genuine and compelling reason to hide their identity. But, crucially, if you have told someone they will not be identified *you must be cast-iron certain they will not be*, either by voice, profile or location.

Sound

You always need more sound than you think. The power of sound is often underrated and much ignored. Most effort goes into chasing the pictures for a story, and the sound is often left as an afterthought. Good sound, allowed to breathe in the edit, will dramatically improve the quality of your report. Natural sound does not have to be extreme. The sound of people's emotions is just as powerful as the sound of shooting in war zones – weeping, shouting, laughing, sighing or simply their silence in certain situations. Consider external sound as well – a radio, a police radio, air traffic control or a telephone ringing. The natural world offers endless possibilities: wind, rain, storms, waves on the shore and so on.

So shoot natural sound. If you find a continuous sound such as singing, music or church bells, then let the camera roll for a good two minutes to guarantee you have an uninterrupted chunk of audio, even while you are changing shot. This can be used to great effect to cover a sequence of pictures or glue together an imperfect series of shots with polish and style. Where you can, get close-up sound – this will heighten the impact of what you're recording and remove any background noise. Think about gathering sound; stop and listen more and use radio mics more often to pick up on atmosphere. Film to work around 'throwaway comments'.

Finally, if you have good audio, give yourself time to edit it properly. Editing sound takes longer than editing pictures. But the polish and natural punctuation marks it creates make it time well spent.

Light

If a camera operator wants time to light something, then give it to them. 'One-man bands' need even more time. You or your camera operator should always have a lighting kit with you in order to have the option to improve your pictures. You can change a boring background to an interesting one with an imaginative use of light and a splash of colour.

If you have learned to use a camera to shoot your own material, the next thing to learn is how to light things. Even if you are not carrying a full lighting kit, carry a portable light on top of the camera. In bright light, such as in tropical Africa, a portable light will make possible the transition from bright daylight to the inside of a hut.

Flat lighting is boring but you can make good use of any available natural light. Even domestic lights and lamps can help create effects and textures. Use what light is available to best effect.

A cautionary tale

Don't get 'out of sync'. This writer was caught with a correspondent and crew at Sarajevo airport when it came under sustained mortar attack. We recorded (or so we thought) the sense of sheer panic – and damage – as the shells rained in on the airport bringing parts of it down.

It was only on returning to base and settling down in the edit room that we realized the cameraman had been shooting 'out of sync' – his camera was off when he thought it was on, and on when he thought it was off. The result (aside from a truly apoplectic correspondent) was roughly fifty-three minutes of footage of the cameraman's shoes running in and out of the airport air-raid shelter. No story.

Remember

- Put a lot of thought into your opening shot and your closing shot, in the same way you do for your opening and closing sentences.
- If you are refused access to somewhere – the gates of a factory, a hospital ward, an army base – then film yourself being refused access. It may become integral to the story.
- Do not switch off too soon; you always need more, and a longer shot

provides more editing options and the possibility of getting something more interesting.

- Avoid over-exposure. Don't rely on automatic settings, especially in high contrast situations – 'ride the iris'.
- Always allow time for a camera to come up to speed before filming.
- Never short change yourself on sound. Carry proper microphones.
- Make sure you are carrying enough tapes and batteries and mark them up.

2.7 you

The difference between a major artist and a minor one
is that a minor one never risks failure.

W.H. Auden

Voice and delivery

In any endeavour, a faulty distribution system will lead to failure.
WTLV-TV news director

Correspondents just don't place enough importance on their voices. You may be good-looking. You may be a brilliant journalist. But a poor voice will always hold you back. Ditto a stilted or 'read' delivery. A good voice and delivery may not make a career, but a weak one will definitely break it. The quality of your voice is every bit as important in communication as your writing. Brilliant and brave journalism can be completely undermined by a poor delivery. Even the most beautifully written script can be killed by a weak voice or a poor delivery – likewise, good delivery can liven up the most mediocre material. Indeed, the best scripts *only* work with the right delivery.

Most often the key to connecting with the audience is a conversational delivery. But the best broadcast voices strike a balance between being conversational and authoritative. And the trick is to achieve the former without compromising the latter – all the time remaining interested in your stories and interesting in your delivery. Conversational delivery doesn't come easy. You must learn how to sound as if you are talking with someone when you're actually reading something you have written. So don't just read your script – tell someone a story. And remember, if you don't sound interested in your script the viewer certainly won't be.

Be yourself. Some correspondents adopt what they think is a broad-cast voice, but it invariably sounds faked and unnatural. Make sure your delivery is your delivery – develop your own style so that you sound natural.

When you track your script, try standing up and using a clip mic. Using your hands and facial expression are all things you do in conversation, and so will make you sound more natural. Try using key words to prompt you rather than reading the script. Experiment with different mics that allow you to move around. Try drinking some water beforehand. All these things will help give your voice light and shade. Find what's best for you.

There are a number of common problems which can arise with correspondents' vocal delivery. Word punching is one of them. Many correspondents have been taught to select certain words from their script and 'punch' them hard. But this technique makes a conversational delivery almost impossible and accentuates the sense of the correspondent 'pretending to be a TV reporter'.

A 'sing-song' or 'bedtime story' delivery can make the reporter sound as if he or she is reading a story to a child. Another common fault is the patterned delivery, where the intonation of the voice is the same in every sentence. Every sentence ends on the same upward or downward beat. And some correspondents are prone to the 'voice of doom' delivery, most commonly over pictures of a disaster or war. In an attempt to empathize with apparent victims, they slow down and put too much emotion into their delivery (and often their writing). Keep it straight – the pictures will tell the story.

Sitting at a computer in an open-plan office may discourage you from reading your script out loud, but if you have not read it out loud you cannot know whether it works or not. When you have laid your voice track – or part of it – on tape, listen to it back to see if it works. You won't win any prizes for doing it in one take unless you're so tight for time that's all you can do. Spend more time listening to your voice, not watching the pictures. Turn your back on the screen and listen to your voice. Many correspondents sound flat or sing-song without actually realizing it.

Help is easily available. Plenty of voice trainers can help with delivery through looking at breathing, intonation, pacing and stress. Whatever the strengths and weaknesses of your voice, if viewers spend time thinking about it, they won't be hearing what you're saying.

Appearance

While it may seem that set design, clothing, cosmetics, hairstyles and accessories have little to do with journalism, they are in some ways identical to the problems of newspaper layout, design and format that confront print journalists. If a newspaper layout is sloppy, confusing, or unattractive, the very message of the story can be damaged. In television news, the story is just as vulnerable to the vagaries of aesthetics.
Frederick Shook, *Television Field Production and Reporting*

There is a view among some correspondents that it's only the quality of your journalism that counts, and not what you look like. If only television news were so simple – or so forgiving. Even the best journalism can be devalued if correspondents don't get their appearance right on screen.

The problem with viewers is that they're human. And when you appear on screen they have formed many, many judgements about you before you have even said a word. Those first impressions are based on your appearance and your body language. A famous piece of research carried out by a professor in the United States broke down how people receive messages from each other:

55 per cent of the message comes from body language
38 per cent of the message comes from tone and attitude
7 per cent comes from the words

So how you look and 'perform' on screen is crucial. Viewers react to your physical presence and appearance far more than you realize. How you look and dress can influence how the viewer thinks not only about you and your story but about your organization as well. Put simply, if you look scruffy or out of place then the viewer will see this as a reflection on your journalism.

In other words, your appearance can enhance your credibility, so it pays to dress appropriately to the story and to your audience. And this is not an issue about age or beauty – it's about authority (indeed, the most beautiful performers can be the least authoritative!) and engaging with your audience. Obviously, there is no single way to dress and every society's dress codes evolve and adapt over time. You must dress in a way that's appropriate to you, the story you're working on and, crucially, the programme you're working for, because what may be right for one programme may be completely inappropriate for another. But you must always dress to reinforce your authority and that of your network.

Put another way, when you have decided what's appropriate, look sharp. If you're going to wear a tie, then make sure you look smart. If you don't, you may be delivering the scoop of the century while the viewer is wondering why you can't put your tie straight or comb your hair. Whatever the story, try to keep your appearance neat and simple and subdue any accessories. If viewers are worrying about your tie or your earrings they'll be missing the story. Try to focus attention on your face, not on your clothes. And you should always keep your hair neat and tidy. It's worth keeping some spare clothes at the office in case of emergencies.

Style

Lucidity is the soul of style Hilaire Belloc

What is style in television news? Well, as Justice Stewart said, about something else altogether (pornography, actually), I can't define it, but I know it when I see it. Some people have style by virtue of their charisma, looks, personality or presence. But these are qualities that, by and large, cannot be learned. Some correspondents regularly have good material to work with, but it's not so easy to make television news about everyday events stylish and engaging. So how do you find style? You don't. You let it find you. Just keep refining your skills, resolve all the small imperfections and your style will come to you.

Chapter Three of this book begins with a Dan Rather quote which sums up how to apply yourself by 'not doing the one big extraordinary thing' but doing 'the routine things extraordinarily well time after time'. Finding a style cannot and must not be your main goal – and if you spend too much time trying to affect a style it will show in your work and it won't reflect well. Your job is to communicate clearly and make sense of things for the viewer. And as you strip away all the things that stand in the way of clarity you'll be left with a style. Concentrate on your ability to tell a story and let your style happen. The best correspondents sound the same on-air as they do off-air.

Watch and listen to other correspondents and by all means wonder what makes the best so good – and so stylish. But, as with developing your voice and delivery, never copy someone else's style. Find your own and, again, be yourself. Don't pretend to be some notion you might have of what a TV correspondent *should* be like – be you.

Seek feedback

Use the phone, use email, use your newsroom computer system, use a pigeon, but *seek feedback*. Don't just wait for 'them' to come to you – go after it. Learning from your previous work is the best way to improve and asking for help is a sign of strength. Talk to the programme editor after the programme or the next day or the next time they are on shift; talk to a line manager. Gather up some recent tapes and book a time to talk through your work with an editor. But whatever you do, seek feedback. A very effective way of getting feedback is to ask an editor to look through your last few pieces. This allows the person viewing them to see consistent themes in the way you work, rather than look at specific aspects of one piece.

View your own work

The greatest of all faults is to be conscious of none. Thomas Carlyle

Very few correspondents ever take the trouble to look at their work, other than watching it go out on a bulletin. Yet viewing your own work critically is one of the best ways to learn.

Of course, feedback from editors and colleagues is crucial in pointing out faults you may not have seen or intended and, hopefully, ways of doing it differently or better. But to a large extent you must teach yourself, spotting your own mistakes or seeing for yourself ways in which you might have done it better. Of course, you can learn from your success, but you can learn far more from working through your failures.

There are three ways to 'view' your own work. Firstly, in the way that anybody watches television, to see how clearly you've explained the story, how you scripted your pictures and used natural sound; secondly, with your back to the screen or your eyes closed, to assess your voice and your delivery; and thirdly with the sound down, concentrating just on how you look, how you come through the screen and the impression you give in your face and body language.

And when you look at your work, these are the questions you should be answering:

the story:
- Is it clear exactly what the story is?
- Did the script contain any jargon or obscure words?
- Have I tightly scripted the top of every sequence of pictures?
- Did I use personal examples and interesting people where I could?
- Have I made the best use of the natural sound available?
- What are the telling phrases, the words with a twist?
- Has my writing made all the sequences 'hold hands' with each other?
- Does the piece 'flow'?
- Was my script as clear and as concise as it could be?
- Did the cue 'sell' the story?
- Did my piece work with the cue?

you:
- Was my delivery conversational?
- Did I sound interested in the story and interesting in my delivery?
- Did I make my piece to camera count?
- Is my appearance the most appropriate and authoritative it could be?

the viewers:
- Am I on the viewers' side – have I approached this from their point of view?
- Have I (or any of my sound bites) assumed too much prior knowledge?
- Will the viewers understand why this story matters?
- Have I raised any questions I haven't answered?
- Have I made all the relevant 'connections' for my audience?
- Did I 'personalize' my script where I could?

Try taking your last five or six pieces, judge them against these criteria and see how well you do. And be honest with yourself. You may learn more than you think.

Attitude

Correspondents seem to have little idea about the way their attitude can affect their reputations, and often their careers. If you're an absolute genius you may be forgiven membership of the tantrum brigade. Otherwise, forget it. Be a team player, and understand what gets things done. As Fergal Keane says earlier in this book, 'you need to achieve the impossible! To match the ambition and toughness necessary to be a real operator with a humility that might allow you to remain a decent human being at the end of the day.'

Help, involve and listen to producers, picture editors, crews and engineers. They can often do as much for your on-screen performance as you can. Don't do it with attitude – do it with humility and flexibility.

Don't oversell your stories. There is a famous children's fable about a boy who kept crying 'Wolf!' for a joke. Every time the villagers ran to rescue him they discovered there was no wolf. So when the wolf really came, the villagers stayed put assuming it was another joke. You are not always the best judge of what you have and how it fits in with the rest of the programme. Don't have programme editors taking account of your reputation for 'overselling' when they're trying to judge your story. Don't cry wolf.

And take responsibility. Correspondents are prone to use every excuse in the book – it was the fault of the cameraman, the producer, the programme editor, the demands of other output, the weather and so on. Almost every package or live report is imperfect in some way. Some are far worse and, yes, TV is a collaborative venture. But in the end your name is on your report – you get the credit when it goes well, so take responsibility when it doesn't. Just do the best you can, and leave the excuses to others.

And finally . . .

Be yourself. You are who you are. Don't try being someone else or adopting someone else's style or the voice of someone you think you should sound like. Learn from others, of course, but you must find out the things that make you unique and work on projecting those.

Vary your approach. There are a wide variety of techniques in this masterclass, all of which can enhance your storytelling, but vary the way you use them. Don't get stuck using the same approach the whole time. Break the formula. Do it differently. Overturn the stereotype.

Question what you're doing. Correspondents have a habit of copying each other. A well-known reporter can do a walking piece to camera, and within weeks everyone's doing them. But don't just follow the herd. Question why you're doing what you're doing. And understand how – or if – you are enhancing your story.

And take the odd risk. The person who never makes mistakes probably never makes anything of any worth. Often, the best make the most presentational mistakes because they're the ones pushing the boat out in order to lift something above the ordinary. So push the boat out occasionally. Try something new with a script or a piece to camera. And get some feedback.

And if you want to win a BAFTA there's one final, important rule: don't be intimidated by rules. Make sure you are always fair, truthful and impartial, but bend or break any of the other guidelines in this book to improve your script or your story. But before you do, take proper notice of T.S. Eliot's advice: 'It's not wise to violate the rules until you know how to observe them.'

part two:
getting in and getting on

I urge you to make a lifetime project of refining and developing your craft while never losing what I like to call 'innocent eyes'. That is, the ability to look upon each new story as if nobody else had ever witnessed such a thing before. I don't mean 'oh, wow' journalism; I mean retaining the ability to see the world freshly every day, while simultaneously deepening your knowledge of the mysteries of the human heart. And tempering what you know with scepticism and irony.

Pete Hamill

3 a career in broadcast news

What moves a career along – not just in journalism – is not doing the one big extraordinary thing, it's doing the routine things extraordinarily well time after time. Dan Rather

ARE YOU SURE YOU WANT TO DO THIS?

The BBC's Director-General, Greg Dyke, once said to me that the trouble with people in news ('you buggers', to be precise) is that they don't realize how exciting their jobs are. And he's right.

But there are certain things you need to know before you start out, and if you are pondering a career in this profession, I hope what you are about to read will help you go into it with your eyes open. Confucius said: 'Find a job you love and you'll never have to work a day in your life.' He obviously never worked in broadcast news. It's not that the vast majority of people don't love their job, because they do, and they wouldn't swap it for anything else. But boy, do they work hard.

There are occasionally surveys which appear in the papers about how workers in the UK do more hours than their counterparts in the rest of Europe. Sometimes, it is said, we in the UK work as many as forty-five hours a week. Well, all I can say is that many broadcast journalists would reply: 'Lord, give me a forty-five-hour week.' Journalism is great fun, it's stimulating and very often rewarding. But short hours there ain't – not in broadcasting, anyway.

A career in broadcast news is not for the faint-hearted. It will stretch your range of emotions – and often those of your friends and family – beyond anything you thought possible. The extreme and intense pressure of working to ludicrously tight deadlines, a programme falling apart in the gallery, operating in conflict zones or live broadcasting; or the boredom and loneliness of the stake-out when the rest of the world's media has gone home for dinner, the endless 'phone-bashing'. In war zones you will witness small acts of dignity that will make you want to cry. In court you will hear of acts of brutality that will make you feel physically sick. The personal compromises are also often considerable. Strained relationships, the mobile phone, cancelled dinner engagements, the mobile phone, the early mornings, late nights, indeed, the all-nights – and the mobile phone.

And then there's the surreal environment in which you will be thrust and where, on a daily basis, you will experience the best and worst of the industry. For each day in a newsroom you will witness your colleagues practise this noblest of callings with grace and skill and yet at the same time you will dance through a carnival of egos to the tune of tantrums. Accepting an award from the Columbia University School of Journalism, the celebrated New York journalist Pete Hamill said of journalism: 'No other work so consistently reminds its practitioners of the persistence of human folly, and mankind's amazing capacity for evil and virtue, stupidity and laughter and the endless weaknesses of men.' He could have been talking about working in a newsroom. Be warned – it's a jungle in here.

Fictional representations of journalists may be fictional, but most are – often uncomfortably – rooted in reality. The film *Broadcast News* is a brilliant reflection of the industry's vices and virtues, and the characters played by William Hurt and Albert Brooks are here in their full glory. So too, in an updated – and hopefully more honest – form, is William Boot from Evelyn Waugh's *Scoop*. And though perhaps rarer, Dustin Hoffman's and Robert Redford's Woodward and Bernstein are here too from *All The President's Men*. And industry executives may be loathe to admit it, but the British satirical spoofs *Drop the Dead Donkey* and *The Day Today* are too often too close for comfort.

But this is just to warn you what you might expect when you arrive, and gently to advise you that wallflowers can wither rather quickly in a broadcast newsroom. Because if you still want to come, and I hope you do, let me tell you something else Pete Hamill said in the same speech: 'Be assured of this: you have chosen a profession that truly matters, a craft that can make human change take place in the real world.'

So my plea is that aspiring journalists should not just ask themselves how they are going to get to the top, but why they want to.

Is it possible to survive a career in this jungle? Here's the BBC's veteran reporter, Brian Barron, who is currently based in Rome for BBC News. During his career he has been a correspondent in the Middle East, Africa, the Far East and the United States and has won several Royal Television Society reporting awards. He would be retired if the word existed in his vocabulary:

Broadcast journalism is something of a high-wire act. Deadlines and pressure lurk there in the wings ready to destabilize even the steadiest practitioner and then there's the competition which (only occasionally, hopefully) can spring a surprise. I've found the actual business of reporting mayhem somewhere, such as war or coup, fairly straightforward because in a hostile environment one's instincts and intuition are tuned right up.

I've reported abroad for the BBC since 1967 – largely ensemble work, which is the most rewarding. Two or three brains are better than one. Radio reporting can be a lonely business. In television journalism, as the decades pass you have to maintain a sense of renewal, otherwise your shelf life runs out and something cushy but ghastly beckons, like PR. Knowing that others want your job concentrates the mind.

I still love the challenge of the tight script, the phrase that captures something true. You can go on polishing that no matter how many conflicts or crises you've witnessed. I watch the domestic news output very closely, especially the BBC Six O'Clock News and the Ten O'Clock. Stylistic changes come via the major news shows through new young editors and correspondents so you have to keep your eyes open.

However, in terms of high-profile news assignments the essentials of television reporting haven't changed in the past thirty years to my mind. Packaging skills are exactly that. They have to be acquired. For years I've rigorously practised composing the stories in my head as the day unfolds – mentally moving the jigsaw bits around; most times that helps because you have a structure already worked out, and often a script as well, when you get back and sit down to edit.

TV journalism can be a rough, tough business but I've never encountered anything that matches it for adrenalin and creativity, so I confess to being an addict. Brian Barron

If none of this has put you off, you may be wondering where to start.

PLOTTING YOUR CAREER

For those trying to get into the industry, three things are required: talent, sheer doggedness and the art of pleasant persistence (as opposed to pain in the neck persistence). The talent speaks for itself. The doggedness is needed to plough on despite the rejections. The pleasant persistence you need to stay on the radar of potential employers without making a nuisance of yourself.

The other obvious requirement is to be completely in tune with all the newspapers, magazines and websites which advertise jobs. You may think that this is teaching grandmother to suck eggs, but it is surprising how often is heard the following lament: 'If I had known that job was coming up, I would have gone for it.' If you're serious about it, you need to read them all, all the time.

It's hard to offer advice about where to get into the industry, other than get in wherever you can however you can, but I would offer one observation by way of context: aside from those who came from newspapers, pretty much every top correspondent or presenter I can think of started in radio.

Radio is a better place to start than television; and local radio the best of all. Radio because, first and foremost, it teaches you to write, but also because if you aspire to reporting or presenting, it helps you find your broadcast voice. It also teaches you to develop ideas. Local radio because you will make the tea, present the programme and everything in between; it is a fast-track experience. There are many who start in radio and happily stay in radio and who would argue that it is more challenging journalistically than its upstart counterpart with pictures.

Even if your heart is set on a career in television, you would be wise not to rush into it. Many of the aspiring correspondents who arrive on my doorstep have started their careers in twenty-four-hour television in some form or other. Indeed, these burgeoning channels are, to a certain extent, replacing radio as the breeding ground for today's broadcast journalists. And broadcast journalism is the poorer for it. This is absolutely not to denigrate twenty-four-hour networks – there are some truly excellent editors, producers and reporters who have made their mark on the industry.

But most twenty-four-hour television networks will not teach you to write, and often the room for developing ideas is limited. The emphasis on live broadcasting means you learn the performance skills more than anything, and the headline nature of most of these networks means that the opportunities to develop your journalism can be limited. By all means work for a twenty-four-hour television network, but don't learn your craft there or, at least, don't imagine they will turn you into the finished product. Too many of the people who come my way can walk and talk, but can't write or think journalistically.

The ability to perform in front of a camera raises another issue – presenting. The huge and increasing number of news networks and niche channels now broadcasting means that if you do look and sound good in front of a camera an offer of presenting may not be far away. But whether you aspire to be a presenter or a correspondent, you should beware. Presentation early in your career is unlikely to help you become a correspondent later, and when you come to make the change from one to the other you will probably have to go back to square one. Conversely, if you want to be a news presenter, you will probably reach a plateau before long unless you have a hinterland of reporting experience.

Of course, it's perfectly possible to be a good presenter without having done a substantial amount of reporting. But at the highest level, this tends to be an exception. Indeed, it's possible to be a brilliant correspondent and a lousy presenter. Of all the career paths in broadcast news, presenting is the most precarious of all. When an editor or executive moves on, the presenter may not be far behind. If the ratings are falling, you'll be the first in the firing line. So, trust me – beware any executive wearing a sincere and earnest look and these words: 'We want to make you the face of the network.'

In a business where you are only as good as your most recent work, you must plot your way through the snakes of any mistakes you make and the ladders of your successes; and with luck, ability and application, you'll hopefully get somewhere near the top of the board. Enjoy your triumphs but keep your feet on the ground, and when reading your own publicity, bear in mind the words of the Italian poet Petrarch: 'Many have not become what they might have because they believed they were what people mistakenly said they were.'

There are doubtless exceptions to the rule of everything I've said here and you must find your own way. What is for certain is that it is easier to move around an organization once you're inside it, so climb aboard wherever you can. Once you are on board, if you want to be on air you should make sure you record all your best work. You will need it for your showreel.

THE ART OF THE SHOWREEL

Showreels have become more important in recent years. The growth of twenty-four-hour channels and cable and satellite networks means it's impossible for anyone in the business of hiring talent to stay across all the output they might want to. So a showreel is a good way of introducing yourself, or rather, a *good* showreel is.

A showreel is an edited highlights tape of your best work which demonstrates your talent and your breadth. You may be making a 'cold call' with a showreel or, as is increasingly the case, you may have to submit one with a job application. Often, showreels are used to shortlist applicants. But they are also used to separate equal candidates at interview. Many a fantastic interview has been let down by a showreel which doesn't match the quality of the candidate's performance in the interview.

As the lucky recipient of many such tapes every week I always find it interesting to see the various techniques reporters – or prospective reporters – use to put them together. Some are fantastic examples of just how to do it. Some are tacky in the extreme. And some are just extreme in the extreme. It's an edit like any other edit in one sense. But it's full of pitfalls, too . . .

If your showreel is worthy and staid (this is the most common complaint), you may look dull and lacking in enthusiasm – but if it's too wacky or 'fluffy' you'll look eccentric or lightweight. You have to show how you appear on screen, so plenty of stand-ups are crucial. But too many implies that you may put looks before journalism and too few leaves the viewer unable to judge how you 'come through the screen'. Then there's the riskiest area of all – showing you have a lightness of touch without filling your tape with puns and gimmicks, which is the biggest turn-off of all.

So what exactly should the ideal news showreel look like? I'd go for something along these lines:

Start on a montage of stand-ups and/or live reports. For the person you're trying to hook, being able quickly to judge voice, body language, eyes and how the camera treats you is immensely useful – don't make the recipient spool through the tape to find out what you look like. You have to make it as easy as possible for the person you are sending it to.

Follow the pieces to camera with two or three packages or treatments. These should demonstrate your live skills, your storytelling skills and your ability to use pictures and sound (don't underestimate the importance of showing you can use good sound). But above all they should demonstrate your ability to write.

Make it a tidy edit. If you can't do whizzy graphics that doesn't matter, but make it clean. If it looks scrappy it implies you're not that bothered.

Keep it short – ten minutes maximum and preferably nearer five.

Don't treat it like a selected highlights 'promo' with no full pieces. You have to demonstrate that you can convert your good journalism into good broadcasting. Use the most recent material you can.

Put it on VHS or whatever format the recipient will have in their office. One way of guaranteeing it will never be seen is to put it on any format that means your intended viewer has to leave their office to view it – they never will. Putting a showreel on a CD-Rom can be an effective way of categorizing your work and allowing the viewer to look at different elements if they wish to see more.

Make sure the tape has your name and phone number on the *spine* – never rely solely on the letter you send with the tape. Any tape that goes up on to a shelf with nothing on the spine will never be viewed again.

Never send your original or only tape. You never get them back.

Read Chapter One in this book on what makes a good broadcast journalist. Can you demonstrate these attributes? Read Chapter Two, the masterclass. Can you show some of these craft skills?

Don't use a news showreel to try to open doors in a features or entertainment programme – no matter how funky you think you may be, they won't. You may need different showreels for different applications.

What are prospective employers looking for? Voice and delivery, good writing and storytelling, good use of sound, character, authority, energy and enthusiasm.

If you are just starting out, then you can't be expected to have a showreel. Indeed, if you have just left college or university, it might be better to have no showreel at all rather than a scrappy one done on poor equipment. And don't worry if you're from a newspaper and don't have a showreel. If a broadcaster is interested enough they will give you a screen test. But as you progress in broadcasting, you should keep copies of your best work so that you can include them in a showreel when you need to. For any senior job you'll be expected to produce a decent tape.

Don't expect people to have jobs waiting for you. It is a very competitive business. I'm always amazed at the number of people that send me a showreel and follow it up with an email and a 'well, do you want me or not?' kind of message. Editors can't magic jobs up out of thin air (well, actually they can, but don't worry, if they're going to they'll call you). And don't expect blow-by-blow feedback. People are too busy. In fact, those who persist in trying to get feedback can get it in the form of shorthand which, though blunt and to the point, will appear to be more hurtful than the sender intended. With a bit of luck you will lodge yourself in the back of someone's head for the next time a job does come up.

Most of the time, the best you can hope for from a showreel is that the viewer will be interested enough to ask you in for a chat or an interview. If that happens then the tape has done its job.

FROM PRINT TO BROADCAST

I've got to admit that, after twenty years in newspapers and magazines, I thought broadcasting would be easy. I'd done some punditry before, but that was all pre-recorded stuff, so I knew if I mumbled and fumbled I could go back and do it again. It's very different when you know the mumbles and fumbles are being broadcast live to the nation. I suddenly realized, this is my career now, not just an add-on. This is it. And it started to freak me out a bit.
Jeff Randall, BBC Business Editor

If he or she can write well, the transfer to broadcasting need not be that difficult for the clever print journalist. But – a very big but – there are two essential things you require before you can even think about it: a good broadcast voice and an engaging and enthusiastic character. You must be a good communicator. It is true that many print journalists make the transition to broadcasting off the back of an expertise in a specialist subject, but only if they have these prerequisites. And there is something else which *you* should look for if you want to transfer to broadcasting from print – an employer who is willing to invest in you and nurture you; who will train you properly and not want instant results. You should insist on plenty of coaching and plenty of feedback. It takes time.

The fact that it takes time can be difficult for both sides. You may have been King of the Castle at the newspaper where you penned your column; and here you are reduced to a trainee again, and one whose every stumble goes out live to six million people. For however confident you are as a human being, you will be petrified during your first attempts at live broadcasting. There will be no notepad, no computer, no spell-check. Just one take; one chance to get it right. And your friends and family will all be watching and most likely wondering, not which angle of the story you took, but why you were speaking in that strange voice and why you wore *that* jacket.

Besides the obvious difference of appearing in person, there are two huge hurdles for print journalists to overcome. The first is learning to condense information. Most newspaper journalists think they do that already, but the extent to which broadcasting demands this can come as a real shock. A live two-way of one minute thirty seconds is just 270 words. A package of the same length, with two interview clips of fifteen seconds each and ten seconds of natural sound will leave you with just 150 words. The second is learning to yield to the primacy of pictures and sound; to keep quiet and back off, using your writing merely to help the sounds and pictures and characters tell the story. This requires huge self-restraint. The short sentences and conversational language of broadcasting also take some getting used to.

These two hurdles can be overcome by close attention to the craft of broadcasting; it can be learned. My own experience of training print journalists is that vocal delivery and 'being themselves' on air are the things they find hardest. Trying to be the articulate, witty and engaging character they are in real life when they have an earpiece carrying instructions through one ear while they talk to an inanimate lens takes a very long time to master. I have heard the sound of rushing air from many a punctured ego during these early stages. Broadcasting does have its attractions – though not necessarily advantages – to outsiders, the main ones being immediacy and impact. Immediacy in that whatever story you have found or developed, you can be on air with it in minutes; and impact in that your journalism will be reaching the often huge audiences of news and current affairs programmes.

The transition from print to broadcast doesn't always work, and if it doesn't, you must be honest with yourself and get out quickly. I have seen a number of excellent print careers ended in order to start mediocre broadcast careers. This is as much the fault of the organization taking them on as the individuals themselves, but too many hang doggedly in there in the hope that they will suddenly become great when it is obvious to those around them that it is not going to happen.

Those who have not made the transition have seen their careers hit the rocks either because they simply failed to learn the craft and wrote first and looked at the pictures and sound as an afterthought. Or they simply couldn't come to terms with the performance aspects of broadcasting and failed to understand that the viewer is engaging first and foremost with you as a human being. You can be a brilliant journalist and even a brilliant writer, but still be a lousy communicator. And probably the most common reason why print journalists, or perhaps any journalists, fail is because of a weak voice. Every time I have employed a journalist whose voice I had doubts about, but which I thought we might make good, I have lived to regret it. Every time.

Some print journalists hold their broadcast counterparts partly in contempt and see only make-up and gimmicks and the search for glory. Some are put off by the very immediacy that attracts others, or the need to work for several programmes or networks at the same time. But more appear to be in awe of what they see as the mysteries of broadcast news. Whatever view you take, plenty of journalists are seeking to transfer from print to broadcast all the time, though surprisingly few go back the other way.

In the end, as with any other craft, the only way you get good at it is to do lots of it. So take your time and play the long game – and the more senior the level you transfer at, the longer you should take in training.

THE SEARCH FOR DIVERSITY

Unlike many other professions, journalism is split equally between male and female. But the profession is also young. According to a report by the Journalism Training Forum, just over two-thirds of all of Britain's journalists are under forty, four out of ten are single, widowed or divorced while, surprisingly, over three-quarters have no dependent children.

To what extent should the make-up of our journalistic workforce reflect the social structure of Britain as a whole? Frankly, a lot more than it does, and this is one of the biggest challenges facing the industry. According to the JTF study, there are some 70,000 journalists working in Britain, with around 10,000 of those in broadcasting. The Forum also estimates there will be 20,000 new jobs in journalism by the year 2010. But of the existing 70,000 a staggering 96 per cent are white. Just 4 per cent of journalists come from ethnic minorities. As the JTF report says, given that so much journalism is concentrated in London and the south-east (more than half of all the UK's journalists are based there) and other urban centres, the number of black and Asian journalists working in Britain is pitifully small.

And what's more, the people becoming journalists are coming from an ever narrower section of society – a section which is almost entirely middle class and, by and large, wealthy enough to fund students through further education, unpaid work experience and subsequent debt. Of those joining the industry, only 3 per cent come from families headed by someone in a semi-skilled or unskilled job. The rest come from families headed by someone in a professional or high level, middle class occupation. Given how competitive it is to get into journalism, and given the way news organizations recruit, this is perhaps not so surprising.

But can a workforce like this properly reflect and understand society as a whole when it is made up of such a narrow section of it? Surely not. So there is a huge desire for greater diversity – a greater proportion of staff from an ethnic background, more regional accents, more social and political diversity. The challenge is to attract and develop talent from all sections of society. The question for many organizations is how. It's clear that not much will change using existing recruitment methods. So the industry as a whole is looking at ways of reaching out to those who might not make it through conventional routes. This is not merely some kind of political correctness – for one thing, there is a clear business need here. Audience research shows that many of the sections of society which are under-represented in our journalistic workforce feel that many of our programmes and much of what we report is irrelevant to them. And this is reflected in audience figures and regional and social breakdowns. It will also be reflected in advertising revenue, as advertisers will want to know that they can reach all audiences.

What is certainly true is that news organizations everywhere are looking for ways of broadening their workforces and making them more diverse. The doors are opening, and the next section looks at starting out on the road to getting through them.

4 the first rung
– education and training

THE TOOLS OF THE TRADE

Before you start, you will need two books: one small, one larger. The small one will last for ever and the larger one will change very frequently. One is very specific, the other can be anything you want. To accompany the smaller one you will need a pen. And here's what you will do:

In the small one you will write down the name, telephone number(s) and email addresses of everyone you meet along the way. Because this is your contacts book. And you will guard it with your life. In this day and age, this small book may be some kind of hand-held mobile device, whatever, but the purpose will be the same. Good contacts are the life-blood of your job.

The second book you will always have on you will change all the time. Novels, biographies, histories, poetry, plays, compilations – mostly nothing to do with journalism, but everything to do with the world we live in and everything to do with provoking thought and loving, living with and working with words. The very best journalists are great writers. And you can't be a great writer unless you're a great reader. And great readers get well beyond newspapers and magazines. All the time.

If the reading bit bores you, stop here. Go find another profession.

WRITING

Do you know the most common criticism journalism courses make about schools? It's this: 'They just don't teach them how to write.' And do you know the most common criticism employers make about journalism courses? It's this: 'They just don't teach them how to write.' The importance of good writing cannot be overestimated. Good writing and good journalism are two sides of the same coin.

But if this is the very beginning of your career, let's be clear what we mean. We are not talking purple prose or winning awards here. We are talking grammar, punctuation and spelling. The ability to write properly punctuated sentences with every word spelled correctly and an understanding of the precise meaning and usage of words is something no good journalist can be without. Newcomers to the profession may wonder what difference or damage the odd spelling mistake makes. But old hands in journalism – many of whom will be judging your early attempts to find a job or get on a course – get very agitated indeed when they encounter poor writing.

Indeed, rightly or wrongly, those same old hands will assume that anyone who can't write properly is careless, or even a bit dim. And this can blight your career in later life too. So when it comes to applying for courses (or jobs) get someone to check your application form. If you don't, you risk your form standing out for all the wrong reasons. In looking at forms for one postgraduate university course I saw some real howlers – 'apoligies', 'seperately' and 'guage' among them.

You must learn these basic skills before you can begin to write with flair and style (see the bibliography for some help here).

WHAT DO YOU KNOW?

A detailed general knowledge is a very good thing. But understanding the way the world works and the major issues facing our planet is an even better thing. In truth, you need both. In his interview for a place on a postgraduate journalism course, one candidate could comfortably name all the key players in the US cabinet – well done to him. But he was completely flummoxed when the interviewer asked which of these politicians were 'hawks'.

It's important to get a grasp of what conflicts like the Middle East and Kashmir are really about. Get to grips with issues like the global water shortage and population trends. Do these seem like remote issues? By the year 2050, 90 per cent of the world's population will live in the developing world, so if you think asylum is an issue now, just wait. Part of your job as a good journalist is to tell people *why* these seemingly remote issues matter to them. Give yourself some breadth. How well do you understand Islam? In a world after 11 September 2001, it is an important thing to try to understand if we are to avoid simply reinforcing stereotypes (another role of the good journalist). With the mass of background information that is available on the internet, it was never easier to research these things, and as a budding journalist another tool of the trade you must have is a total grasp of how to use internet search engines. There is no excuse.

Above all, understanding these issues demonstrates a genuine interest in news and current affairs. So, when you are reading the newspapers, look at the leader pages and read the commentaries. Understand the arguments and the debates as well as simply what's happened. The best columnists and leader writers are there to provoke debate and argument and reading them will get you beyond mere details.

These two quotes, both from senior editors, sum up the feelings of many who sit through interview panels:

'Don't even bother if you don't read the papers/watch TV news/ listen to radio news most days, and lots. Your lack of hinterland will soon be exposed.'

'I've interviewed so many people over the years now and the biggest problems are lack of general knowledge, lack of hinterland, and then basic writing skills.'

STARTING FROM SCHOOL

If you're still at school and feel that a career in journalism beckons, there are a number of things you can do now. Practise your writing at every opportunity – school magazines, essays, articles for the local paper; and read as much as you can. Great writers are great readers. Absorb words – look up every new word you come across. Having some writing to show potential employers or courses could well give you the edge over other candidates.

There are other areas you can get involved with. School councils or, if your school has one, the debating society. Volunteer to work in the community. News is about ordinary people, and doing this will broaden your horizons and develop your communication skills. Use every opportunity you can to make videos. Involvement in drama can certainly help you in a career in broadcast news. Computer literacy is also vital for journalists. If you are considering a technical career in television, then maths and science will be helpful, if not crucial.

Watch and listen to television and radio news programmes, read newspapers and look at websites. Look at how the major stories are treated.

This is how a recent postgraduate student gained experience:

The careers teacher at school actively discouraged me from journalism declaring, 'It's too hard to get into,' and 'It's very competitive.' That failed to put me off. So while studying I wrote articles and contributed to everything from the school magazine and a French newsletter to the local newspaper's letters page. I even wrote a few features for the WH Smith company newsletter, where I worked as a Saturday girl.

GET A DEGREE

If you are a school leaver with an eye on entering journalism, broadcast or otherwise, there are a number of routes open to you. But the best thing to do is to go to university. It really doesn't matter what you do. If you have a strong desire to do journalism as a first degree then do it, but you don't have to. You'll do as well – and probably better – doing the degree subject that interests you most and then doing a postgraduate course in journalism or heading straight for a job.

Many BA or first degree courses involving journalism are what's known as 'joint degrees' – journalism with another subject such as English, modern languages, modern history, politics and so forth. The upside of this is obvious. You get to study (and, hopefully, practise) journalism while gaining some depth in another subject. The potential downside is that you don't study either with the kind of depth that you would if you were studying just one subject. You have to go and have a look around the course and judge for yourself.

It is by no means impossible to get into broadcasting without specific journalism training or attending a journalism course. A particular skill, some specialist knowledge or strong language skills can all help you find a niche. Either way, if you are still at school and want to go into journalism, read this statistic: 98 per cent of all journalists have a degree. That has to be the starting point. As it happens, nearly two-thirds of journalists have a journalism qualification as well. It is a well-educated profession. A degree won't guarantee you a place in the industry, but it's a good start. Whatever financial woe you go through to get a degree – or indeed most training – it's almost certainly worth it. If you decide not to go into journalism, then you still have a degree under your belt.

You will be saddled with debt when you emerge from education and attempt to enter the world of work. But that will be the case whatever profession you enter, and the debts incurred studying to go into journalism don't appear to be significantly worse than any other profession.

WORK EXPERIENCE

One of the most important factors in clinching a place on a course or even a job is the ability to demonstrate that you've had some relevant work experience. It also demonstrates your commitment to a career in journalism. Get as much work experience as possible – however you can, whenever you can. Work experience can mean many things, and can happen in many ways. Many college and university courses have work placements built into them. The BBC accommodates 120 students accredited to BJTC courses by finding placements for them in BBC local radio.

Many journalism courses have work experience built into them through their own radio networks, like Channel M at Salford University and Angel FM at City University. These provide invaluable experience, and tapes that demonstrate it. In many organizations it is a case of the cold call – letters and calls to ask for work experience. Not all work experience is unpaid, but the vast majority is. Perseverance and the skills of the salesman are crucial. As are the funds. Whatever you do, keep trying – you'll get there in the end.

Some companies, such as Sky and the BBC, have formal schemes to which you can apply. The BBC jobs website has details of its formal work experience scheme. The BBC scheme was established in part to avoid friends of the bosses getting work experience over other, often better qualified, candidates. But, sadly, it is still the case that knowing someone in the industry is more likely to give you a head start with work experience than anything else.

Think carefully about where to do your work experience. The bright lights of a London newsroom may seem alluring, but the larger the office is, the less useful experience you'll get. In a big newsroom you'll make calls, make tea and log tapes. In a small office or a foreign bureau you can end up doing anything and everything. Go to the smallest place you can find. Work as hard as you can. Volunteer for as much as you can. Get to know everyone. Be nice to everyone. You may be working with people who will give you your first references.

Being able to demonstrate work experience is crucial. Here's a recent graduate on doing work experience:

While studying, I've managed to successfully balance academic commitments, paid employment and unpaid work placements. I've organized and completed work placements at local and regional newspapers, commercial radio stations, BBC TV and radio. So what have I gained from work placements? The highs have been seeing articles printed, getting opportunities to interview and meet some of the most fascinating people – and some who are not so interesting, too! I've experienced so much, from booking and interviewing the great and the good, politicians, the public etc. to wackier things like spending a weekend with the Fat Club.

Most of all I value the opportunities I've had to learn from and work alongside professionals who are where I aspire to be. You may not take home a pay cheque, but this is invaluable. While at

BBC Wales, I was motivated by the constant challenges each day brought, like trying to book an English-speaking Italian for an early morning news programme to talk about the re-opening of the Leaning Tower of Pisa (which the Italians are not keen to publicize anyway). Then ringing anyone and everyone in the Middle East trying to book a guest the producer just had to have on the programme and being constantly told, 'He's a bit busy at the moment – we're in the middle of a war, you know.' As one news reporter told me, 'You will either love the atmosphere of a newsroom or you'll hate it. Come along and see what you think.' There is no greater feeling than a busy newsroom. The rewards in terms of job satisfaction are endless even when you're working for free. My advice to students would be to go along and find out for themselves what floats their boat.

There are lows to work placements. It's not a nice feeling when someone takes on your ideas as their own because they know you're just passing through. But constantly remind yourself an idea that's not shared is not worth having. The art of getting the most out of work placements is to be keen and get on with everything your asked to do. I've had some of the best opportunities and met amazing people while boiling the kettle or running around delivering heavy bags of tapes to edit suites. At one work placement, I leapt a few rungs up the ladder in a matter of hours, went from being the post girl to working on programme ideas. This I achieved through showing I was genuinely interested, asking questions, talking to everyone without getting in the way and listening to people. Something I learnt at BBC Wales was to make opportunities to spend time with everyone, TV in particular is a real team effort. I got a greater sense of the place from spending time with not just reporters but with graphic designers, camera people etc.

CHOOSING THE RIGHT COURSE

For any newcomer starting out there is an extremely confusing array of ways into the industry. There has never been so much choice, so much training, so many courses, so many routes in. There are literally hundreds of courses you might do to help you begin or further your career in broadcast news. And the number of courses is still growing. So you must check them out to make sure they're not over-egging their particular pudding.

What you do depends on where you are trying to get to and what time and money you have available. Courses come in all shapes and sizes – longer, academic courses with a mixture of theory and practice (BAs and MAs in journalism and related studies) ending in exams and shorter, entirely vocational courses ending with some form of industry assessment.

Having just finished a postgraduate journalism course I can honestly say it's one of the most challenging things I have ever done. For anybody thinking of taking one on, my advice would be to enter into it with your eyes wide open. It's not like the previous three/four years you've just spent having cosy tutorials and a definite structure and timetable. For the nine months, you'll be juggling academic study, assignments, practical modules, work placements and job applications. Then there are the technical aspects which you need to grasp with great speed. Things often go wrong and there is often no one to troubleshoot, so be prepared to turn things around for yourself.

It'll take over your life. There are often not enough hours in the day – the schedule can be punishing but it's worth it. Just be sure you want to do it badly enough before you set out on the adventure. It's expensive too, and there's no money-back guarantee (remember, they make a lot of money from these courses). The government will give you £6,000 to train to be a teacher. Train to be a journalist and you'll leave with a debt possibly in excess of £10,000 and possibly still have to work for free at the end. It's not the easy option but the rewards in terms of opportunities are endless, and in my opinion it's the best decision I ever made. Recent postgraduate journalism student

But in order to find the right course for you, and in order to avoid wasting time, energy and money on the wrong course, you must put in some serious work to sort the wheat from the chaff. At some point, a brochure or prospectus will plop through your letterbox. It may be colourful, it may be seductive and it may promise you an exciting career in journalism. But don't believe it. You would not expect a good journalist to take the marketing hype at face value – so nor should you. A healthy dose of journalistic scepticism is called for. The following quote, from a senior reporter, appeared in the Journalism Training Forum report, 'Journalists at Work': 'Sixth formers and college students should be much better informed about what editors consider credible courses. Too many youngsters are given bad advice about courses and finish three years of hard work still ill-equipped to get a job. There are some very good courses, but many do not offer the professional skills needed to enter the workplace.'

Here's what you should do:

- You must go to see the course. Try to look around on a normal working day for the course. As with finding schools, don't end up judging the quality of the 'open day' rather than the course itself. Talk to current students.
- If you know anyone in the industry, ask them what reputation the course has.
- Look at the course website.
- Research the tutors. How many are still working in the industry? How many used to?
- Find out how much exposure you'll get to industry insiders (lots in some cases).

- Is it located in a 'media hub' or city with plenty of media activity and plenty of news?
- What's happened to recent graduates? What did they think?
- What do they do to help you find a job?
- How much access to equipment will you get?

One recent graduate told me the equipment on her course was terrible, but that the access to good tutors and industry insiders was excellent. Another explained: 'Well, the technical facilities are often not that great and feedback is sometimes lacking which can be frustrating. But there's no point in grumbling – you haven't got the time. The best advice I could give to anyone who's in the position I was in a year ago, wanting to pursue a postgraduate broadcast journalism diploma course, is to go into it with a clear idea of what you need from the course and then make it work for you.'

You need to find these things out:

- What are the facilities like?
- Does the course offer work placements? Can they say where they are? Are they guaranteed? Do you have to organize them yourselves?
- Have they got their own radio network?
- Compare the student numbers per tutor with other courses. Are there too many students?
- Do you come out with a showreel? Are there any examples you can see?
- What are the costs? (As with everything else in life, expensive doesn't always equate with the best.)
- Is it a commercial course or is it funded somehow?
- Are there any hidden costs along the way?
- What funding is available for you to do projects?
- Will it broaden the skills you already have?

- What are the entry qualifications?
- Does it help you into the branch of journalism in which you're most interested (a word of caution here, though – don't decide too early what sort of journalist you want to be). A broadcast course will prepare you more specifically for a job in broadcasting, but the principles of journalism are much the same and will apply across the board. And employers recognize this.

It all requires the kind of tenacity, perseverance and curiosity that it takes to be, well, a good journalist . . . And even then you may well end up trying to get on the one course that everybody else is trying for. But it's like that when you're applying for jobs, so get used to it. The key here is perseverance. Unless you are almost uniquely lucky, there will be many courses and even more jobs that you will go for and not get. It goes with this industry.

University journalism courses are often massively oversubscribed. Sheffield University had around 850 applicants for sixty places. But you shouldn't – indeed, you can't – let this put you off. All of these courses still need good applicants. Many applicants get on to the course of their choice and then don't go because they get work placements or can't afford it.

Many courses have expanded rapidly, particularly joint degrees, to accommodate the increasing interest in journalism. But you must also be clear that, on the course you are looking at, journalism is not being used to shore up other subjects and merely increase the numbers. You should be aiming to study at a centre of excellence, not a sausage factory.

For many potential students, the extra time and debt mean that undertaking a postgraduate course is a huge decision for them. This email was from a budding journalist whose work experience had turned into regular work, but who had also been offered a place on a postgraduate course (I've withheld the name of his employer):

> *Dear Mr Ray, I'm writing to ask you for some advice. I've been working at 'X' News for the last seven months, writing scripts and editing footage. My ambition is to be a broadcast journalist at the BBC. I was wondering how necessary you felt it was for me to do a broadcast journalism course, given the experience I'm getting at the moment.*

My reply:

> *It's impossible for me to judge and it would be improper for me to advise – because it could go wrong either way! On the one hand, turning down an opportunity to do a course where you can get to grips with all the issues may be a mistake – it's the only chance of its kind you'll get. It's a long-term investment. On the other hand, the BBC would employ you because it thought you were good, not because you'd done a course. So you must judge for yourself. If you stay at 'X' News, make sure they're committed to you for a good while. You're young enough not to be too short-termist.*

THEORY OR PRACTICE?

In considering what you want from a course you must weigh up what the course offers in the amount of theory relative to the amount of practice; the amount of 'education' relative to the amount of 'training'. If you want to go into broadcast news you have to get some element of practice. As a general rule, media studies give more of a theoretical perspective, while journalism courses are slightly more practical (though check that the courses you are looking at have the equipment to allow you to be practical).

The truth is that you need a balance of both: between theory and practice, between education and training. Anyone entering journalism should have a broad sense of the moral and ethical issues surrounding what they do. They must be able to place their craft in the broader context of the society they are serving. But too much theory at the expense of practice will leave them ill-equipped for the realities of what they are about to do ('Unable to tell one end of a camera from another,' as one of my less charitable colleagues put it). Most jobs in broadcast news combine the editorial and the technical. Some understanding of the technology and a sense of having worked in a team are also essential.

APPLYING

Selection procedures vary enormously from place to place. But because of the huge number of applications, many first degree courses are choosing not to interview for places, but to decide on two criteria: the application form and exam results. I can't help you with your exam results, but I can tell you this: a well written, well supported application form is crucial.

Your form – most commonly the UCAS form – has to be relevant to your journalistic ambitions. Your personal statement should not be too broad. It should be single-minded in demonstrating your enthusiasm and ambition to get into journalism. It should be clear and *very* well written. Use bullet points if you want to get things across simply.

Crucially, your reference should be relevant to your ambitions to be a journalist. It needs to get beyond what a nice, studious person you are and say why you might fare well in the world of journalism. Because if you are applying to a course that isn't going to interview you, your form and reference are all they have to go on. Get a second opinion (as well as a spelling check) before you send it off.

Some courses will ask you to interview someone and send the tape or disc with the application. If you are asked to do this, don't think you have to interview someone famous. Just make sure it's an interesting interview – you don't need someone famous to achieve that.

INTERVIEWS FOR JOURNALISM COURSES

When you have chosen where you want to go and sent in your (beautifully written) forms you may be lucky enough to get an interview. The procedure will vary from place to place, but for most postgraduate courses the interview day will involve a mixture of tasks – a one-to-one interview, a group discussion or editorial meeting, a news quiz or general knowledge test, a spelling test, some form of writing test and sometimes a voice test.

For the interview, the university will be looking for you to demonstrate your enthusiasm for news. They will want you to expand on what relevant experience you have had – any writing you've done, any college, university or hospital radio broadcasting or any work placements. What travel have you done? Some questions will be obvious, like why you want this particular course and where else you have applied. You may be asked which story you would really like to work on at the moment or which most interests you. Or who your role model is – who you would aspire to be. Read Chapter Six about editorial interviews. The interviewers are looking for these things: clear enthusiasm, a demonstrable interest in news and current affairs and focused answers – and all of these things backed up by what you've done with your life so far.

General knowledge tests may be just that: the kind that ask questions like 'Who is the vice-president of the USA?' But they may be more sophisticated, asking questions like 'Why is x in the news this week?' So you need to know your cabinet ministers but you also need to be bang up to date with what's happening in the world. This may be tough if you've just sat your finals, but your interviewer will still expect it.

Sometimes group discussions will be part of your test and marked as such. The BBC sponsorship scheme, which funds successful candidates through postgraduate courses, uses group sessions in this way as part of its selection procedure. Here are the comments an interviewer wrote down after watching a successful candidate in a group session:

- Identifies one person who hasn't yet spoken and asks for ideas.
- Makes good suggestions which were inclusive of the group.
- Supports other people's ideas ('Oh, that's interesting').
- Listens and looks at who's speaking – good body language.
- Makes the group laugh and laughs at other jokes.
- Identifies what is needed from the exercise and lets people know. (We've only got five more minutes', 'All we need to do is to identify a story to develop.')
- Creates a good environment – is funny, allows quieter ones to have their say, doesn't talk over them, stays focused.
- Argues clearly for and against stories. Sticks with his own opinion even when the majority of the group disagreed.
- Thinks of good ways to develop a story even though he didn't think it should run.
- Visually describes the pictures to be used in pieces.
- Talks about what radio and the tabloids were running with.

Not all organizations will mark group sessions. Some will get candidates into groups, but only as a way of dividing up a running order or a certain amount of work between them. Teamwork is a fundamental part of broadcast journalism and, whether a group discussion is marked or not, interviewers will certainly take note of any signs of candidates being unable to work as part of a team.

The writing test could be one of a number of exercises. You may be given agency copy about a range of stories, asked to choose your top three, write them up and put them into a running order. You may be given one story and asked to write a television script with pictures and interviewees. You may be given five stories, asked to put them into an order and then write them into a summary. There are many variations, but the test is essentially the same – can you write engaging scripts which tell a story in a powerful and simple way? Try and show some flair and imagination, without resorting to clichés. And understand this: broadcast news is all about what you leave out – don't try to pack all the facts in, otherwise flair and imagination will be impossible. Part of the test is to see if you can select the salient facts, leave out the less important and then write it in a way that really engages the listener. The single most common mistake is to try to pack too much in.

If you are given a voice test, don't make the mistake of trying to 'put on' a broadcast voice. The best broadcasters are those who sound the same on-air and off-air. Try not to worry too much about a voice test. The majority of people in broadcast news do not appear on air; and those that do often take years to 'find' their broadcast voice or writing style.

Practise writing some scripts. Read the masterclass in this book, then take some newspaper articles and write them into fifteen, thirty and forty-five second radio scripts (three words per second). Then practise reading them aloud. Record some on tape and see how conversational and engaged you sound.

TRAINEE SCHEMES

Internal trainee schemes are not as common as they once were. ITN has ended its scheme altogether. The BBC's news trainee scheme no longer exists in the same form and has been replaced by a sponsorship scheme where a number of students are funded through a postgraduate diploma in journalism. Entry-level schemes are few and far between and even those that do exist are almost absurdly oversubscribed. So never go into them (or any other application for that matter) half-heartedly.

The BBC gave up its news trainee scheme because it found that the candidates that went through it would probably have got into the corporation anyway. Channel 4 funds training for those in the independent sector via Skillset, and some ITV companies run local training schemes. Check out the Skillset website to see what it funds.

TRAINING RATHER THAN EDUCATION . . .

Another option for those who have long been out of school or university and are seeking more of a career change than a first job is to look at some of the huge variety of shorter vocational courses. There is also a greater acceptance now that people can come in at a later stage in their life. The BBC has recently taken on an investment banker, a forty-year-old teacher and a thirty-nine-year-old policeman and trained them to be broadcast journalists. So don't think that because you're not a journalist and you're not trained as a journalist that it's too late. Exceptional writing or presentational skills or a deep expertise in a specific area are still regarded as assets.

THAT ELUSIVE FIRST JOB . . .

According to the JTF study, just under a third of journalists got their first job through an advertisement, while a similar number got there by making contact or writing to an employer. Somewhat reassuringly, only one in ten got in through a friend or relative. A small but significant number said their first job followed work experience.

Should you just 'get your foot in the door' or wait until the right job comes along? The risks with the latter approach are obvious – the ideal job for you is just as ideal for the huge number of other, possibly better qualified, candidates. So getting a foot in the door somewhere in an organization can seem like a good idea. But there are risks with this approach, too. If you join as a secretary, the culture of some organizations is such that you may not be thought of as someone with any potential beyond that; and some managers get very frustrated having appointed someone to a job, only for that person to immediately try to move on out of it. Nonetheless, plenty of people have fared well by getting a foot in the door and gradually moving on.

The following was written by a senior BBC correspondent, and describes a fictitious ideal candidate arriving for an interview for her first job:

> I will try to describe the type of person I think the BBC would be likely to hire, and the attributes I would advise her to push.
>
> The candidate 'has lived a bit'. Though still in her early twenties, she has clearly shed the naïvety and unworldliness that many new graduates exhibit. She didn't waste the time between school and university or further education. She has travelled – in this period or in university vacations. Even if she hasn't done any further education she still travelled. On her own. And this was travel to interesting places, not just sitting by Uncle Buck's pool in Cape Town with a large gin. In the course of this, she worked abroad for a short while as well. This makes the candidate interesting to the BBC. She knows a bit about the countries she's visited; they aren't just abstract names to her. She has shown through travelling, and maybe learning a language or two along

the way, that she's got a curious mind; that she's willing to learn and continue learning through adult life; that she likes doing things first hand rather than reading about others doing them; and she's willing to put in hard work to make sure what she's set as her goals become reality.

She shows by the way she answers the panel's questions that she can listen, consider a problem, and suggest an answer. She can understand and appreciate both sides of a story, and develop an argument. She is ready to talk about a few stories that have really 'got under her skin' and which she has pursued further. She is a self-starter. Socially, she's a good mixer, able to start a friendship or good working relationship quickly with all comers. She knows where to strike the balance between shocking older hands with her youthful arrogance and hiding in the corner like a mouse. The questions she asks show she's thought through the issues, and she comes across as genuinely interested in the answer. She watches/listens to our programmes, and has sensible observations to make about them. She has a little of the maverick about her – not a gratuitous flouting of authority; just that she's prepared to challenge, to question, and think her way round problems in an original way. She can penetrate bullshit, gobbledygook, jargon and pseudo executive-speak.

Her work experience portfolio shows that she's immersed herself in as much journalism as she could during her time at university and/or since. There's also variety in the work experience she's completed. If by the end of her academic course she was starting to be paid by these newsrooms/publications, get stuff aired on network radio or into national newspapers, then the interviewers can be fairly sure this is likely to be a successful journalistic career. The candidate brings one or two aspects to the interview that are fairly unique: her newspaper experience wasn't just with the Dartley Ditcher *... she did a fortnight's unpaid work with the* Tehran Times *when she was visiting Iran, etc.*

She still got a respectable degree/FE qualification, nothing stunning, but enough to show that she didn't neglect her studies. She's computer literate, a voracious user of the Internet, and probably has her own website (or at least knows how to build one). She's likely to own a DV camera, and might have edited home movies or reports of her own on a PC. She is enthusiastic about undergoing further training, and has identified which skill areas she most needs to develop. She has a sense of humour, which comes across during the interview. She is relaxed and confident, without being smug. She speaks naturally, and not as if reciting a pre-written speech. She has interests/pastimes about which she is passionate which have nothing whatsoever to do with journalism.

I could only add one thing to this description – that this fictitious character has read a huge variety of books. Not just because she wants to broaden her mind, but because she understands that (and I know I have said this before) it is only by becoming a great reader that she can become a great writer.

STICK AT IT

I was thirty years old before the BBC finally realized what it had been missing out on all those years and let me in. I got a three-month contract as a sub-editor in the teletext service, CEEFAX. My first task was to compile the television listings (and there are doubtless those who would say it's the most useful thing I ever did in the BBC!). I was lucky that a job came up during those three months and infinitely luckier that I got it. But the point is this: I had been turned down time after time. Perseverance and an ability not to get despondent are crucial qualities.

You will often hear people use the phrase, 'You have to make your own luck,' but what does this mean? It means working hard, trying to get yourself in the right place at the right time. Doing the overnight shifts and the weekend shifts that others don't want to, because at some point you'll be the only person around when the big story drops and then you'll have your stage on which to perform. You will have made your own luck. Keep an eye on the press and relevant magazines and websites – this is where jobs, trainee schemes, careers fairs and the like will be advertised.

And even as your career progresses, never stop training. Never stop getting coached. Never stop getting feedback. There is a tendency for everyone in broadcast news to be trained when they start out, but never again revisit the fundamentals of what they do. Most practitioners never reflect – or never get time to reflect – on what they do. They never go back to basics in a way that really questions what they are doing. That's a mistake. They can't and shouldn't do it constantly, but from time to time they should stop, think, question themselves, go back to basics and start again.

You know you're becoming an old fart when people start writing to you asking for advice about how to get into journalism. Nowadays, I get at least one letter like that every week. Some of them even ask me to endorse them, as if they were a can of baked beans. Cheeky buggers. Actually, the fact that they write at all shows they've got one of the assets useful in a journalistic career, the readiness to tackle anyone on any subject.

So, if you're an aspiring broadcast journalist, please don't write to me asking for an endorsement of a career plan which takes you to the top. If you've got a journalistic temperament, you don't endorse anything you cannot personally vouch for. And if you would never have thought of writing to someone with a brassy CV and a presumptuous letter, don't worry. It would never have occurred to me either.

Jeremy Paxman, BBC *Newsnight* presenter

From this day on – if you are lucky, and persistent, and go out to work in the places where news is gathered – your true education will begin. If you hope to be any good, as journalists and as human beings – the roles are not mutually exclusive – that part of your education will last for the rest of your life.

Pete Hamill, speaking at a graduation day for journalism students at Columbia University

5 'how I got there' – journalists on getting from school to their first job

WHAT ADVICE WOULD YOU GIVE TO PEOPLE STARTING OUT?

Check your shoes. If they're too clean, begin to worry. The key thing, in my view, is to get some mud and dust on your shoes, to get out into the field. Get a tape recorder/camera, go somewhere, hit 'record' and get cracking. Simple as that. Someone somewhere will take the story. Doesn't matter where it is, just so long as your shoes get scuffed about and you find some stories.
James Reynolds, BBC Middle East Reporter

Be determined. Don't be disappointed if you keep being rejected – if you persevere you'll make it. A lot of it, I think, has to do with being in the right place at the right time. So keep trying!
Steve Rosenberg, BBC Moscow Correspondent

In my day Asian people became doctors, pharmacists or lawyers. Indeed, my father wanted me to be a doctor. When it came to careers advice my teachers told me that only people who went to Oxford or Cambridge joined the BBC. By the time I'd joined the sixth form my head of year told me to forget the idea: 'Look, you're Asian, do what you're good at . . . it's a career in science for you . . . anyway, you can't write, it's too flowery!' Keep your mind on your dream. It will come true. Barnie Choudhury, BBC correspondent

Do as much work experience as possible whatever stage of your education you're at. Do a postgraduate course rather than an undergraduate course – a wider knowledge is better and it's good to have something to fall back on.

Looking for your first job? Concentrate on building a rapport with one or two places instead of writing to dozens. Learn about the industry, how it works and who the players are – broadcasting is a small world.

Don't turn down jobs just because they aren't ultimately what you want to do. Do, however, make sure the jobs you take are relevant to your goal – don't take endless producing jobs if you want to report, as there is a tendency to pigeonhole people.

Have lots of ideas – broadcasting needs to evolve and bosses are always looking for someone with innovative ideas. Be aware that you do need to have some natural talent! Luisa Baldini, BBC *Breakfast* reporter

Have a great time at university and don't be too calculating about what you want to do career-wise.

Do the 'right' job rather than the best-paid job.

Try, at some stage, to work in print.

Build up your journalistic credibility before you even begin to worry about your profile.

Never try to over-sell a crap story.

Never, never brown-nose.

Do your best work and hope someone notices.

Be patient.

Cover the stories which interest you most, rather than the ones which you think can get you 'on'. Nick Bryant, BBC Washington Reporter

Don't take no for an answer, especially when you're asking for work experience. But be sensible about what you apply for. Newsnight *might sound more glamorous than local radio, but you won't get to do anything except watch Jeremy Paxman sharpen his wit. Local radio is so stretched – if you're keen and you've got half a brain they'll let you loose on the airwaves. Don't be too proud. We all started doing the jobs no one else wanted to do.*
Chris Hogg, BBC Health Correspondent

My advice to anyone wanting to get into radio or television would be to get as much experience as you can of either medium before you get to the stage of

applying for jobs or courses. Those interviewing you will want some evidence of both talent and commitment. The best way to find both is to get some experience at a local TV or radio station. If you offer yourself up as a free assistant (accept the fact that you are NOT going to be paid for this, at least initially) and you are willing to be flexible, very few places will turn you away forcefully.

If you have a specialism or expertise in a topic — sport, music, architecture — try to find an outlet where you can be genuinely useful, either a particular programme, or a particular network (though the big networks get flooded with requests by people who want experience, and will be more difficult to get into). Don't be afraid to use contacts in the business mercilessly! That is the approach you will need for a career in journalism anyway, so you might as well start as you mean to go on. Friend of a friend who answers the phone on Midlands Today/Newsnight/Grandstand? *Call them and get them to give you an introduction to* The Boss. Richard Lister, BBC correspondent

WHAT'S IT LIKE APPLYING FOR COURSES?

While I was at university I got myself work experience at a London radio station and asked everyone there for advice. The general consensus was that I would have to do a postgraduate after my finals, so I applied for several. The competition to get in was fierce. At one day of interviews for one particular college, we were in a group of thirty to start with. After every round of tests, people were asked to leave because they'd failed. Some had travelled across the country to be there at 9.00am and by 10.00am they were back on the train! It was a humiliating process. By the end of the day, there were just three of us, with only two places left on the course. I was the only one who didn't make the last round. I was very happy, however, to start a postgrad at Falmouth College of Arts in 1996. The course was invaluable. I didn't have a clue about media law, local government or how to write for broadcasting. It gave me time to develop from a student into a potential reporter.
Luisa Baldini, BBC *Breakfast* reporter

I did the the broadcast journalism course at Cardiff University. Getting on to it was a total nightmare. I'd applied for two or three courses and the interview process was the same for them all. It felt as though the people who shouted the loudest impressed, rather than those who'd be best for the job. All the interviews were done in a group. For some it was just a chance to show off. I chose Cardiff for one reason really – its facilities. As well as a journalism tutor it had someone who taught technology. They had everything – we saw Avid/Cool Edit in its early stages and had Basys in our student newsroom. I'm never convinced there's much journalism to be learnt on these courses but Cardiff equipped us all with the technical skills. The course was also a ticket to work experience. The course had excellent links with BBC Wales and HTV. Again invaluable. We were all in the newsrooms there on a regular basis. It was the best way to learn and build confidence.
Daniela Relph, BBC Sports Correspondent

I had to send a tape in so I made a feature specially – about nuns and Bosnian refugees I think. I got an interview at Cardiff. Thankfully I'd spoken to someone who had done it the day before so I knew what to expect. The interview was tough. We were all interviewed in a room together and every-one else there was keen to make a big impression. Some were probably too keen as they never made it on to the course.
Chris Hogg, BBC Health Correspondent

DO YOU HAVE TO DO A JOURNALISM COURSE?

There are a large number of media degrees around now but I would say you certainly don't need to get on to that kind of course to pursue a career in broadcasting. If you intend to go into a career in journalism perhaps that's a good reason to do something else for your degree. A postgraduate scheme is sufficient to learn the necessary law and get the basic training you need to start applying for jobs. I knew at university that it would be competitive to get on to a journalism course and I would have to prove my interest in the subject. So I got some work experience at BBC Radio WM during the summer vacation and wrote for a university paper. I know that experience did count when applying for a place at the London College of Printing and for a bursary from the BBC. People want to know you are serious and for you to show you know a little about what you are going into. Ben McCarthy, BBC presenter

Did I lose out by not going on a journalism course or working my way up through local radio? Yes and no. There have been times when I've felt that some of the basic skills don't come as naturally to me as they do to journalists who've had formal training, but, overall, I think that the most important skills – such as persistence or the ability to spot interesting stories and tell them creatively – are better learnt on the job. The one time that I have felt my lack of training was a handicap was when I tried to make the leap from locally hired fixer in Moscow to the London newsroom. Even with the backing of the Moscow correspondents, I found editors unwilling to take me on, without formal skills. I suspect there is greater flexibility these days, but, if I'm asked, I tell people that a certain amount of training – as long as there is a practical element to it – can only be useful.
Jamie Coomarasamy, BBC World Affairs Reporter

I went off to Leeds University to study . . . Russian! In my first term I did a week of work experience at BBC Radio Leeds, but after that the Russian took over and I concentrated on the degree. Why Russian? Easy answer – it was interesting and a bit different (Gorbachev had just come to power, perestroika was underway, it was a pretty exciting time). In other words, if you want to work in journalism, you don't have to study journalism at college or university. I think whatever you choose to study (whether it's English lit, law, whatever) will come in useful in a media job. But I'd certainly recommend getting some work experience, either in a local paper, or a local TV or radio station.
Steve Rosenberg, BBC Moscow Correspondent

HOW IMPORTANT IS WORK EXPERIENCE?

Get some work experience and make sure it's what you really want to do. The work experience I'd done at university and at Cardiff got me my first job – at GWR Radio in Bristol. I got my first BBC job a few months later in Brighton. I was lucky. Getting a place at Cardiff and the amount of work experience I'd done helped me get those first jobs. In interviews it meant I could talk about what I'd done already rather than talk about what I hoped to do. I had real experience, examples, dilemmas to discuss.
Daniela Relph, BBC Sports Correspondent

However good a CV you have, the truth is that the person who is about to employ you will want to know what you are like doing the job for real. Work placements as part of a course are great. I think they were probably my way in. I did placements at BBC Radio Kent and ended up freelancing there. And my work there led to my first staff job with the BBC because people at Beds knew those in Kent and were able to recommend me. I still had to do an interview but at least to some extent I was a 'known quantity'. One of the most important things in the early days is getting hands-on experience. The great thing about local radio is that you get to do everything. Writing, editing, producing, reporting, live work and packaging. These are all skills you will use throughout a career in news. Then when you move on to national radio and TV at least you will have done all these things before.
Ben McCarthy, BBC presenter

DOES A SPECIALISM OR LANGUAGE HELP?

Lessons for would-be journalists from my rather unconventional early career experiences? Well, if my first job was about being in the right place at the right time (Russia), it also showed that local skills, such as a language, can be

a great way to get into the industry – certainly in foreign news. In the long run, it may be more important to know how to exploit others' local knowledge, but don't forget about exploiting your own. I also think that working in an area where you already have expertise helps develop your reporting and broadcasting confidence early in your career.
Jamie Coomarasamy, BBC World Affairs Reporter

I'd love to say that I always knew I'd be a journalist, that I edited my school magazine, that I slaved away at journalism school then worked my way up through local papers to land my dream job at the BBC. But sadly it wasn't that glamorous. My first love – and my ticket into what I think is one of the most rewarding careers you can have – was economics. I loved writing at school, but there was never any doubt that it was economics that I wanted to focus on. I studied it at King's College, Cambridge – and aside from what at the time seemed a gruelling schedule of eighteen essays a term – I didn't do any writing in my entire three years there. In fact, it's a wonder I got into this business at all.

When I left Cambridge I went straight to the Bank of England where I worked as an economist in the International Division. After about eighteen months I went on a three-week trip to the US with my boss – my job was to write up the meetings we went to and produce a lengthy paper on the US economy when we got back. I loved it. A month later I applied to Reuters to their graduate training scheme. I got in largely on the strength of my economics and my enthusiasm. So I'd say find a specialism – it worked for me. Lots of people can write, lots can broadcast. I think if you can offer something different, in-depth knowledge of a subject, it'll give you a valuable head start.
Jenny Scott, BBC Economics Correspondent

WHAT WAS YOUR EXPERIENCE OF APPLYING FOR JOBS?

Pretty mixed. After the trainee scheme I started work at the BBC in Nottingham in June 1997. After three months I managed to get a staff job as a broadcast journalist – the most junior position on the roster, but it was a start. I then started to apply for jobs at the BBC in London, all with a view towards working abroad as a foreign correspondent one day. I applied for six junior level positions in London. Each rejected me without an interview. Then, on 11 March 1998 the South America job was advertised. That was the chance I'd been looking for. I was given an interview and then, luckily for me, I was given the job. James Reynolds, Middle East Reporter

Everyone on the course started to panic about jobs around Easter time. I decided to apply for local radio jobs and for the BBC's national and regional training schemes. I got a job at Radio Northampton, my second interview. My Cardiff course had a good reputation which stood me in good stead. In the end, though, it was all about ideas. I think that's what they've been after in every job I've applied for. The day I started work there, I heard I had interviews for the national and regional trainee schemes. My boss in local radio persuaded me to stay. I don't think that was a mistake. Local radio may not be the most glamorous place to work but again it gives you great experience. I would argue it's a better grounding in the basics of reporting than a trainee scheme where you rarely leave Television Centre. In the end it depends where you want to end up. If you want to edit The World at One, *it probably makes sense to come to network asap and get stuck into national politics. If you want to report you're better off learning your trade on the road in local radio and TV first.* Chris Hogg, BBC Health Correspondent

FIRST JOBS AND LUCKY BREAKS

I had studied Modern Languages – Russian and French – and about ten months after leaving university, I decided to head out to the Soviet Union, where I'd spent part of my year abroad in 1988–89, with my heart set on getting into journalism of some kind. I took a plane to Moscow, a fortnight after the August coup of 1991, armed with a two-week visa courtesy of some Russian friends. I had the contact name of a friend of a friend who worked as a locally hired fixer in the BBC bureau. That person wasn't there, but the new correspondent, Ben Brown, picked up the phone and offered me a few days work. I stayed rather longer. I worked in the bureau for nearly two years, fixing and field producing. This was my Rolls Royce journalistic training – working in a high profile BBC bureau, covering one of the major geopolitical stories of the end of last century.
Jamie Coomarasamy, BBC World Affairs Reporter

I did as much work experience as I could around my course – at the local radio stations, Westcountry Television and at News Direct Radio in London. It was there that I decided to concentrate my efforts as I knew it would be the best place to get my grounding. So instead of applying for loads of different jobs, I offered to work there unpaid several times and made it clear from the start I really wanted to work there and nowhere else. My determination paid off – I was offered a reporter's job at the end of my course. I was very green but very keen. Some of the staff resented me being a college leaver so it was incredibly difficult for some six months until I'd really proved myself. It was an invaluable lesson – you have to have a tough skin and believe in yourself. Luisa Baldini, BBC *Breakfast* reporter

I had just graduated in Russian at Leeds. Then, at the time of the 1991 coup in Moscow, I went there to work – not in the media, but as an English language teacher at the Moscow Machine Tool Construction Institute. It paid peanuts, the hostel where I stayed was full of cockroaches, but at least it got me a visa to Russia. On arrival I started scouring foreign news bureaux looking for part-time work, and I was really lucky – the American network CBS needed someone to monitor Soviet television news bulletins in the evenings. So that was my foot in the door! I did that for six tumultuous months, as the USSR and communism collapsed. Then I was 'promoted' to answering the phones and booking tickets etc – desk assistant. I was still teaching English, but the job at CBS was becoming more time consuming and eventually they took me on. Steve Rosenberg, BBC Moscow Correspondent

When I left university, I started writing on a freelance basis for The Times *and the* Independent, *but then the* Daily Mail *just rang up one day and offered me a job. It was never the paper that I thought I'd end up writing for, but it was a top place to learn the ropes. They sat me across from a chain-smoking industrial correspondent, who had spent most of the Iranian revolution in a Tehran jailhouse (he was still living off the over-time) and left me to it. I was no fan of the paper, but marvelled at the professionalism which lay behind it – still do. The* Mail *was especially good at teaching you to write for your audience. Did I find it hard to break into the industry? I seemed to be lucky, but I remember organizing face-to-face meetings with a bunch of people during my final months at Oxford. Then, I'd get them to recommend a few other people for me to speak to. In a few months, I'd built a pretty useful contact base. The job at the* Mail *basically came about because an editor there knew someone I had spoken to at the* Standard. *In truth, I'm completely crap at 'networking' – I still hate it. But I forced myself to do it, and it worked. People usually want to help, especially if you see them in person.*
Nick Bryant, BBC Washington Reporter

I didn't write for the school magazine, nor did I volunteer for hospital radio or for local papers. Instead I spent much of my time involved in theatre and in public speaking. My real entry into broadcasting came during my second year at university – I made a thirty-minute programme for Radio 4's Tales from the Back of Beyond *series, based on an expedition some friends and I made to a Tibetan refugee camp in northern India in August 1994. Doing this programme was my first break – it really helped me to get into the broadcasting industry.* James Reynolds, BBC Middle East Reporter

The first step was applying for every BBC training course going, and getting interviewed for quite a few. First interview was to be a VT Editor (so wound up I couldn't remember Desmond Tutu's name when shown his picture during a recognition test). Then for a Sound Engineer trainee place (I was not able to assemble a working speaker from a cardboard box, a roll of wire and various other Blue Peter-*style objects). Finally, the Local Radio Trainee Reporter Scheme, where I managed to get in. It was a marvellous training in that, (unlike the more cosseted network trainee scheme) we had to learn to do absolutely everything, from reading the news, to editing tape, to working a sound desk. It stood us in very good stead for working at a series of under-resourced local stations, where we had to do all of those things, very quickly indeed. Having done a BBC course, the way was clear for a job with the Beeb.*
Richard Lister, BBC correspondent

FREELANCING

I found after nearly two years in local radio I was keen to move on, but even though I applied for lots of jobs in London I didn't get an interview – too many people chasing too few jobs and I had too little experience. I decided to go freelance. It has none of the security of the staff job I was giving up. Many places are happy to have people in for a couple of shifts just to try them out. I had little television experience, but Sky News, then a newcomer in the business, was happy to give me some work. It's much easier from the inside to show what you can do and I managed to convince the bosses that I had some potential. My first proper TV reporting job was for Sky in Birmingham. There was no interview – I was just asked to do it and didn't look back.
Ben McCarthy, BBC presenter

LEARN FROM OTHERS

One hugely important thing to remember is to learn from those around you. I had no producer in my first television job, but the cameramen I worked with taught me an enormous amount. Often the crew will have far more experience than the reporter and it is a mistake not to draw on this. The more you trust them to do their job, explain what you are trying to do and ask for advice, the more you will get out of them. In my experience at three news networks there are very few difficult cameramen in the business, and their support will make all the difference. Most go out of their way to help. Just don't pretend you know what you are talking about when you don't . . . that really gets on their nerves! As a reporter you must always remember that. It should always be 'we' and not 'I'. That way you'll get the best out of each other and the most important thing is that it will be great fun. Ben McCarthy, BBC presenter

THINK LATERALLY

I did an American Studies degree at Manchester University, which was influential in two ways – first, because it involved a year at Penn State University, where I presented a live radio comedy show at the local station, and second because the course involved a dissertation in which I compared The Times'*s and the* New York Times'*s coverage of events in Nicaragua during President Reagan's term. That was what made me interested in journalism. When I graduated I sent a demo tape of my efforts at Penn State to every local station in the UK, and got an audition to be a DJ at an independent station in Cleveland. Having never been a radio DJ in my life, my audition was, shall we say, less than polished. Obviously I didn't tell the Station Manager, who would have almost certainly pulled the audition, so I spent fifteen minutes familiarizing myself with the desk ('it is a little different from the one I am used to') and dived in. Thankfully, no tape exists . . .* Richard Lister, BBC correspondent

6 interviews for jobs in journalism

There are many books which offer a huge amount of doubtless invaluable information on how to go about interviews. There are even more websites devoted to the theory of interviews – many with really excellent advice on them. So there is no point in my repeating what is available in abundance elsewhere. But what you're about to read is based on the experience of conducting many hundreds of interviews for jobs at every level of one of the biggest news organizations in the world.

Every question quoted in this chapter comes up regularly in interviews for editorial jobs. Some are more basic than others. Some are more likely to come up in interviews for senior jobs; others for more junior jobs. But they all come up regularly. Because, if the truth be told, interviews are remarkably formulaic. There may be some sort of formal test occasionally, but for those 'in the know', the line of questioning follows a very familiar pattern. Well, you are about to join those 'in the know'. But before we get on to what you might face, let's consider for a minute the role of the interviewer.

THE INQUISITORS

The people sitting before you are most likely to be very busy people who would otherwise have many things to do. They hate wasting their time. Interviewing is a peculiarly draining experience. Have you ever experienced the feeling of exhaustion after you've been sunbathing all day? Well, interviewing is a bit like that. Sitting in the same chair all day, asking the same questions, often hearing the same answers and trying to be as fair to the last candidate as you were to the first. Here's another (tough, but true) analogy – sometimes when you are looking at a property you think you might want to buy, you know as soon as the front door opens that it's not for you. But you spend the next thirty minutes looking around and making interested noises, all the time waiting for the ordeal to end. Interviewing can be a bit like that, too. It is genuinely hard work.

In one interview for the post of Washington Correspondent, a reporter – now a well-known figure – was stopped in his tracks by a noisy interruption from one of the interviewers, now a very senior manager. Was this the manager launching a barbed riposte? Or a piercing intervention in response to some waffle? Sadly, it was neither. The manager in question had fallen asleep and crashed sideways off his chair into a desk next to him. Needless to say, the correspondent didn't get the job (and the manager went on to much greater things!).

The point is this: you have to engage the interviewers. You must have something to say – and preferably something they didn't know or hadn't thought of before. Like many things in life, there is no substitute for planning and preparation. But before you can prepare to answer the questions, you have to prepare *yourself*.

FILLING IN FORMS

The application form and, possibly, a showreel are all you have to secure an interview. So you must take care filling the form in. Do it on a computer if you can; if you have to write it by hand, make sure it's neat. Appearances matter. Your form will have to be copied for the interview panel and sometimes faxed as well. If it's hard to read in the first place, it will be all but illegible by the time it gets to the interviewers. Fill it in properly. Don't just print off a CV and attach it.

The application can be approached in a number of ways: you might want to enlarge on your experience; explain in more detail why you want the job and why you should get it; talk about the job itself and how you would approach it; or talk about the brief. For instance, if applying to be a health correspondent you might want to offer a summary of the big health issues of the day and likely developments.

Any and all of these approaches are legitimate. It's an opportunity, not a chore, and it offers two opportunities in particular. The first is to make good any obvious holes in your CV. If you are applying for a job in Africa, for example, and there's nothing on your form to suggest any previous connection with Africa, then this is the place to explain that you were brought up there, or wrote your thesis about it, or spent your gap year there.

The second opportunity for the clever applicant is to direct the interviewers to ground on which you feel strongest. Offer some opinions about the current coverage, about the future direction of the story, about the way the job could be done differently. Not fully developed arguments, just some outlines. With a bit of luck, someone on the panel will be sufficiently alert to pick you up on these ideas and ask you to expand on them. In this way, you are wresting back a little of the initiative and setting your own agenda.

Whatever you write, just use the space provided. Don't write a pamphlet. The place to make your pitch in full is the interview itself.

STOP SHAKING, YOU'LL BE OKAY

There is one thing that is perhaps worth establishing before we go any further. You are not going to die as a result of this interview. Let's get this in perspective. It's a conversation with one person or a few people.

It's an interview, not a firing squad. You will not be physically hurt. Your family and friends will still be there that half-hour later when you emerge. It's okay.

I have never witnessed a full-on panic attack in an interview (though they have been known to happen), but I have seen people shaking violently, sweating profusely, literally unable to speak through nerves and, sadly, crying with anxiety. You may be one of the lucky ones who are not afflicted with nerves before interviews. Good for you. For the rest of us, there are a number of things we can do.

First and foremost, prepare as thoroughly as you can. Preparation breeds confidence. The feeling that you couldn't have done more to prepare than you did will help you cope with the interview. Three other things you can do if your nerves are shredding: breathe in through your nose and out through your mouth; sip water; and try holding something – preferably not a teddy bear, but perhaps a pen, a pad, or some notes.

Most importantly, let go. Nerves and tension are an important part of an interview. And many books advise candidates to let go straight after the interview. But my advice is to let go *before* the interview. Be happy that you could not have prepared any better; if you don't get this, something else will emerge, and at least you got an interview. You will have learned something in the preparation and in the interview itself. Letting go beforehand will help you relax and come across confidently rather than desperately.

Interviewers want you to do well – ninety-nine per cent are friendly. They want good candidates. The worst thing that can happen is that you won't get the job, and if you don't, the chances are it wasn't right for you anyway. It is perfectly natural to fear rejection, and many people worry that they might make a fool of themselves. But statistically, your chances of getting the job are always going to be slim, so congratulate yourself for getting an interview. The more you fear rejection the more desperate you are. The more desperate you are the more nervous you are. The more nervous you are the less you can think clearly. The less you can think clearly the more you waffle. You can see where I'm going here . . .

If you don't get the job, move on. It's easy to begin to feel defeated and for this in turn to affect your confidence and self-esteem. Rejection hurts, but you must learn from the experience and move on. Understand too that there may be many reasons why you didn't get the job which are not immediately obvious – factors well beyond your control. Further on in your career you will be going for jobs which you and your colleagues believe are 'stitched up' for someone else. Thinking this may help you cope with any rejection but understand this: it's not true. If there is a deceit in interviewing it is not that the winner is known in advance, but that too many people are interviewed who have no chance of getting the job.

If the interviewers know you and your work then they will take that into account. So you won't be discarded simply on the basis of a poor performance on the day; but nor will you necessarily be appointed solely on the basis of a brilliant interview. Some of the BBC's most established correspondents have sat in my office – sometimes in tears – thinking that their careers are finished or irreparably blighted because they did not get a job. Some of them are now household names. All of them went on to rewarding jobs. It's very hard in the immediate aftermath of a rejection, but recovery is swift.

EVERY INTERVIEWEE'S ENEMY – WAFFLE

The most common offence committed by interviewees is waffle – overlong, unfocused answers. Or answers to questions that haven't been asked. Many candidates are prone to trying to demonstrate how much preparation they have put into an interview. But the interviewers are looking for people who can synthesize what they have learned into clear, focused answers.

Listen carefully to the question. Briefly talk round the issue so that the interviewers see you understand it, then answer the question. And the key word in the sentence you have just read is this: briefly. Demonstrate that you know the issues then focus on the answer.

This section is very short, but, believe me, it is important. Do not waffle. Keep your answers focused.

> Don't throw yourself alive into the board pit. I used to specialize in digging a shallow hole because I misunderstood the question, usually through nerves, then proceeding to dig deeper and finally not be satisfied until I had smoothed the earth over my head. My advice now is if you realize or suspect you have misheard, or if you are digging that grave, just stop and tell the board that you may have misunderstood and that you want to take the question again.
>
> Do give answers that are a reasonable length. If you go on and on and on you don't demonstrate your knowledge, you just demonstrate your inability ever to do a two-way to time, or even contribute to an ideas meeting without everyone dropping off to sleep. You should be able to sub yourself. Senior BBC manager

DOS AND DON'TS

Before we get on to the questions you will be asked, here are some other tips:

Do the work beforehand, nothing beats good preparation. A little humour is a good thing – humility and a touch of self-deprecation too can be engaging. But my advice is to avoid jokes. And, above all, avoid being flippant and too 'chummy'. Sometimes candidates, often through sheer nerves, come across as 'cocky' – you do not want to do this. You are aiming to come across as intelligent, imaginative, professional, enthusiastic and quietly self-confident.

> *I had made a big effort to know what I was talking about and to have some ideas and it worked. The board went better than average, I thought. At the very end, the guy in charge asked, as he should, did I have any questions? I didn't and I said so. He then said he had one final one for me: 'How tough are you?' I hadn't heard this one before and wasn't sure where he was coming from (although it later became apparent he was concerned about how able I'd be dealing with longer serving correspondents and the like), so I gave the natural Scottish response: 'Try me.' There was a pause for a moment while this settled, then everyone smiled. I got the job.* David Mackie, BBC Home News Assignments Editor

Have a few key points you want to make but don't memorize entire answers. Don't hand out bits of paper in the middle of the interview. You can't expect the interviewers to listen to you carefully and read at the same time. If you absolutely have to hand out story ideas then do it at the end of the interview. Otherwise put anything else in your application.

After a candidate has just walked out, interviewers often say: 'He/she was just telling us what he/she thought we wanted to hear.' Don't just say what you think they want to hear. Leastways, don't *only* say what you think they want to hear.

> *Do have an opinion about how stories will develop. I did a ridiculous interview with someone who wanted to be Tokyo correspondent covering all of East Asia. When I asked about how*

*things would develop in any story, the interviewee refused to
answer on the basis that she had been trained to be an objective
journalist not to have opinions on anything as that would compro-
mise her art. She didn't last long.* BBC editor

Tell them something they don't know. And this could mean telling
them something that may seem blindingly obvious. Here's a question
from an interview for Arts Correspondent: 'What is arts coverage –
what do you think should fall into the remit of this job?' 'That's for
you to decide' is not the answer. Often managers are looking for ideas
of how to change for the better and use interviews to provoke some
thought. Don't open a door you can't walk through – be prepared to
back up what you say. Your interviewers will want to test what you're
saying. Follow-up questions have a habit of exposing 'surface knowledge'.

To some extent, there are many parallels with doing a live report –
read the section on live reporting in the masterclass on page 102. Read
the trade magazines and get to know the big issues, themes and gossip.
Practise beforehand, out loud. Don't be afraid to ask a friend or a
colleague to do a mock interview with you. This will help you decide
which things you want to say whatever happens. You may discover
some nice turns of phrase you want to use. Take in notes by all means,
but make sure they are key words or bullet points – definitely not
anything you end up reading out.

*Have a small card with you with the main points you want to
make. Especially any programme ideas. I find you forget any ideas
you have as soon as you walk in unless you jot them down.*
BBC correspondent

Ask yourself this – if I were one of the interviewers, what would I ask and what would I be looking for? Write down twenty questions they may ask. Then write down the answers. Never, never lose your temper in an interview. You may as well walk out there and then if you do. If you are going for a job in a high pressure atmosphere, your interviewers may try to see how cool you can remain, despite their provocation (often by asking a question and then reading a book or magazine while you try to answer). It's rare, but not unknown.

> *Don't be put off by the interviewer. One editor I worked with used to ask a question and then look out of the window when you answered. And another doodled so ostentatiously through my last interview I began to lose my nerve because I assumed I was only being seen out of courtesy. But I took a deep breath and got myself on track. And got the job.* BBC editor

You will probably be asked questions about things that have been the subject of discussion and dispute for years. If there were any simple answers, they would have been found long since. No one will expect you to produce a miracle solution and there will not necessarily be a 'right' answer. But what will be expected is that you can show an awareness of the issues and an informed assessment of the arguments on either side.

At the end of the interview, you'll be asked if you have any questions. You may want to seek clarification of something that was said during the interview, or to refer back to one of your earlier answers, to amend or to expand it; or there may be something you wanted to say but had no opportunity to say it. But if there's nothing you want to ask, then don't ask anything. You'll be prolonging the interview to no good purpose. And this is certainly not the time to ask about what the job is. Do the work beforehand. Nothing beats good preparation.

So now that you're calm, focused and prepared, let's look at the questions you will face. There are many things that can come up at an interview, and some of them you can't prepare for. But many, if not most, of them are really quite predictable.

THE QUESTIONS YOU WILL BE ASKED

Questions about you

It may sound like a cliché, but the most common opening question in interviews is 'So, tell us, why do you want this job?' The first impression you make is very important, so it's worth thinking hard about what you will say in response. It is surprising how many candidates have not thought about it. 'I'm bored where I am' or 'It's about time I moved' are just two of the many limp and anodyne answers which are often given. Interviewers are looking for positive and enthusiastic candidates. And this is your chance to sell yourself.

Other questions you may face are 'What story would you most like to work on at the moment?', 'What's the best story you've worked on ... why?', 'What's the thing or story you're most proud of?' and 'What's the best "exclusive" story you've done?' All questions designed to find out about you and what interests you.

A common question is 'What will you bring to this job?' and another is 'Give us your assessment of your strengths and weaknesses.' Think through what is unique about what you can offer, then think through how you can describe that without appearing to be too arrogant. The reasoning behind this line of questioning is to get a sense of how you assess yourself and how open and honest you are. It might help to say how other people have assessed your strengths in the past. And if you are going to reveal a weakness, it's advisable to make it something you are working on getting better at, and not something irreparable. For example, 'I think my live work could be better. So I've started using key words to prompt myself and I think my answers are beginning to get shorter and more focused. At the moment I'm recording all my work to look back over it.' This is better than 'I do have a habit of losing my temper occasionally. But I've been like that since I was a kid and I think my strengths more than compensate for it.'

Some jobs, in a small office or team or bureau, require you to work very closely with the same people all the time. 'How will you organize yourself in this job?' or 'How will you share out the work with the others?' are both common questions. These questions will probe your organizational skills and, more importantly, your sense of teamwork. Answers like 'I'm as good a team player as you can get, but Fred's going to have to understand that when the bomb goes off it's me who will be in the driving seat' are bound to alarm some editors, who have enough problems without adding you to their list. In this kind of situation, it's worth trying to find out as much as you can about the set-up and expectations for the job before the interview.

'How did you prepare for this interview?'

You may be asked how you prepared for the interview. In one sense this is an easy opening question; in another sense it is a way of seeing how you approached finding out more about the programme, network or organization you want to work for. A lot of research is infinitely easier with the advent of the Internet – but that makes it easier for those you are competing with too.

It is always worth asking if you can go and have a look around before the day of the interview. Not every organization will let you. But doing this can help you pick up what the current issues are or what the audience figures are and how the competition is doing. This kind of 'insider' information can be invaluable; there are some things you will only ever learn by talking to those 'in the know'. If you are applying for a job where you are already working, you may get marked down if you *don't* go and look around and ask what a programme is looking for. Don't worry if you can't, but it's always worth trying.

Nothing infuriates interviewers more than people who clearly don't know what they have applied for, or who, at the end of the interview, ask for basic information about the job. Try to find out how the job fits into an overall programme or network strategy, or hierarchy, how well it's functioned in the past; and what plans or aspirations there are for it in the future.

Who have you talked to in preparation? Look at the questions outlined below and talk to others about them in the context of the job you are going for. In a recent interview for an arts correspondent, one candidate spoke about having talked to a number of well-known authors about story ideas and what they thought of existing arts coverage. This allowed her to, in effect, say: I've got good contacts, here are some story ideas and here is something you don't know – what some prominent authors think of our arts coverage.

Surprise your interviewers with your initiative and with how diligent you've been. And if you have been diligent but you are not asked how you prepared for the interview then drop a few things in along the way: 'Well, I talked to so-and-so about that because I was coming for an interview and they had an interesting take on this issue . . .'

What do you know about where you're applying to work?

There are two really common offences committed by interviewees. As we have already seen, one of them is giving long, unfocused answers. The other is a failure to watch or listen to the output.

No matter what the organization or programme or network you are applying to you must watch or listen to the output beforehand. One of CNN's senior executives told me: 'I never cease to be amazed at the number of applicants who simply have not watched the output.' An ITN editor agreed: 'If people haven't watched the programme it automatically rules out asking them a whole range of questions, and then you can't judge them against other candidates. So you rule them out.'

> Don't even bother if you haven't seen the programme or channel you are applying for, assuming it's not a start-up. At ITN, the Head of Human Resources would stop interviews there and then if they hadn't. When I was Editor of World News on the Channel 4 Daily we advertised for a news editor. If the applicants hadn't bothered to watch the show they were politely asked to leave.
> Rachel Attwell, Deputy Head of BBC Television News

Get the point? The questions themselves are fairly predictable.

'What did you think of last night's programme?'

There is one answer to this question that is tantamount to saying, 'Stuff your job, I didn't want it anyway.' And it is this: 'I don't know – I didn't see it.' This will not wash. You must watch the output. If you can't watch it live, record it. But make sure you watch it.

Was it the right lead? Was the balance of stories right? Did we give undue prominence to some stories and not enough to others? Were there stories we missed? Looking at the way the papers have developed stories today, should we have done anything differently? What did the opposition do differently? What stood out as excellent – or dismal?

There is often no right answer to these questions, but you must show an appreciation of the issues. Watch as much as you can. Take notes while you're watching. Have a view.

'What did you think about the way we handled the story about (. . .)?'

This question is about a particular story and can often be translated as: 'I think we cocked this up. What do you think?' Again, you'll need to have watched closely. Looking at how the story was done elsewhere will often help. Did the story merit a place in the programme in the first place? Was the story clear? Were there any elements missing, or that confused the story and needn't have been there? Were the interviews the right ones? Did the reporter make the best use of pictures and sound? And so on. Constructive criticism is the key.

'What do you think of our coverage of (. . .) story over the past year?'

This can come up at any time, but it's especially likely to come up when the job is in a specialist area. Most news organizations live for the day – yesterday was a long time ago, tomorrow's another day. But it is perfectly possible to get a long-running story right day after day and still get it wrong over a long period of time. This is mostly about the benefit of hindsight. But it's not only that. The coverage may have concentrated (perfectly fairly in itself) on one aspect of the story and ignored another, slowly creating the wrong impression over time. It may have been too hasty to jump to conclusions – best guesses at the time – and been proved wrong. Or simply devoted a disproportionate amount of time to a story that turned out to be much less of an issue than was expected.

So if you were going for a job in, say, environment, you would be expected to have a view about coverage of the long-running foot-and-mouth crisis. Was it objective? Was there the right balance between analysis and first-hand reporting? Was there too much emotive reporting of the farmers' plight and not enough context? Was there enough to reassure consumers about what they were buying? Was there enough about the science? Was the government's policy put under enough scrutiny? And so on. Interviewers understand you can't watch and listen to everything, but again, you need to demonstrate an understanding of the issues.

'How can we make our programme better?'

Interviewers will often draw you into this question with phrases like 'Come on, be frank' or 'within these four walls', inviting you to draw your verbal dagger from its scabbard and get stuck in. Don't. Much as editors and professionals think they can take it, they can't. Nobody likes some new kid on the block taking their precious work to pieces.

These situations require the precious art of constructive criticism – with the emphasis on the word constructive. 'Clearly the programme's got a long way to go' or 'Frankly, I don't know where to start' is unlikely to endear you to your interviewers. 'Clearly the programme's in good shape. I especially like x, y and z. I guess if you wanted to build on that you could . . .' Same thing said, but the latter will take you a little nearer that job.

Conversely, those who say the programme is so good it's beyond improvement are also not doing themselves any favours. If you can't make it better what use are you? Have something to say. Alluding to the strengths and weaknesses relative to the competition will show you appreciate the differences between various programmes and networks.

'Have we got the balance right between interviews and packages (or whatever)?'

This question can come in a variety of forms, but it is ultimately about the style and feel of the programme rather than the content. Does the set work? What do you think of the presenter? If there are two presenters, how do they work together? Is the programme surprising or predictable? Are there too many live interviews with correspondents?

Or too few? Do the graphics work? Should there be more textual graphics or 'straps'? Does the programme cross-trail its website effectively? Are the headlines effective or are they too long or too many? Is the programme 'teased' properly – does it make the viewer want to stay with it all the way through? Does the handover to the weather work? And so on.

'What's your assessment of the competition?'

One of the best ways of assessing the programme or network you're applying to is by looking at it against the competition. Of course, to do this you must first understand what the competition is. If you are applying for a job at Sky News, your interviewers will want to know what you think of BBC's News 24, ITV's News Channel or CNN. What do they do better than the programme you're applying to? How do the presenters compare? Or reporters? Or the sets? Or storytelling techniques? Or the scheduling of programmes? And so on. If you appreciate the nature of the opposition, your interviewers will appreciate you.

'How do you see the difference between programme x and programme y?'

This is a difficult question, and you ought to be prepared for it. Many programme and network editors have a very clear idea in their head of how their programme is different from everybody else's. And so they should – that's their job. Trouble is, the differences are often much clearer in the editor's head than anywhere else. So this is a question about agenda – what a programme is trying to achieve. It may be a question about differences between programmes within the same organization, like ITV's early evening and nightly news; or opposing programmes, like Channel 4 News and *Newsnight*.

Generally, the nearer the programme is to the beginning of the day, the more likely it is to want to try to set the agenda, to look ahead to the day. The nearer the end of the day, the more likely it is to want to sum up the day's events.

There are many ways of looking at what a programme is trying to do. What subjects does it focus on and why? Are the story treatments and techniques different? What is it trying to do differently from the competition? What is the balance between news and analysis? Between foreign and domestic news?

But more often that not, the key to understanding the agenda of a programme or network is understanding the audience.

'What do you think is the profile of our audience?'

Some things about audiences are fairly obvious. How many people watch or listen, and what is the audience 'share' (two different things)? What time does the programme go out and what are people likely to be doing at that time? What kind of people will be watching or listening at that time?

Most news organizations now have an increasingly sophisticated sense of who their audiences are and how they are made up – how old they are, how interested in news they are and what other forms of media they consume. Even down to what kind of holidays they take. They know how many people are watching at the beginning of the programme and at the end. How many people switch from other networks to your programme and vice versa.

So, in terms of agenda, a programme with a much older audience is likely to be more interested in a story about hearing aids; one with a much younger audience might concentrate more on a particular entertainment story. A twenty-four-hour network will tend to look more at live coverage or fast turnaround headline sequences.

It's important to try to get a sense of the make-up of the audience for the programme or network you are trying to get a job with. This information may not be easily at hand to anyone outside the company to which they are applying. But if you can't find specifics, try and get some general information. For instance, the BARB and RAJAR websites are full of useful information.

'What do you think about this or that technique of storytelling?'

This is a question about which methods of storytelling work best for which stories. Programmes are determinedly less predictable than they were a few years ago. A lot of thought is given to which particular technique is the best vehicle for any given story – straightforward packages, a two-way (a live interview with a correspondent), a two-way with interview clips played into it, a two-way with pictures floated over it, a studio interview with a correspondent, a studio 'big board' or videowall where a correspondent uses graphics and video to explain a story.

It's perfectly possible (indeed, in some radio programmes, more common) to cover stories without a correspondent at all, using interviews with guests or getting a typical 'player' in a story – a teacher or a nurse perhaps – to do a film of their own (a technique that needs careful handling and plenty of context but one which can be very effective). The role and benefit of graphics is also a source of much debate. Should any graphics sit in the presenter's 'intro' to the story or within the body of the correspondent's piece? And many of these techniques can be used to do 'new readers start here' pieces which bring audiences up to date with long-running stories.

Using a variety of techniques can give a programme pace and surprise, but none should be deployed merely for the sake of using them. They should be used because they are the best method for telling a particular story. Nothing will engage a viewer more than strong pictures and sounds (or in radio, vivid sounds and/or voices). If you have these, then a straightforward correspondent report is all that's needed to make the best of them.

But many stories or issues are blighted with being both complicated

to explain and without interesting pictures and sound. The adminis-
tration of the railways, perhaps, or pension reform – both vitally
important stories but ones which need a lot of work before they achieve
the Holy Grail of telling the whole of the story in a way that is both
clear and engaging. So an editor will put a lot of thought into which
technique will work best for which story. Again, you need to watch the
output to have a view about what works well and what doesn't.

Story ideas

The ideal way to walk out of an interview is to leave those left behind
in the room thinking, 'Wow, that was a great idea – I'd love to see that
on air.' And the easiest way to do that is by having great story ideas.
There is no substitute for good story ideas and treatments. More
interviews – particularly as you move up through an organization – are
won more by good, original story ideas and treatments than anything
else. They illustrate that you are a creative thinker, able to take an idea
or an issue and turn it into something people will relate to.

What do we mean by story ideas? In essence, there are two types –
original ideas that you have researched or come across, and original
ways of looking at stories we already know are coming up. So you need
to have done your homework, to have read beyond the obvious enough
to have discovered some good stories tucked away in books, the
Internet, newspapers or magazines or through people you have spoken
to.

A common question in interviews is this: 'If you get the job, what
are the first three story ideas you're going to offer me?' And this is your
chance to dazzle the panel with your ideas. If you come up with three
ideas the interviewers already know about, your rejection letter will be
in the post. Good story ideas are crucial. But, as we shall see, the treatment is as important as the story itself.

Story treatments

The following three questions come up very frequently in interviews for editorial jobs, in one form or another:

- 'If you get this job, what are the big themes and trends you think you'll be covering in the next two or three years?'
- 'What stories can you do to illustrate those big issues?'
- 'Talk me through how you would do that story.'

How you would do the story is the treatment. For some interviews, it's worth remembering this story triangle, which stems from the three questions above:

Big themes and trends in the years ahead;
stories to illustrate them;
treatments.

A simple example could be this:

big theme: The perceived clash between Islam and the Western world.

story: The education of two young boys in Islamic schools, or *madrassas*, one in Pakistan, where the education is radical and one in more moderate India. This is the tale of two ten-year-old boys and what they are being taught.

treatment: Start in Pakistan with boy. Try and get some shots of him alone, some close-ups – something that illustrates that this is a ten-year-old. Then in school. Clip of him. What is he taught? Clip of teacher. School again. Piece to camera bridging from Pakistan to India. Inside Indian school. Look at the differences between India and Pakistan using the Indian boy as the vehicle. Closing shot back on boy in Pakistan. What will become of him?

This is how we take the micro to illustrate the macro. In this instance, we look at the perceived clash between Islam and the Western world through the eyes of two ten-year-old boys (and all the time fighting against reinforcing stereotypes). You could be looking at the prevalence of truancy in Nottingham through the eyes of one family – the principle is the same.

But be careful. If you have a story idea you must have a treatment. Here's why you should be careful – listen to this: 'I'd talk to the headmaster of a local secondary school, talk to a truant, talk to his or her parents and maybe talk to a social worker.' This is: you talking to a variety of people. This is not: a story treatment.

The ability to translate a story or an issue into an engaging piece of television or radio is one of the most important things the interviewers are looking for. They want to know what they would see and/or hear; what the script would say; where you might do a piece to camera; who you would talk to; the feel of the piece. Yet many people, when asked how they would treat a story, simply reel off a list of people they would talk to.

Remember that the treatment needs to relate to a specific pro- gramme – certain programmes or networks might want you to do the report live with interviewees or with a demonstration of a location or a piece of equipment. If you are applying to a twenty-four-hour network with an emphasis on live coverage, then your treatment should be appropriate to the network.

Here's another common problem: 'I'd do a comparison with other countries – look at truancy in France and China and see how it compares with Nottingham.' To which the interviewer replies: 'Yeah, fantastic idea – but the story only broke this morning and I want a piece for tea-time.' Which illustrates another fundamental truth about interviews: your answers must be realistic. What you are suggesting must be achievable in terms of the time available and, crucially, within the budget available. A world tour will look great on your passport, but suggesting it at an interview won't get you a job.

Same story – different programme

This is a question about understanding different programme styles and audiences. It could also be about doing the same story for a different medium. If you're doing a story about police reform, how would you do it differently for breakfast television and prime-time evening news? How would you do it differently for television and radio? If you were doing it for television and radio, how would that affect the way you gathered your material for the story? How could you do it for an online outlet?

This raises many issues: live work versus packaging, gathering sound, good interview guests, possibilities for interactivity, and so on. Again, you must look at or listen to the output as much as you can and try to get as much information about the programmes' audiences and styles.

You must do your homework on the network, programme and department you're trying to get on to or into. Watch or listen to the programmes, read the papers, show you know about the people currently working there. Give some reasoned analysis, pro and con, of some recent items. Don't insult the panel by not appearing to have bothered enough to do some serious home-work. Have thought-through ideas for programmes or items – not just headlines (anyone can do that) – and give some idea of how you'd treat the topic, a shot list for TV, some idea of the sound for radio. Sound enthusiastic, not just as if you'd learned the right answers by rote. Try to have something really different and original to unveil and wow the interviewers.

Malcolm Downing, BBC World News Assignments Editor

What's on the diary?

It doesn't – or it shouldn't – take a brain surgeon to realize that there will quite likely be questions about stories that are happening either that day or coming up soon. So make sure you have a good look at a news diary before the interview. Make sure you understand the background to stories coming up. One of the most common questions in interviews for editorial jobs is: 'So-and-so is happening today. How would you approach that story?'

For general reporting jobs you need a very broad, general sense of what's going on, though you can still be faced with a situation akin to that A-level revision nightmare: turning the paper over and realizing you've revised the wrong things. For specialist jobs (health, education, business, etc.) and foreign postings it is easier to predict the questions about current and forthcoming stories and issues, so you should go through the diary for the weeks ahead accordingly. But for these jobs, interviewers will absolutely expect you to have a very clear grasp of what's coming up (indeed, they will absolutely expect you to tell them something they didn't know).

In every case, remember the programme style and the audience. Explain enough of the story and the issues around it for the interviewer to see you know what you're talking about, then explain your treatment for that story. As ever, stay focused.

Anyone going for a specialist job should use the story triangle laid out above. First of all, you must understand all the big themes and trends in this particular area. Then you must think about how to translate those themes into stories. In personal finance, for example, the collapse in endowments covering mortgages may be a big theme. What stories could you illustrate that with? In environment, the future of genetically modified crops in the developing world will be a huge issue. Which specific stories will help engage the audience with this theme?

Beware the interviewer's elderly mother

'Explain that in terms my elderly mother (or an eight-year-old) would understand . . .' This seemingly innocuous question has been the undoing of more candidates than you can imagine. When telling stories or explaining issues, being able to assume some knowledge on the part of the audience is a wonderful luxury. Too many correspondents assume too much knowledge too often.

'Can you explain to me the issues around the introduction of the Euro?' is one question. 'Can you explain to me the issues around the introduction of the Euro without any jargon and in terms my elderly mother could understand?' is a different question altogether. And the latter has an uncanny habit of exposing those who don't have the grasp of detail they should – or who understand the detail but can't unpack it. Trust me: beware this question.

'How can you make that story relevant to my elderly mother in her flat in Bognor?'

A variant of the previous question, and it's about making connections. Maybe you are very excited about the US economy going into depression. You've read the cuttings, looked on the Net. You explain with confidence that repeated interest rate cuts have not had an effect, that manufacturing is suffering, that New York cabbies are complaining. Indeed, you are really rather pleased with yourself.

And then the interviewer says, 'Why should my audience care about that? Make that relevant to someone sitting at home in Preston.' And this seemingly innocuous question completely floors some candidates. Because it's not just about what the story is – it's about why it matters. It's about making the connection between the story and our daily lives. It's about relevance. Much good journalism is about making what is significant interesting and relevant.

Explaining simply how companies and jobs in Britain depend on the

US, how the performance of your pension fund may be affected by a recession over there – these kinds of things make the story relevant to a UK audience. And they show that you have a depth of understanding beyond the cuttings. That you understand the processes and connections. Always think about why stories matter (something that will stand you in good stead for the rest of your journalistic career).

'Fred Bloggs has just died in a car crash'

This is the obituary question (and many a candidate has rested in peace after attempting to answer it). 'A prominent person has just died. You're asked to put together his obit. What would you put in it and what would you want to say?'

In some ways these obituary questions test your breadth of knowledge. Can you prepare for this question? To an extent, yes. Sorry if this sounds ghoulish, but are there any prominent people who are ill? You had better know about them if there are. For a local radio job you would be expected to have some knowledge of your local MP's life, particularly if he or she is well known. If you are going for Middle East Correspondent, understanding Ariel Sharon's life is fundamental to understanding the Middle East conflict. It's not just about what the person did. Who should we interview who could speak with authority about their life? Who knew them? In television, what are the key images you would want to include? The key sound bites? What would you conclude about their life?

It is worth remembering here, particularly when starting out, that your interviewers can often be considerably older than you are. During a recent round of interviews for a sports reporter some members of the panel became quite indignant that a couple of candidates could not describe the life history of the footballer George Best. On the one hand, the reality was that Best had stopped playing before some of the candidates were even born. On the other, he was a seminal figure in the sport.

'The big interview'

'You land an interview with so-and-so. What are you going to ask them?' Like the obituary question, this is about understanding the key players and understanding the issues around them. Hearing which questions you would ask is another way of the interviewers assessing whether you understand a story.

If you were going for a job on a local London network, for example, you might be asked what you would ask the mayor if you had an interview. So you need to know what the current issues are in order to answer this. Think about any interviews relevant to the job you are going for and then think about which questions you would ask. This is more relevant to jobs with a patch or a specialism, but it still might come up in an interview for a general job.

'Which guests should we get on the programme?'

This question comes up more with producer or specialist jobs (i.e. health, education etc.) and involves not your treatment of a story, but a sense of who the key players are or which interviewees could best bring the story to life in a discussion. So the question might be: 'We want to do a studio discussion on the crime figures which come out tomorrow. Which guests should we get in?' Again, this is partly about a broad general knowledge. But it's also about your sense of what makes great and illuminating broadcasting.

'What would you lead on?'

When two really significant stories break on the same day, malicious wags in the newsroom will often be heard to say, 'Classic interview question – which would you lead on?' The first thing to say on this is don't worry, everyone gets things wrong.

If you get an obvious one, like the Ethiopian famine versus talks to resolve a minor element of an industrial dispute then that's fine. Easy. But if, say, Sir Robin Day and Sir Alec Guinness had died on the same day, which would you lead with? An internationally renowned, award-winning actor against one of the most prominent broadcast journalists the UK has ever known. You would probably say Sir Alec Guinness and I would probably agree with you. Except they did die on the same day and BBC television bulletins led with the death of Sir Robin Day.

There are no easy answers. If you get this question, try to sum up the relative merits of each story – their significance, their relevance to the audience and which one would seem the most important looking back from ten years hence. And then just make a decision.

Oh, and the Ethiopian famine thing? Get this: Michael Buerk's 1984 report on the Ethiopian famine – probably the most influential piece of television news ever broadcast – ran halfway down the BBC's lunchtime news. The programme led on talks to resolve the NACODS dispute in the mines and a state visit by the French president.

'What if . . . ?' Hypothetical questions

Hypothetical questions are fantastic levellers and many a candidate going along well has been unhinged by them. They could be about a whole range of issues, but they are designed to test how quickly you can think. Here's an example:

It's eleven o'clock in the morning. You have gone with a crew to cover a speech by a minor politician in a town hall. No big deal – there's just you and the camera operator. But as you are setting up to cover the speech you get a call from the newsdesk to say there has been a huge train crash at the station on the other side of town. You have gone from covering a speech that may or may not make a story to the lead item. And the programme is on at one o'clock. What do you do?

Just as if the situation were real, you need to think quickly. The obvious answer, and the one which most people give, is: 'I'd just get the hell down there and start filming.' This may be the right answer, but only in part. There are many issues to consider and among them are these: is it true? Is one o'clock the first deadline you need to meet? If you work for more than one programme (and many correspondents do these days), which one has priority? Where do you feed from? Is a satellite truck on its way? Is there a feedpoint or a friendly broadcaster in town? Is there a picture editor? Can the camera operator edit? Should you attempt to feed track and rushes (very tight with such a short turnaround)? Should you just feed the rushes to be edited at base and go for a live two-way? Are there any other crews in the area? Can you share pictures with anyone? Where are the injured being taken? How can you get pictures from the hospital? And so on. As you can see from this list of things to think about, this kind of question can be as much about an understanding of the logistics as anything else.

Hypothetical questions like the one above work very well for interviewers because they separate those who you could rely on in a crisis – the 'operators' – from those who are better suited to something a little less stressful. In other areas, like law for instance, hypothetical questions can effectively test not just whether you know your stuff but whether you know how to apply it. Many interviews are decided on the answers to hypothetical questions.

Hypothetical questions can only test how quickly you can think in an interview; they don't test how quickly you act in real situation. So be prepared for this question: 'Tell me about a story where you faced a really difficult situation and how you got around it.' This will test whether you have in the past done what you say you can do.

'Who's your favourite correspondent? Who do you most admire?'

This question is often a way into a discussion about craft skills, because your answer will immediately be followed by this question: 'Why?

What makes them stand out from the rest? What is it that makes them good?' Is it their writing? What about their writing? Is it their ability to make things easy to understand? Their enthusiasm? Their live reporting?' It is worth thinking this through before the interview – it's good to have role models anyway.

This is a question about how you assess other people's craft skills, and it's also about how much news you watch or listen to. It always amazes me that some people struggle to name anyone at all. Others name presenters when you're asking about correspondents. It quickly exposes people who don't watch much news.

The classy answer? 'I like Fred Smith's investigative work on Channel X and I think Joanna Bloggs's live work on Channel Y is also top rate. But the person I most admire is Fred Bloggs on Channel Z who combines all of these things but also writes like a dream.' You quickly show you have breadth and then focus on the answer.

Ethics and the law

An understanding of journalism law is absolutely fundamental. There is nothing worse for an editor than a nagging doubt that you may land your organization in court through a legal slip. But most interview questions about law take the form of hypothetical questions probing whether you understand issues such as when a court case becomes active, reporting restrictions, injunctions, sexual offences and cases involving children. Legal issues have probably become even more important since the advent of twenty-four-hour news, which means correspondents often have less time to think about what they are going to say.

The law as it affects journalism is quite straightforward. Applying it is altogether more complicated. When one interviewee walked out of the room recently, one of the interviewers was moved to remark, 'She's a lawsuit waiting to happen.' This you do not want. Your editor must be able to trust you – not least because it will be his or her job on the line if you mess up.

Ethical issues often emerge as hypothetical questions too, around areas such as freedom of speech versus privacy, protection of sources, 'doorstepping', anonymous interviewing and so on. When is it appropriate to doorstep someone? How and when would you shoot an anonymous interview? Candidates are often given a hypothetical story and asked whether they would run it.

The law you must learn for yourself, but many companies have guidelines which set out their ethical policy. The BBC, for instance, has its 'Producers' Guidelines' which are available publicly (and worth reading wherever you are applying). Try to find out whether the company you are applying to has any of its own guidelines. Again, if you are asked a question in this area, briefly explain the issues involved and then answer the specific question.

A TYPICAL INTERVIEW

Here are some of the questions asked in a forty-five-minute interview for the post of Environment and Science Correspondent for BBC1. Nearly all of them would be followed up with subsidiary questions:

- Imagine you are reporting for *Newsround* (the children's news programme). Explain what the internet is and how it works.

- Can you explain in terms anyone could understand, without jargon, what a black hole is?

- Imagine Richard Dawkins has died. What would you say about him in your obit? Who would you talk to?

- With the benefit of hindsight, what did you think of our coverage of the foot-and-mouth crisis?

- With the benefit of hindsight, was the government's approach to foot-and-mouth the right one?

- Can you explain the issues around whether global warming is man-made or not?

- What do you think of the science coverage on the *Ten O'Clock News*?

- The World Summit on Sustainable Development in Johannesburg is next month. If you were in this job, what would you seek to do to report it? Do you think you should go to the summit?

- What would be the first two or three original or 'off-diary' stories you would like to do if you got the job? How would you treat those stories?

- What are the three or four big themes or trends you would expect to cover over the next two years?

- A UN report this week paints an apocalyptic vision of the environmental future of our planet. Isn't it odd that it didn't feature more prominently in the media? Should we have done more to cover it? If not, why not?

- Isn't science incompatible with television news? If not, what would you do to get more on?

TESTS

Plenty of interviews for entry level jobs, and some further up the ladder, will involve formal tests. These can take a variety of forms: general knowledge tests, specific or specialist knowledge tests, writing and subbing tests or, for on-air jobs, screen and 'live two-way' tests.

Knowledge tests depend on your preparation and background reading. Subbing exercises test your ability to take a lot of information, decide on the crux of the story, filter out what you don't want and write up the rest in a clear and engaging way. The mistake most people make is to try to include too much information, which makes their writing cramped and difficult to understand.

Read the masterclass in this book, particularly the section on live reporting if you know you'll have a screen test. And read the section on making good showreels.

There are three bits of advice I regularly give people who call me about jobs.

Assume nothing about your interviewers – the interview is an opportunity to shine and you must do so – even if everyone in the room knows you and your work.

It's easier to shine if you know what you are talking about. You must know enough about the job and how it's done to prove you can do it, so know your facts and try not to make things up (I'm amazed at how often candidates do this).

Your ideas should be plentiful and you should know how to execute them. Candidates often seem to have the idea and then say, for example, 'I'd speak to him/her/them and film this and that,' but haven't thought what the opening shot of their package or live event might be. David Mackie, BBC Home News Assignments Editor

In conclusion

TOP TEN INTERVIEW TIPS

- Understand this: preparation is all.

- Don't waffle. Give clear, focused answers.

- Watch or listen to the output beforehand – and that of the competition.

- Learn as much as possible about the programme, network or organization you are applying to join.

- Have a broad and completely up-to-date, in-depth understanding of all the main stories in the news at that moment.

- Have some great, original story ideas, backed up by equally good treatments.

- Be prepared to back up everything you say.

- Tell the interviewers something they don't know. Have a view.

- Read the masterclass in this book before the interview.

- If you don't get the job, don't give up – persevere.

There was a young aspiring reporter in Belfast, being interviewed by the indomitable Robin Walsh, who could be a ferocious and forensic inquisitor on BBC 'boards'. Walsh had recently broken his ankle playing cricket, and his plastered leg was resting on the table between the panel and the interviewee. The exchange went as follows:

Walsh: You are walking along the Falls Road with your tape recorder, and you see me. I am Seamus Twomey, reputed to be the Chief of Staff of the IRA. What do you do?

candidate: I interview you.

Walsh: Good. [Emphatically] What's your first question?

candidate: Er, how's the leg coming along then, Seamus?

panel erupts with laughter.

bibliography

Atkinson, Max, *Our Masters' Voices*
(Methuen, 1984)
BBC Producers' Guidelines (BBC)
Block, Mervin, *Broadcast Newswriting: The RTNDA Reference Guide*
(RTNDA and Bonus Books, 1994)
Block, Mervin, *Writing Broadcast News – Shorter, Sharper, Stronger*
(Bonus Books, 1997)
Everton, Neil, *The VJ Handbook*
(CBC Training and Development, 1998)
Journalists at Work: Their Views on Training, Recruitment and Conditions
(The Journalism Training Forum, 2002)
Kerrane, Kevin and Yagoda, Ben, (ed.), *The Art of Fact*
(Simon and Schuster, 1988)
Llewellyn, Shiona, *Career Handbook for TV, Radio, Film, Video and
Interactive Media* (Skillset, A&C Black, 2001)
Mayeux, Peter E., *Broadcast News: Writing and Reporting*
(McGraw-Hill, 1996)
Papper, Robert A., *Broadcast News Writing Stylebook*
(Allyn and Bacon, 1995)
Peck and Coyle, *The Student's Guide to Writing*
(Palgrave Study Guides, 1999)
Shook, Frederick, *Television Field Production and Reporting*
(Longman, 1996)
Utterback, Ann S., *Broadcast Voice Handbook: How to Polish Your On-air
Delivery* (Bonus Books, 1995)

White, Ted, *Broadcast News Writing and Reporting*
  (St Martin's Press, 1993)
Wilson, John, *Understanding Journalism: A Guide to the Issues*
  (Routledge, 1996)

part three: database of contacts

7 news organizations

Terrestrial TV

If you are trying to contact the news department and there is no contact name listed here, ask for the News Editor.

BBC Television

BBC News Division
BBC Television Centre
Wood Lane
London
W12 7RJ
Tel: 020 8743 8000
www.bbc.co.uk/news

Director of News: Richard Sambrook; *Deputy Director:* Mark Damazer; *Head of Current Affairs:* Peter Horrocks; *Head of Newsgathering:* Adrian Van Klaveren; *Head of News Interactive:* Richard Deverell; *Head of Political Programmes:* Fran Unsworth; *Head of Radio News:* Stephen Mitchell; *Head of Television News:* Roger Mosey; *Chief Operating Officer:* Peter Phillips; *Deputy Head of Newsgathering:* Vin Ray; *Deputy Head of*

Television News: Rachel Attwell; *Head of News Resources and Technology:* Julia Nelson; *Head of News Publicity:* Alison Kelly.

Television
Director of Television: Jana Bennett; *Head of Television News:* Roger Mosey; *Editor, One O'Clock News:* Chris Rybczynski; *Editor, Six O'Clock News:* Jay Hunt; *Editor, Ten O'Clock News:* Mark Popescu; *Editor, Newsnight:* George Entwhistle; *Editor, Breakfast News:* Richard Porter; *Editor, Breakfast With Frost:* Barney Jones; *Head of News, World TV:* Caroline Howie.

BBC1
Television Centre
Wood Lane
London
W12 7RJ
Controller, BBC1: Lorraine Heggessey.

BBC2
Television Centre
Wood Lane

London

W12 7RJ

Controller, BBC2: Jane Root.

BBC3

Television Centre

Wood Lane

London

W12 7RJ

Controller, BBC3: Stuart Murphy; *Editor, BBC3 News:* Colin Hancock.

BBC4

Television Centre

Wood Lane

London

W12 7RJ

Controller, BBC4: Roly Keating; *Editor, BBC4 News:* Amanda Farnsworth.

BBC Nations and Regions

BBC Nations and Regions Headquarters

Portland Place

London

W1A 1AA

Tel: 020 7580 4468

Director, Nations and Regions: Pat Loughrey.

Northern Ireland

BBC Northern Ireland Headquarters

Broadcasting House

Ormeau Avenue

Belfast

BT2 8HQ

Tel: 028 9033 8000

Fax: 028 9033 2576

www.bbc.co.uk/northernireland

Controller: Anna Carragher; *Head of Programme Operations:* Stephen Beckett; *Head of News and Current Affairs:* Andrew Colman; *Head of Marketing and Communications:* Peter Johnston; *Head of Public Affairs and Secretary Northern Ireland:* Rosemary Kelly; *Head of Finance and Business Affairs:* Crawford McLean; *Head of Broadcast:* Tim Cooke; *Head of Entertainment, Events and Sport:* Mike Edgar; *Head of Factual and Learning:* Bruce Batten; *Head of Drama:* Robert Cooper; *Managing Editor, Foyle:* Ana Leddy.

Programmes include *Newsline 6:30, Hearts and Minds* and *Country Times.* Radio stations: BBC Radio Foyle and BBC Radio Ulster.

Scotland

BBC Glasgow National Headquarters
Queen Margaret Drive
Glasgow
G12 8DG
Tel: 0141 338 2000
Fax: 0141 334 0614
www.bbc.co.uk/scotland
Controller: John McCormick; *Head of News and Current Affairs:* Blair Jenkin. Centres in Aberdeen, Dundee, Edinburgh and Inverness. Programmes include *Reporting Scotland* and *Sportscene* on TV, and *Good Morning Scotland* and the *Fred MacAulay Show* on radio.

Aberdeen
Broadcasting House
Beechgrove Terrace
Aberdeen
AB9 2ZT
Tel: 01224 625233
Head of North: Andrew Jones.

Dundee
Nethergate Centre
66 Nethergate
Dundee
DD1 4ER
Tel: 01382 202481

Edinburgh
Broadcasting House
Queen Street
Edinburgh
EH2 1JF
Tel: 0131 225 3131

Inverness
7 Culduthel Road
Inverness
IV2 4AD
Tel: 01463 720720
Headquarters for Radio Nan Gaidheal, the Gaelic radio service serving most of Scotland (*Editor:* Isabel MacLennan).

Wales

BBC Cardiff National Headquarters
Broadcasting House
Llandaff
Cardiff
CF5 2YQ
Tel: 029 203 2000
Fax: 029 2055 2973
www.bbc.co.uk/wales
Controller: Menna Richards; *Head of News and Current Affairs:* Aled Eurig. Centres in Bangor, Aberystwyth, Carmarthen, Wrexham and Swansea. Programmes include daily news programme *Wales Today*, *Wales on Saturday* and *Pobol y Cwm* on television

and *Good Morning Wales, Good Evening Wales, Post Cyntaf* and *Post Prynhawn* on radio.

Bangor
Broadcasting House
Merion Road
Bangor
Gwynedd
LL5 2BY
Tel: 01248 370880
Fax: 01248 351443
Head of Centre: Marian Wyn Jones.

BBC English Regions

English Regions HQ
and BBC West Midlands
Pebble Mill Road
Birmingham
B5 7QQ
Tel: 0121 432 8888
Fax: 0121 432 8847
Controller: Andy Griffee.

BBC East Midlands (Nottingham)
East Midlands Broadcasting Centre
London Road
Nottingham
NG2 4UU
Tel: 0115 955 0500
Head of Regional and Local Programmes: Alison Ford; *Output Editor:* Liz Howell.

BBC East (Norwich)
St Catherine's Close
All Saint's Green
Norwich
Norfolk
NR1 3ND
Tel: 01603 284405
Head of Regional and Local Programmes: David Holdsworth.

BBC London
35 Marylebone High Street
London
W1M 4AA
Tel: 020 7224 2424
Fax: 020 7486 2442
Executive Editor: Jane Mote (BBC *London Live* and *Newsroom South East*); *Editor, Newsgathering:* Sandy Smith.

BBC North/BBC North West/BBC North East and Cumbria
The regional centres at Leeds, Manchester and Newcastle make their own programmes on a bi-media approach, each centre having its own head of regional and local programmes.

BBC North (Leeds)
Broadcasting Centre
Woodhouse Lane
Leeds
LS2 9PN

Tel: 0113 244 1188
Fax: 0113 243 9387

Head of Regional and Local Programmes:
Colin Philpott; *Editor, Newsgathering:*
Jake Fowler; *Editor, Look North:* Kate
Watkins; *Producer, North of Westminster:*
Rod Jones; *Producer, Close Up North:* Ian
Cundall; *Producers, Look North:* Denise
Wallace, Nicola Swords.

BBC North West (Manchester)

New Broadcasting House
Oxford Road
Manchester
M60 1SJ
Tel: 0161 200 2020
Fax: 0161 244 4999

Head of Regional and Local Programmes:
Martin Brooks; *Editor, Newsgathering:*
Barbara Metcalf; *Producers, Northwest
Tonight:* Tamsin O'Brien, Jim Clark;
Producer, Close Up North: Deborah van
Bishop; *Producer, North of Westminster:*
Liam Fogarty.

BBC North East and Cumbria (Newcastle Upon Tyne)

Broadcasting Centre
Barrack Road
Newcastle upon Tyne
NE99 2NE
Tel: 0191 232 1313

Head of Regional and Local Programmes:
Olwyn Hocking; *Editor, Newsgathering:*
Andrew Hartley.

BBC Newcastle

Barrack Road
Newcastle upon Tyne
NE99 2NE
Tel: 0191 232 1313
Fax: 0191 221 0112

BBC Nottingham

London Road
Nottingham
NG2 4UU
Tel: 0115 955 0500
Fax: 0115 955 0501

BBC South East (Tunbridge Wells)

The Great Hall
Mount Pleasant Road
Tunbridge Wells
Kent
TN1 1QQ
Tel: 01892 670000
Fax: 01892 549118

Head of Regional and Local Programmes:
Laura Ellis (responsible for BBC South
East TV); BBC Radio Kent and BBC
Southern Counties Radio: *Editor,
Newsgathering:* Rod Beards; *Executive
Producer, First Sight:* Dippy Chaudhary.

BBC West/BBC South/BBC South West

The three regional television stations,
BBC West, BBC South and BBC South
West, produce the nightly news magazine

programmes, as well as regular thirty-minute local current affairs programmes and parliamentary programmes. Each of the regions operates a comprehensive local radio service.

BBC West (Bristol)
Broadcasting House
Whiteladies Road
Bristol
BS8 2LR
Tel: 0117 973 2211
Head of Regional and Local Programmes:
Andrew Wilson.

BBC South (Southampton)
Broadcasting House
Havelock Road
Southampton
Hampshire
SO14 7PU
Tel: 023 8022 6201
Fax: 023 8033 9931
Head of Regional and Local Programmes:
Eve Turner.

BBC South West (Plymouth)
Broadcasting House
Seymour Road
Mannamead
Plymouth
Devon
PL3 5BD

Tel: 01752 229201
Fax: 01752 234595
Head of Regional and Local Programmes:
Leo Devine.

BBC Sports
BBC White City
Wood Lane
London
W12 7RJ
Tel: 020 8743 8000
Director, Sport: Peter Salmon; *Head of Programmes and Planning:* Pat Younge; *Head of Major Events:* Dave Gordon; *Head of Radio Sport:* Gordon Turnbull; *Head of New Media, Sports News and Development:* Andrew Thompson; *Head of General Sports:* Barbara Slater; *Head of Football and Boxing:* Niall Sloane; *Director, Sports Rights and Finance:* Dominic Coles.

Independent Television

Anglia Television
Anglia House
Norwich
Norfolk
NR1 3JG
Tel: 01603 615151
Fax: 01603 761245
Regional newsrooms:
Norwich: 01603 753400
Cambridge: 01233 467076

Chelmsford: 01245 357676
Ipswich: 01473 226157
Luton: 01582 729666
Northampton: 01604 624343
Peterborough: 01733 269440
www.angliatv.com
angliatv@angliatv.co.uk
Controller of News: Guy Adams.
Owned by Granada; covers the East of
England. Regional news programme:
Anglia News East/West.

Border Television plc
The Television Centre
Durranhill
Carlisle
Cumbria
CA1 3NT
Tel: 01228 525101
Fax: 01228 541384
www.border-tv.com
Head of News: Ian Proniewicz.
Owned by Border Television; covers the
Scottish borders, the Lake District and
the Isle of Man. Regional news
programmes: *Look Around, Border News.*

Carlton Television (London Region)
101 St Martin's Lane
London
WC2N 4AZ
Tel: 020 7240 4000
Fax: 020 7240 4171
www.carlton.com

*Director of Programmes, Carlton
Productions:* Steve Hewlett.
Has four regional ITV licences which
include the London region; Carlton
Central Region – covering the east, west
and south Midlands; Carlton West
Country Region; HTV Wales and HTV
West, covering the south west of England.

Carlton Broadcasting, Carlton Central Region
Gas Street
Birmingham
B1 2JP
Tel: 0121 643 9898
Fax: 0121 634 4240
www.carlton.com/central
dutyoffice@carltontv.co.uk
Programmes include *Central Weekend*
and *Asian Eye.*

Carlton Broadcasting, Carlton West Country Region
Language Science Park
Western Wood Way
Plymouth
Devon
PL7 5BG
Tel: 01752 333333
Fax: 01752 333444
www.carlton.com/westcountry
Director of News and Current Affairs:
Brad Higgins.

Central Television

Central Broadcasting

Gas Street

Birmingham

B1 2JT

Tel: 0121 643 9898

Fax: 0121 634 4240

www.carlton.com

Controller of News and Operations:
Laurie Upshon. Regional news
programme: *Central News East/South/*
West.

Channel 4

124 Horseferry Road

London

SW1P 2TX

Tel: 020 7396 4444

Fax: 020 7306 8356

www.channel4.com

Editor Channel 4 News: Jim Gray; *News,*
Current Affairs and Business: David
Lloyd; *Sport:* David Kerr.
Channel Four's flagship news and current
affairs programme, *Channel 4 News*, is
presented by Jon Snow.

Channel Five

22 Long Acre

London

WC2E 9LY

Tel: 020 7550 5555

Fax: 020 7550 5554

www.channel5.co.uk

Editor, Channel Five News: Gary Rogers.
Nightly news programme *5 News*
presented by Kirsty Young.

Channel Television

The Television Centre

La Pouquelaye

St Hellier

Jersey

Channel Islands

JE1 3ZD

Tel: 01534 816816

Fax: 01534 816817

Regional newsrooms:

Guernsey: 01481 241877

Jersey: 01534 816688

www.channeltv.co.uk

broadcast@channeltv.co.uk

Regional news programme: *Channel*
Report.

GMTV

London Television Centre

Upper Ground

London

SE1 9TT

Tel: 020 7827 7000

Fax: 020 7827 7249

www.gmtv.co.uk

talk2us@gmtv.co.uk

Director of Programmes: Peter McHugh;
Executive Producer: Martin Frizell.
Holds the national breakfast time slot
from 0600 to 0925 daily.

Grampian Television
Queen's Cross
Aberdeen
Grampian
AB15 4XJ
Tel: 01224 846846
Fax: 01224 846800
www.grampiantv.co.uk
Head of News and Current Affairs:
Henry Eagles.
Regional news programme: *North Tonight.*

Granada Television Manchester
Quay Street
Manchester
M60 9AE
Tel: 0161 832 7211
Fax: 0161 953 0283
www.granadamedia.co.uk
Controller of Current Affairs and Features: Jeff Anderson.
Covers north-west England. Regional news programme: *Granada Tonight.*

Granada Television London
London Television Centre
Upper Ground
London
SE1 9LT
Tel: 020 7620 1620
Fax: 020 7261 3307

Granada regional newsrooms:
Blackburn: 01254 690099
Chester: 01244 313966
Liverpool: 0151 709 9393
Manchester: 0161 832 7211

HTV Wales
The Television Centre
Culverhouse Cross
Cardiff
CF5 6XJ
Tel: 029 2059 0590
Fax: 029 2059 7183
www.htvwales.co.uk
news@htvwales.com
Controller/Director of Programmes:
Elis Owen.
HTV News is the regional news programme.

HTV West
Television Centre
Bath Road
Bristol
BS4 3HG
Tel: 0117 972 2722
Fax: 0117 972 2400
www.htvwest.co.uk
news@htvwest.com
Controller, HTV West and Director of Regional Programmes: Sandra Jones.
HTV News is the regional news programme.

ITN (Independent Television News Ltd)
200 Gray's Inn Road
London
WC1X 8XZ
Tel: 020 7833 3000
Fax: 020 7430 4868
www.itn.co.uk
contact@itn.co.uk
Chief Executive: Stewart Purvis; *Editor, ITV News:* David Mannion; *Editor, Channel 4 News:* Jim Gray; *Editor, Channel Five News:* Gary Rogers.
Provides main national and international news for ITV, Channel 4 and Channel Five and radio news for IRN.

LWT
The London Weekend Television Centre
Upper Ground
London
SE1 9LT
Tel: 020 7620 1620
Tel: 020 7827 7700 (newsroom)
Fax: 020 7621 1290
www.lwt.co.uk
Regional news programme is *London Today*, supplied by London News Network.

Meridian Broadcasting
Television Centre
Southampton
Hampshire
SO14 0PZ
Tel: 023 8022 2555
Fax: 023 8033 5050
Regional centres:
Tel: 01622 882244 (Hythe, Kent)
Tel: 01635 522322 (Newbury, Berkshire)
www.meridiantv.com
viewerliason@meridiantv.com
Director of News Strategy: Jim Raven.
Programmes include *Meridian Tonight*, *Countryways* and *Grass Roots*.

S4C
Parc Ty Glas
Llanishen
Cardiff
CF14 5DU
Tel: 029 2074 7444
Fax: 029 2075 4444
www.s4c.co.uk
s4c@s4c.co.uk
Heno is the nightly Welsh language current affairs programme.

Scottish Television
200 Renfield Street
Glasgow
G2 3PR
Tel: 0141 300 3000
Fax: 0141 300 3030
www.scottishtv.co.uk

Head of News: Paul McKinney; Factual and Sport: Dennis Mooney. Regional news programme is Scotland Today. Covers the central Scotland area and the south-west Highlands.

Scottish Television (London Office)
20 Lincoln's Inn Fields
London
WC2A 3ED
Tel: 020 7446 7000
Fax: 020 7446 7010
www.scottishtv.co.uk

Tyne Tees Television
Television Centre
City Road
Newcastle upon Tyne
NE1 2AL
Tel: 0191 261 0181
Fax: 0191 261 2302
www.granadamedia.com
tyne.tees@granadamedia.com
Head of Network Features: Malcolm Wright; Editor, Current Affairs and Features: Jane Bolesworth; Head of Sport: Roger Tames.
The regional news programme is North East Tonight. Covers north-east England and the North Yorkshire area.

UTV (Ulster Television)
Havelock House
Ormeau Road
Belfast
BT7 1EB
Tel: 028 9032 8122
Fax: 028 9024 6695
www.utvinternet.com
info@utvplc.com
Head of News and Current Affairs: Rob Morrison.
The regional news programme is called UTV Live at Six. Covers Northern Ireland.

West Country Television
Weston Wood Way
Language Science Park
Plymouth
PL7 5BQ
Tel: 01752 333333
Fax: 01752 333444
www.westcountry.co.uk
info@westcountry.co.uk
Controller of News: Brad Higgins.
The regional news programme is West Country Live. Covers the Cornwall, Devon, west Dorset and south Somerset area.

Yorkshire Television
The Television Centre
Leeds
West Yorkshire
Tel: 0113 243 8283
Fax: 0113 244 5107
www.granada.media.com

Yorkshire Television (London Office)
96–108 Great Suffolk Street
London
SE1 0BE
Tel: 020 7578 4304
Fax: 020 7578 4320
www.granadamedia.com
Head of News and Current Affairs:
Clare Morrow.
Documentary and current affairs
programming.

Satellite, Cable and Digital TV

BBC News 24
Television Centre
Wood Lane
London
W12 7RJ
Tel: 020 8743 8000
Deputy Head of Television News (and
Editor, News 24): Rachel Attwell.

BBC World TV
Television Centre
Wood Lane
London
W12 7RJ
Tel: 020 8743 8000
Deputy Head of Television News (and
Editor, World TV): Rachel Attwell; *Head
of News:* Caroline Howie.

BBC3
Television Centre
Wood Lane
London
W12 7RJ
Controller, BBC Choice: Stuart Murphy;
Editor, BBC3 News: Colin Hancock.

BBC4
Television Centre
Wood Lane
London
W12 7RJ
Controller, BBC4: Roly Keating; *Editor
BBC4 News:* Amanda Farnsworth.

Bloomberg Television
39–45 Finsbury Square
London
EC2A 1PQ
Tel: 020 7330 7500
Fax: 020 7392 6000
www.bloomberg.com/uk
Covers business news and financial news
stories with multiscreen format.
Broadcasts ten channels around the
world in eight languages. Available on
cable, satellite and Sky Digital.

**British Sky Broadcasting Ltd
(BSkyB)**
6 Centaurs Business Park
Grant Way

Isleworth

Middlesex

TW7 5QD

Tel: 020 7705 3000

Fax: 020 7705 3030

www.sky.com

Chief Executive: Tony Ball; *Managing Director, Sky Sports:* Vic Wakeling; *Director of Broadcasting and Production:* Mark Sharman; *Head of Sky News:* Nick Pollard.
Over 200 channels delivering Sky News, Sky News Active and other services.

Cable and Wireless

Caxton Way

Watford Business Park

Watford

Herts

WD1 8XH

Tel: 020 7528 2000

Fax: 020 7315 5000

www.cwplc.com

Develops interactive services in partnership with other broadcasters.

Cable News Network International

CNN House

19–22 Rathbone Place

London

W1P 1DF

Tel: 020 7637 6700

Fax: 020 7637 6910

www.cnn.com

London Bureau Chief: Tom Mintier; *Vice President and Managing Editor for Europe/Middle East/Africa:* Tony Maddox. International twenty-four-hour network.

CNBC

10 Fleet Place

London

EC4M 7QS

Tel: 020 7653 9300

Fax: 020 7653 9333

www.cnbceurope.com

feedback@cnbceurope.com

President: Rick Cotton.
Twenty-four-hour business and financial news service provided by NBC and Dow Jones.

EuroNews

BP 161–60, chemin de Mouilles,

69131 Lyon Ecully cedex

France

Tel: +33 4 7218 8000

Fax: +33 4 7218 9371

www.euronews.net

Twenty-four-hour network covering Europe in seven languages.

GMTV2

The London Television Centre

Upper Ground

London

SE1 9TT

Tel: 020 7827 7002
www.gmtv.co.uk

ITV News Channel
200 Gray's Inn Road
London
WC1X 8XZ
Tel: 020 7833 3000
www.itn.co.uk
Twenty-four-hour news network.

ITV News Channel – Wales
Parc Ty Glas
Llanishen
Cardiff
CF4 5DU
Tel: 029 2074 7441
www.s4c.co.uk

NBC Europe
Unit 1/1
Harbour Yard
Chelsea Harbour
London
SW10 0XD
Tel: 020 7352 9205
Fax: 020 7352 9628
www.nbc.com
Chairman: Patrick Cox; *Director of Programming:* Bernhard Bertram. European news-based twenty-four-hour information and entertainment service in English, with extra programmes in

German and advertisements in English and German.

S4C2
Parc Ty Glas
Llanishen
Cardiff
CF4 5DU
Tel: 029 2074 7444
Fax: 029 2074 1457
www.s4c.co.uk

Radio

If you are trying to contact the news department and there is no contact name listed here, ask for the News Editor.

BBC National Radio Stations

BBC Radio Headquarters
Broadcasting House
Portland Place
London
W1A 1AA
Tel: 020 7580 4468
www.bbc.co.uk
Director of Radio and Music: Jenny Abramsky; *Controller, Radio One:* Andy Parfitt; *Controller, Radio Two:* James Moir; *Controller, Radio Three:* Roger

Wright; *Managing Editor:* Brian Barfield; *Controller, Radio Four:* Helen Boaden; *Managing Editor:* Wendy Pilmer; *Controller, Radio Five Live:* Bob Shennan; *Controller, Radio Sports Rights* and *Deputy Controller, Radio Five Live:* Mike Lewis; *Head of Radio News:* Steve Mitchell; *Managing Editor, Radio News Programmes:* Bill Rogers; *Editor, Today programme:* Kevin Marsh; *Editor, The World at One/World This Weekend/PM/ Broadcasting House:* Richard Clark; *Editor, The World Tonight:* Prue Keely; *Head of News, Five Live:* Ceri Thomas; *Editor, World Service News Programmes:* Mary Hockaday.

BBC Radio One
Broadcasting House
Portland Place
London
W1A 1AA
Tel: 020 7765 4575
www.bbc.co.uk/radio1
Frequency 97–99 FM.

Radio Two
Broadcasting House
Portland Place
London
W1A 1AA
Tel: 020 7765 4330
www.bbc.co.uk/radio2
Frequency 88–91 FM.

Radio 3
Broadcasting House
Portland Place
London
W1A 1AA
Tel: 020 7765 5337
www.bbc.co.uk/radio3
Frequency 90–93 FM.

Radio 4
Broadcasting House
Portland Place
London
W1A 1AA
Tel: 020 7765 5337
www.bbc.co.uk/radio4
Frequency 92–95 FM and 198 LW.

Radio Five Live
Television Centre
Wood Lane
London
W1A 1AA
Tel: 020 8576 1694
www.bbc.co.uk/fivelive
Frequency 693 and 909 AM.

BBC Asian Network
BBC Pebble Mill
Epic House
Charles Street
Leicester
LE1 3SH

Tel: 0116 251 6688

Fax: 0116 253 2004

www.bbc.co.uk/asiannetwork

Managing Editor: Vijay Sharma.
Broadcasts to a Midlands audience during
the day, with nationwide coverage in the
evening. Programmes in English, Bengali,
Gujarati, Hindi, Punjabi and Urdu.

BBC World Service

PO Box 76

Bush House

The Strand

London

WC2B 4PH

Tel: 020 7240 3456

Tel: 020 7557 2941 (publicity office)

Fax: 020 7557 1900

www.bbc.co.uk/world service

Frequency depends on where you live and
is either FM or MW.

Director World Service: Mark Byford;
Deputy Director World Service: Nigel
Chapman; *Head of Go Digital project:*
Benny Ammar; *Director English Networks
and News:* Phil Harding; *Head of
European Region:* Zdenka Krizman; *Head
of Africa and Middle East Region:* Jerry
Timmins; *Head of Eurasia Region:*
Behrouz Afagh Tabrizi; *Head of Americas
Region:* Lucio Mesquita; *Head of Online:*
Chris Westcott; *Head of Asia and the
Pacific Region:* Barry Langridge; *Editor,
World Service News Programmes:* Mary
Hockaday.

The World Service broadcasts in English
and forty-two other languages.

Independent National Radio
Stations

Classic FM

7 Swallow Place

London

W1B 2AG

Tel: 020 7343 9000

Fax: 020 7344 2700

www.classicfm.com

enquiries@classicfm.com

Classical music and news.
Owned by the GWR Group.
Frequency 99.9–101.9 FM.

TalkSport

18 Hatfields

London

SE1 8DJ

Tel: 020 7959 7900

Fax: 020 7959 7802

www.talksport.net

Output includes a combination of news
and sport.
Owned by the Wireless Group.
Frequency 1053, 1089, 1107 and 1071 AM.

Virgin 1215

1 Golden Square

London

W1R 4DJ

Tel: 020 7434 1215
Fax: 020 7434 1197
www.virginradio.co.uk
reception@virginradio.co.uk
Output includes news, music and sport.
Owned by SMG Plc.
Frequency 1215, 1197, 1233, 1242 and 1260 AM.

BBC Local Radio

BBC Radio Berkshire
PO Box 104.4
Reading
Berkshire
RG94 8FH
Tel: 0645 311444
Fax: 0645 311555
www.bbc.co.uk/radioberkshire
Editor: Phil Ashworth.

BBC Radio Bristol
Broadcasting House
Whiteladies Road
Bristol
BS99 7QT
Tel: 0117 974 1111
Fax: 0117 973 2549
www.bbc.co.uk/radiobristol
radio.bristol@bbc.co.uk
Editor Newsgathering: Ian Cameron.

BBC Radio Cambridgeshire
Broadcasting House
104 Hills Road
Cambridge
CB2 1LD
Tel: 01223 259696
Fax: 01223 460832
www.bbc.co.uk/radiocambridgeshire
cambs@bbc.co.uk
News Editor: Andrew Tomlinson.

BBC Radio Cleveland
Broadcasting House
Newport Road
Middlesbrough
TS1 5DG
Tel: 01642 225211
Fax: 01642 211356
www.bbc.co.uk/radiocleveland
radio.cleveland@bbc.co.uk

BBC Radio Cornwall
Phoenix Wharf
Truro
Cornwall
TRU 1UA
Tel: 01872 75421
Fax: 01872 40679
www.bbc.co.uk/radiocornwall
radio.cornwall@bbc.co.uk
Editor: Pauline Causey.

BBC Coventry and Warwickshire
Holt Court
1 Greyfriars Road
Coventry
CV1 2WR
Tel: 024 7686 0086
Fax: 024 7657 0100
www.bbc.co.uk/coventrywarwickshire
Managing Editor: Keith Beech.

BBC Radio Cumbria
Annetwell Street
Carlisle
CA3 8BB
Tel: 01228 592444
Fax: 01228 511195
www.bbc.co.uk/radiocumbria
radio.cumbria@bbc.co.uk
Editor: Nigel Dyson.

BBC Radio Cymru
Broadcasting House
Llandaff
Cardiff
CF5 2YQ
Tel: 029 2032 2000
Fax: 029 2055 5960
www.bbc.co.uk/cymru
radio.cymru@bbc.co.uk
Editor: Aled Glynne Davies; *Editor, Radio
Cymru News:* Rhian Gibson.
Welsh and English language
programmes.

BBC Radio Derby
PO Box 269
Derby
DE1 3HL
Tel: 01332 361111
Fax: 01332 290794
www.bbc.co.uk/radioderby
radio.derby@bbc.co.uk
Manging Editor: Mike Bettison.

BBC Radio Devon
PO Box 5
Broadcasting House
Seymour Road
Mannamead
Plymouth
Devon
PL3 5YQ
Tel: 01752 260323
Fax: 01752 234599
www.bbc.co.uk/radiodevon
radio.devon@bbc.co.uk
Managing Editor: John Lilley; *Head of
Programmes:* Matthew Price; *Head of
News:* Sarah Solthley.

BBC Essex
198 New London Road
Chelmsford
Essex
CM2 9XB
Tel: 01245 616000
Fax: 01245 492983

www.bbc.co.uk/essex
essex@bbc.co.uk
News Editor: Tim Gillett.

BBC Radio Foyle
8 Northland Road
Londonderry
BT48 7JD
Tel: 028 7126 2244
Fax: 028 7137 8666
www.bbc.co.uk/northernireland
Managing Editor: Ana Leddy; *News Producers:* Eimear O'Callaghan, Paul McFadden.

BBC Radio Gloucestershire
London Road
Gloucestershire
GL1 1SW
Tel: 01452 308585
Fax: 01452 309491
www.bbc.co.uk/radiogloucestershire
Editor: Bob Lloyd Smith.

BBC GMR
PO Box 951
Oxford Road
Manchester
M60 1SD
Tel: 0161 200 2000
Fax: 0161 236 5804
www.bbc.co.uk/gmr
gmr@bbc.co.uk
Managing Editor: Karen Hannah.

BBC Radio Guernsey
Commerce House
Les Banques
St Peter Port
Guernsey
GY1 2HS
Tel: 01481 728977
Fax: 01481 713557
www.bbc.co.uk/radioguernsey
radio.guernsey@bbc.co.uk
Managing Editor: Robert Wallace.

BBC Hereford and Worcestershire
Hylton Road
Worcester
WR2 5WW
Tel: 01905 748485
Fax: 01905 748006
www.bbc.co.uk/herefordandworcester/
bbchw@bbc.co.uk
Managing Editor: James Coghill.

BBC Radio Humberside
9 Chapel Street
Hull
North Humberside
HU1 3NU
Tel: 01482 323232
Fax: 01482 621403
www.bbc.co.uk/radiohumberside
radio.humberside@bbc.co.uk
Editor: Helen Thomas.

BBC Radio Jersey
18 Parade Road
St Helier
Jersey
Channel Islands
JE2 3PL
Tel: 01534 870000
Fax: 01534 732569
www.bbc.co.uk/radiojersey
james.filleul@bbc.co.uk
Managing Editor: Denzil Dudley; *Senior Producer:* James Filleul.

BBC Radio Kent
The Great Hall
Mount Pleasant Road
Tunbridge Wells
Kent
TN1 1QQ
Tel: 01892 670000
Fax: 01634 830573
www.bbc.co.uk/radiokent
radio.kent@bbc.co.uk
Managing Editor: Steve Tabchini.

BBC Radio Lancashire
26 Darwen Street
Blackburn
BB2 2EA
Tel: 01254 262411
Fax: 01254 680821
www.bbc.co.uk/radiolancashire
radio.lancashire@bbc.co.uk
Managing Editor: Steve Taylor.

BBC Radio Leeds
Broadcasting House
Woodhouse Lane
Leeds
LS2 9PN
Tel: 0113 244 2131
Fax: 0113 242 0652
www.bbc.co.uk/radioleeds
radio.leeds@bbc.co.uk
Managing Editor: Ashley Peatfield;
Newsgathering Bureau Editor: Tim Smith.

BBC Radio Leicester
Epic House
Charles Street
Leicester
LE1 3SH
Tel: 0116 251 6688
Fax: 0116 251 1463
www.bbc.co.uk/radioleicester
radio.leicester@bbc.co.uk
Editor: Liam McCarthy.

BBC Radio Lincolnshire
PO Box 219
Newport
Lincoln
LN1 3XY
Tel: 01522 511411
Fax: 01522 511726
www.bbc.co.uk/radiolincolnshire
Managing Editor: Charlie Partridge.

BBC London Live
PO Box 94.9
London
WC2B 4QH
Tel: 020 7224 2424
Fax: 020 7208 9210
www.bbc.co.uk/londonlive
londonlive@bbc.co.uk
Managing Editor: David Robey.

BBC Radio Merseyside
55 Paradise Street
Liverpool
L1 3BP
Tel: 0151 708 5500
Fax: 0151 794 0988
www.bbc.co.uk/radiomerseyside
Editor: Mick Ord.

BBC Radio Newcastle
Broadcasting Centre
Barrack Road
Newcastle upon Tyne
NE99 1RN
Tel: 0191 232 4141
Fax: 0191 261 8907
www.bbc.co.uk/radionewcastle
radio.newcastle@bbc.co.uk
Editor, Newsgathering: Andrew Hartley.

BBC Radio Norfolk
Norfolk Tower
Surrey Street

Norwich
NR1 3PA
Tel: 01603 617411
Fax: 01603 633692
www.bbc.co.uk/radionorfolk
norfolk@bbc.co.uk
Editor: David Clayton.

BBC Radio Northampton
Broadcasting House
Abington Street
Northampton
NN1 2BH
Tel: 01604 239100
Fax: 01604 230709
www.bbc.co.uk/radionorthampton
northampton@bbc.co.uk
Managing Editor: David Clargo.

BBC Radio Nottingham
London Road
Nottingham
NG2 4UU
Tel: 0115 955 0500
Fax: 0115 902 1983
www.bbc.co.uk/radionottingham
radio.nottingham@bbc.co.uk
Editor: Kate Squire.

BBC Radio Oxford
269 Banbury Road
Oxford
OX2 7DW

Tel: 0645 311444
Fax: 0645 311555
www.bbc.co.uk/radiooxford
Managing Editor: Phil Ashworth.

BBC Radio Scotland (Dumfries)
Elmbank
Lover's Walk
Dumfries
DG1 1NZ
Tel: 01387 268008
Fax: 01387 252568
dumfries@bbc.co.uk
Senior producer: Willie Johnston.

BBC Radio Scotland (Orkney)
Castle Street
Kirkwall
Orkney
KW15 1DF
Tel: 01856 873939
Fax: 01856 872908
Senior Producer: John Fergusson.

BBC Radio Scotland (Selkirk)
Municipal Buildings
High Street
Selkirk
TD7 4JX
Tel: 01750 21884
Fax: 01750 22400

BBC Radio Sheffield
54 Shoreham Street
Sheffield
SY1 4RS
Tel: 0114 273 1177
Fax: 0114 279 6699
www.bbc.co.uk/radiosheffield
radio.sheffield@bbc.co.uk
Station Editor: Gary Keown.

BBC Radio Shetland
Pitt Lane
Lerwick
Shetland
ZE1 0DW
Tel: 01595 694747
Fax: 01595 694307
www.bbc.co.uk/radioshetland
Senior Producer: Richard Whitaker.

BBC Radio Shropshire
2–4 Boscobel Drive
Shrewsbury
Shropshire
SY1 3TT
Tel: 01743 248484
Fax: 01743 237018
www.bbc.co.uk/radioshropshire
radio.shropshire@bbc.co.uk
Editor: Tony Fish.

BBC Radio Solent
PO Box 9000
Portfolio House
Princes Street
Dorchester
DT1 1TP
Tel: 01305 269654
Fax: 01305 250910
www.bbc.co.uk/radiosolent
radio.solent@bbc.co.uk
Managing Editor: Chris Van Schaick.

BBC Somerset Sound
14 Paul Street
Taunton
TA1 3PF
Tel: 01823 252437
Fax: 01823 332539
www.bbc.co.uk/radiobristol/somerset
Richard.austin@bbc.co.uk
Editor: Jenny Lacey.
Part of Radio Bristol.

BBC Southern Counties Radio
Broadcasting Centre
Guildford
GU2 5AP
Tel: 01483 306306
Fax: 01483 304952
www.bbc.co.uk/southerncounties
southern.counties.radio@bbc.co.uk
Managing Editor: Mike Hapgood.

BBC Radio Stoke
Cheapside
Hanley
Stoke-on-Trent
ST1 1JJ
Tel: 01782 208080
Fax: 01782 289115
www.bbc.co.uk/radiostoke
radio.stoke@bbc.co.uk
Managing Editor: Mark Hurrell.

BBC Radio Suffolk
Broadcasting House
St Matthews Street
Ipswich
IP1 3EP
Tel: 01473 250000
Fax: 01473 210887
www.bbc.co.uk/radiosuffolk
suffolk@bbc.co.uk
Editor: Keith Beech.

BBC Three Counties Radio
PO Box 3CR
Luton
Bedfordshire
LU1 5XL
Tel: 01582 637400
Fax: 01582 401467
www.bbc.co.uk/threecounties
3cr@bbc.co.uk
Managing Editor: Mark Norman.

BBC Radio Ulster
Broadcasting House
Ormeau Avenue
Belfast
BT2 8HQ
Tel: 028 9033 8000
Fax: 028 9033 8800
Head of Broadcasting: Tim Cooke; *Head of Production:* Paul Evans.

BBC Radio Wales
Broadcasting House
Llandaff
Cardiff
CF5 2YQ
Tel: 029 2032 2000
Fax: 029 2032 2674
www.bbc.co.uk/wales/radio
radio.wales@bbc.co.uk
Editor: Julie Barton; *Editor, Radio Wales News:* Geoff Williams.
Programmes include *Good Morning Wales, Good Evening Wales, Wales at One, Adam Walton* and *Kevin Hughes.*

BBC Wiltshire Sound
Broadcasting House
Prospect Place
Swindon
SN1 3RW
Tel: 01793 513626
Fax: 01793 513650

www.bbc.co.uk/wiltshiresound
wiltshire.sound@bbc.co.uk
Editor: Tony Wargon.

BBC Radio WM
BBC Broadcasting Centre
Pebble Mill Road
Birmingham
B5 7SA
Tel: 0121 432 8888
Fax: 0121 414 8900
www.bbc.co.uk/radiowm
radio.wm@bbc.co.uk
Managing Editor: Keith Beech.

BBC Radio York
20 Bootham Row
York
YO3 7BR
Tel: 01904 641351
Fax: 01904 610937
www.bbc.co.uk/radioyork
Editor: Barrie Stephenson; *Senior Broadcast Journalist:* William Jenkyns.

Independent Local Radio

2CR FM
5 Southcote Road
Bournemouth
Dorset
BH1 3LR

Tel: 01202 259259
Fax: 01202 255244
www.koko.com
newsbournemouth@creation.com
News, weather, sport and local
information. Owned by the GWR Group, it
covers the Dorset, west Hampshire area.
Frequency 102.3 FM.

2-Ten
PO Box 2020
Reading
RG31 7FG
Tel: 0118 945 4400
Fax: 0118 928 8513
www.koko.com
liz.gameson@creation.com
News, weather, sport and local
information. Owned by the GWR Group,
it covers the Reading, Basingstoke,
Andover area.
Frequency 102.9FM and 103.4 FM.

Active 107.5 FM
Lambourne House
7 Western Road
Romford
RM1 3LD
Tel: 01708 731643
Fax: 01708 728486
www.activefm.co.uk
sales@activefm.co.uk
News, weather, sport and local
information. Owned by the UKRD Group,

it covers the East London and west Essex
areas.

96.3 Radio Aire FM/Magic 828
53 Burley Road
Leeds
West Yorkshire
LS3 1LR
Tel: 0113 283 5500
Fax: 0113 283 5501
www.airefm.com
Music-based programming with news.

Alpha 103.2
Radio House
11 Woodland Road
Darlington
County Durham
DL3 7BJ
Tel: 01325 255552
Fax: 01325 255551
www.alpha1032.net
mail@alpha1032.net
News, weather, entertainment and local
information for Darlington and Newton
Aycliffe area. Owned by the Radio
Investments Group.

Amber Classic Gold
47–49 Colegate
Norwich
NR3 1DB
Tel: 01603 630621

Fax: 01603 666353
www.classicgolddigital.com
News, weather and sport for the Great
Yarmouth, Norwich area.
Frequency 1152 kHz.

Argyll FM
27–29 Longrow
Campbelltown
Argyll
PA28 6ER
Tel: 01586 551800
Fax: 01586 551888
www.argylfm106@aol.com
News and sport for Kintyre, Islay and
Jura.
Frequency 107.1, 107.7 and 106.5 FM.

Asian Sound
Globe House
Southall Street
Manchester
M3 1LG
Tel: 0161 288 1000
Fax: 0161 288 9000
www.asiansoundradio.co.uk
info@asiansoundradio.co.uk
News and information for the Asian
community covering the
east Lancashire area.
Frequency 1377 and 963 AM.

Bath FM
Station House
Lower Weston
Ashley Avenue
Bath
BA1 3DS
Tel: 01225 471571
Fax: 01225 471681
www.bathfm.co.uk
studio@bathfm.co.uk
Music, news, travel, sport, weather and
local information for Bath.
Frequency 107.9 FM.

The Bay
PO Box 969
Lancaster
LA1 3LD
Tel: 01524 848747
Fax: 01524 848787
www.thebay.co.uk
information@thebay.co.uk
Music, news, travel, sport, weather and
local information provider.
Owned by the CN Group, it covers the
Lancashire and South Cumbria area.
Frequency 96.9, 102.3 and 103.2 FM.

BCR FM
PO Box 1074
Bridgwater
Somerset
TA6 4WE

Tel: 01278 444211

Fax: 01278 444211

www.bcrfm.co.uk

info @bcrfm.co.uk

Music, news, travel, sport, weather and local information for the Bridgwater area. Frequency 107.4 FM.

Beacon FM/WABC Classic Gold Digital

267 Tettenhall Road

Wolverhampton

WV6 0DE

Tel: 01902 461383

Fax: 01902 461299

www.koko.com

Music, news, travel, sport, weather and local information for the Black Country, Shrewsbury. Owned by the GWR Group. Frequency 97.2 and 103.1 MHz; 990 and 1017 AM.

FM 102 The Bear

Banbury Road

Stratford upon Avon

Warwickshire

CV37 7HX

Tel: 01789 262636

Fax: 01789 263102

www.thebear.co.uk

studio@thebear.co.uk

Music, news, travel, sport, weather and local information for Stratford upon Avon

and surroundings. Owned by the CN Group.

Beat 106

Four Winds Pavilion

Pacific Quay

Glasgow

G51 1EB

Tel: 0141 5666106

Fax: 0141 5666110

www.beat106.com

info@beat106.com

Music-based station with news, sport and entertainment. Owned by Capital Radio, it covers central Scotland. Frequency 105.7 MHz and 106.1 MHz.

106.3 Bridge FM

Cambria House

Wyndham Street

Bridgend

CF31 1EY

Tel: 01656 647777

Fax: 01656 673611

www.bridgefm.co.uk

newsroom@bridgefm.co.uk

News, sport, weather, traffic and local information for Bridgend and the surrounding area. Owned by the Tindle Radio Group.

96.4 FM BRMB

Nine Brindley Place

4 Oozells Square

Birmingham
B1 2DJ
Tel: 0121 245 5000
Fax: 0121 245 5245
www.brmb.co.uk
info@brmb.co.uk

Music-based station with news, sport and entertainment. Owned by Capital Radio, it covers the Birmingham area.
Frequency 96.4 FM.

Broadland 102.4 FM

47 Colegate
Norwich
Norfolk
NR3 1DB
Tel: 01603 630621
Fax: 01603 666353
www.broadland102.co.uk
sales@broadland102.co.uk

Music, news, travel, sport, weather and local information. Owned by the GWR Group, it covers the Norwich/Great Yarmouth area.
Frequency 102.4 MHz and 1152 kHz.

Broadland 102.4 FM/Classic Gold Digital Amber

47–49 Colegate
Norwich
Norfolk
NR3 1DB
Tel: 01603 630621
Fax: 01603 630892 (newsroom)

www.koko.com
sales@broadland102.co.uk
Part of the GWR Group. Popular music programmes and local news only.

The Buzz

Media House
Claughton Road
Birkenhead
CHY41 6EY
Tel: 0151 6501700
Fax: 0151 6475427
www.thebuzz.co.uk

Owned by the Marcher Radio Group, it covers the Wirral area.
Frequency 97.1 MHz.

95.8 Capital FM/Capital Gold

30 Leicester Square
London
WC2H 7LA
Tel: 020 7766 6000
Fax: 020 7766 6100
www.capitalfm.com
www.capitalradiogroup.com
info@capitalradio.co.uk

Music-based station with news bulletins, sport, entertainment and celebrity interviews. Owned by Capital Radio, it covers the London area.
Frequency 95.8 MHz (Capital FM); 1548 kHz (Capital Gold).

1152 Capital Gold, Birmingham
BRMB Radio Group
Nine Brindley Place
4 Oozells Square
Birmingham
B1 2DJ
Tel: 0121 245 5000
Fax: 0121 245 5245
www.brmb.co.uk
info@capitalgold.co.uk
Music-based station with news bulletins,
sport, entertainment and celebrity
interviews. Covers the Birmingham area.
Frequency 1152 AM.

Capital Gold, Brighton
Radio House
Franklin Road
Portslade
BN41 2SS
Tel: 01273 430111
Fax: 01273 430098
www. brmb.co.uk
info@southernradio.co.uk
Music-based station with news bulletins,
sport, entertainment and celebrity
interviews. Owned by Capital Radio.
Covers Brighton, Southampton,
Portsmouth.
Frequency 1323 kHz (Brighton), 1170 and
1557 kHz (Portsmouth, Soton).

Capital Gold, Cardiff
West Canal Wharf
Cardiff
CF10 5XL
Tel: 029 2066 2066
Fax: 029 2066 2060
www.capitalfm.com
news@reddragonfm.co.uk
Music-based station with news bulletins,
sport, entertainment and celebrity
interviews. Owned by Capital Radio.
Frequency 1359 kHz (Cardiff) and 1305
kHz (Newport).

103.1 Central FM
201High Street
Falkirk
FK1 1DU
Tel: 01324 611164
Fax: 01324 611168
www.centralfm.co.uk
mail@centralfm.co.uk
Broadcasts music, sport and local news
to central Scotland. Covers the Stirling
and Falkirk area on frequency 103.1 MHz.

101.6/102.4 Centre FM
5–6 Aldergate
Tamworth
Staffordshire
B79 7DJ
Tel: 01827 318000
Fax: 0870 000 1024

www.centrefm.com
studioone@centrefm.com
News and local information.
Covers the south-east Staffordshire
area.
Frequency 101.6 MHz and 102.4 MHz.

Century 105.4 FM

Laser House
Waterfront Quay
Salford Quays
Manchester
M5 2XW
Tel: 0161 400 1054
Fax: 0161 400 1105
www.centuryfm.com
info1054@centuryfm.co.uk
Music-based station with news bulletins,
sport, entertainment and celebrity
interviews. Owned by Capital Radio, it
covers the North West.
Frequency 105.4 MHz.

Century 106 FM

City Link
Nottingham
NG2 4NG
Tel: 0115 910 6100
Fax: 0115 910 6107
www.century106.com
info106@centuryfm.co.uk
Music-based station with news bulletins,
sport, and entertainment and celebrity

interviews. Owned by Capital Radio,
it covers the East Midlands area.
Frequency 106 MHz.

CFM

PO Box 964
Carlisle
Cumbria
CA1 3NG
Tel: 01228 818964
Fax: 01228 819444
www.cfmradio.com
studio@cfmradio.com
Music, news and information station
covering Cumbria.
Frequency 96.4 FM (Carlisle), 102.5
(Penrith), 102.2 FM (Workington) and
103.4 FM (Whitehaven).

Champion 103 FM

Llys-y-Dderwen
Parc Menai
Bangor
LL47 4BN
Tel: 01248 671888
Fax: 01248 671971
www.championfm.co.uk
International, national and local news,
sports and entertainment for Caernarfon.
Owned by the Marcher Radio Group.
Frequency 103 MHz.

Channel 103 FM

6 Tunnel Street
St Helier
Jersey
JE2 4LU
Tel: 01534 888103
Fax: 01534 887799
www.channel103.com
firstname@channel103.com

News and information service.
Owned by Tindle Radio, it covers Jersey.
Frequency 103.7 MHz.

Chiltern 96.9 FM

55 Goldington Road
Bedford
MK40 3LT
Tel: 01234 272400
Fax: 01234 218580
www.koko.com
studio@bedford.musicradio.com

News, travel, weather, sport.
Owned by the GWR Group, it covers
Bedfordshire, Hertfordshire and
Cambridgeshire.

96.9 Chiltern FM/Classic Gold

Chiltern Road
Dunstable
Bedfordshire
LU6 1HQ
Tel: 01582 676200
Fax: 01582 676241 (newsroom)
www.koko.com

News, travel, weather, sport.
Owned by the GWR Group, it covers the
Bedford, Luton area.
Frequency 97.6 MHz (Chiltern FM), 792,
828 kHz (Gold).

Choice 96.9

291–299 Borough High Street
London
SE1 1JG
Tel: 020 7378 3969
Fax: 020 7378 3911
www.choicefm.net
info@choicefm.net

Music and news provision. Owned by Soul
Media, it covers the south London area.
Frequency 96.9 and 107.1 MHz.

Choice 107.1

291–299 Borough High Street
London
SE1 1JG
Tel: 020 7378 3969
Fax: 020 7378 3911
www.choicefm.net
info@choicefm.net

Music and news provision. Owned by Soul
Media, it covers the north London area.
Frequency 107.1 MHz.

City Beat 96.7

PO Box 927
Belfast
BT9 6BN

Tel: 028 9020 5967
Fax: 028 9020 0023
www.citybeat.co.uk
citybeat96.7@dnet-co.uk
News, sport, entertainment and local
information. Owned by the CN Group, it
covers the Belfast area.

Clan FM

Radio House
Rowantree Avenue
Newhouse
ML1 5RX
Tel: 01698 733107
Fax: 01698 733318
www.clan-fm.co.uk
clanfm@aol.com
Music and news. Owned by the UKRD
Group, it covers North Lanarkshire.
Frequency 107.5 and 107.9 FM.

Classic Gold 828

5 Southcote Road
Bournemouth
BH1 3LR
Tel: 01202 259259
Fax: 01202 255244
www.classicgold828.co.uk
sales@musicradio.com
Music and news. Owned by the GWR
Group, it covers Dorset and West
Hampshire.
Frequency 828 kHz.

Classic Gold 1260

PO Box 2020
1 Passage Street
Bristol
BS99 7SN
Tel: 0117 984 3200
Fax: 0117 984 3202
www.classicgold1260.co.uk
name@classicgold.musicradio.com
Music and news. Owned by the GWR
Group.
Frequency 1260 kHz (Bristol), 936 kHz
(West Wilts), 1161 kHz (Swindon).

Classic Gold 1332

PO Box 225
Queensgate
Peterborough
PE1 1XL
Tel: 01733 460460
Fax: 01733 281445
www.classicgolddigital.com
Music and news. Owned by the GWR
Group, it covers Peterborough.

Classic Gold 1359

Hertford Place
Coventry
CV 3TT
Tel: 024 7686 8200
Fax: 024 7686 8202
www.classicgold.musicradio.com
jeff.harris@classicgolddigital.com

Music and news provider. Owned by the GWR Group, it covers Coventry and Warwickshire area.

Classic Gold 1431
PO Box 2020
Reading
RG31 7FG
Tel: 0118 9454400
Fax: 0118 9288513
www.2-tenfm.co.uk
musicmix@twotenfm.musicradio.com
Music and news provider. Owned by the GWR Group, it covers Reading.

Classic Gold 1557
19–21 St Edmund's Road
Northampton
NN1 5DY
Tel: 01604 795600
Fax: 01604 795601
www.classicgold.co.uk
reception@northants96.musicradio.com
Music and news provider. Owned by the GWR Group.

Classic Gold Digital Amber
47 Colegate
Norwich
Norfolk
NR3 1DB
Tel: 01603 630621
Fax: 01603 666353

www.broadland102.co.uk
sales@amber.radio.co.uk
Music and news provider. Owned by the GWR Group, it covers Norwich and Great Yarmouth.
Frequency 1152 kHz.

Classic Gold Gem
29–31 Castle Gate
Nottingham
NG1 7AP
Tel: 0115 952 7000
Fax: 0115 912 9333
www.classicgold.co.uk
Music and news provider. Owned by the GWR Group. Covers Nottingham and Derby.
Frequency 999 and 945 kHz.

Radio Clyde/Clyde 1 FM/Clyde 2 AM
Clyde Business Park
Clydebank
G81 2RX
Tel: 0141 565 2200
Fax: 0141 565 2265
www.clydeonline.co.uk
info@clyde.com
info@clyde1.com
info@clyde2.com
Local news and information.

96.3 Coast FM
Media House
41 Conwy Road

Colwyn Bay
LL28 5AB
Tel: 01492 533733
Fax: 01492 535248
www.coastfm.co.uk
info@coastfm.co.uk
News and local information. Owned by
the GWR Group, it covers the North
Wales coast.
Frequency 96.3 MHz.

96.4 Compass FM
Witham Park
Waterside South
Lincoln
LN5 7JN
Tel: 01522 549900
Fax: 01522 549911
www.compassfm.co.uk
enquiries@compassfm.co.uk
Owned by Lincs FM, it covers the Grimsby
area.

Connect FM
Unit 1
Robinson Close
Kettering
NN16 8PU
Tel: 01536 412413
Fax: 01536 517390
www.connectfm.co.uk
info@connectfm.co.uk

Music, news, entertainment. Owned by
Forward Media, it covers the Kettering,
Corby, Wellingborough, Rushden area.
Frequency 97.2 and 107.4 FM.

97.4 Cool FM
PO Box 974
Belfast
BT1 1RT
Tel: 028 9181 7181
Fax: 028 9181 4974
www.coolfm.co.uk
music@coolfm.co.uk
Music and news for Belfast.
Frequency 97.4 MHz.

1566 County Sound Radio
Dolphin House
North Street
Guildford
GU1 4AA
Tel: 01483 300964
Fax: 01483 531612
www.ukrd.com
eagle@countysound.co.uk
Music, news and local information for the
Guildford area.

106 CTFM Radio
16 Lower Bridge Street
Canterbury
Kent
CT1 2HQ

Tel: 01227 789106

Fax: 01227 785106

www.ctfm.co.uk

reception@ctfm.co.uk

Music, news and local information for
Canterbury, Whitstable and Herne Bay
area.

Delta FM 97.1/102

65 Weyhill

Haslemere

Surrey

GU27 1HN

Tel: 01428 651971

Fax: 01428 658971

www.ukrd.com

studios@deltafm.freeserve.co.uk

Music and news, local information.
Owned by the UKRD Group, it covers the
Haslemere area.
Frequency 97.1 MHz and 102 MHz.

Downtown Radio

Newtownards

County Down

Northern Ireland

BT23 4ES

Tel: 028 9181 5555

Fax: 028 9181 5252

www.downtown.co.uk

programmes@downtown.co.uk

Owned by Scottish Radio Holdings.
Frequency 1026 kHz (Belfast), 102.4 MHz

(mid Antrim), 96.4 MHz (north), 96.6 MHz
(west), 103.1 MHz (South Down).

Dream 100 FM

Northgate House

St Peters Street

Colchester

CO1 1HT

Tel: 01206 764466

Fax: 01206 715102

www.dream100.com

info@dream100.com

Owned by Tindle Radio.
Frequency 100.2 FM.

107.9 Dune FM

The Power Station

Victoria Way

Southport

PR8 1RR

Tel: 01704 502500

Fax: 01704 502540

www.dunefm.co.uk

Owned by the Forward Media Group.
Covers the North Merseyside and west
Lancashire area.

The Eagle 96.4

Dolphin House

North Street

Guildford

GU1 4AA

Tel: 01483 300964

Fax: 01483 531612
www.ukrd.com
eagle@countysound.co.uk
Music, news and local information.
Owned by the UKRD Group, it covers the
west Surrey and north-east Hampshire
area.

Essex FM/Breeze
Radio House
Clifftown Road
Southend on Sea
Essex
SS1 1SX
Tel: 01702 333711
Fax: 01702 345224
www.koko.com
studio@essexfm.co.uk
News, travel, weather, sport. Owned by
the GWR Group.
Frequency 96.3 MHz (Southend), 102.6
MHz (Chelmsford).

107 FM The Falcon
Brunel Mall
London Road
Stroud
Gloucestershire
GL5 2BP
Tel: 01453 767369
Fax: 01453 757107
www.thefalcon.org
info@thefalcon.org

Music, news and local information.
Owned by the UKRD Group, it covers
southern Gloucestershire.
Frequency 107.9 MHz and 107.2 MHz.

107.6 FM The Fire
PO Box 1234
Bournemouth
BH1 1DJ
Tel: 01202 318100
Fax: 01202 318110
www.clickfire.net
Music, news and local information.
Owned by Radio Investments, it covers
Bournemouth, Poole and Christchurch.

Forth AM/Forth FM
Forth Street
Edinburgh
EH1 3LF
Tel: 0131 475 1226
Fax: 0131 475 1221
www.forthonline.com
scott.wilson@fortham.co.uk
david.bain@forthfm.co.uk
News stories welcomed from freelancers.
Music-based programming.
Frequency 97.3, 97.6 and 102.2FM (Forth
One), 1548 AM (Forth 2).

Fosseway Radio
Suite 1
1 Castle Street
Hinckley

Leicestershire
LE10 1DA
Tel: 01455 614151
Fax: 01455 616888
www.fossewayradio.co.uk
enquiries@fossewayradio.co.uk
Music and news. Owned by Lincs FM, it covers Hinckley and Nuneaton. Frequency 107.8 FM.

Fox FM
Brush House
Pony Road
Oxford
OX4 2XR
Tel: 01865 871000
Fax: 01865 871037 (news)
www.fox.co.uk
fox@foxfm.co.uk
Music, news and entertainment for Oxford and Banbury. Owned by Capital Radio.
Frequency 102.6 and 97.4 FM.

Fusion Radio 107.3
Astra House
Arklow Road
New Cross
London
SE14 6EB
Tel: 020 8691 9202
Fax: 020 8691 9193
www.fusion1073.com

Music and news for the Lewisham area. Owned by the Fusion Radio Group.

Fusion 107.9
Westgate Centre
Oxford
OX1 1PD
Tel: 01865 724442
Fax: 01865 726161
www.fusion1079.com
Music and news for the Oxford area. Owned by the Fusion Radio Group.

Galaxy 101
Millenium House
26 Baldwin Street
Bristol
BS1 1SE
Tel: 0117 901 0101
Fax: 0117 901 4666
www.galaxy101.co.uk
Music and news. Owned by the Chrysalis Group. Covers south Wales and the West.

Galaxy 102
5th Floor
The Triangle
Hanging Ditch
Manchester
M45 3TR
Tel: 0161 279 0300
Fax: 0161 279 0301

www. galaxy102.co.uk
mail@galaxy102.co.uk
Music and news. Owned by the Chrysalis
Group, it covers Greater Manchester.

Galaxy 105
Joseph's Well
Hanover Walk
Leeds
LS3 1AB
Tel: 0113 213 0105
Fax: 0113 213 1055
www.galaxy105.co.uk
mail@galaxy105.com
Music and news. Owned by the Chrysalis
Group, it covers Yorkshire.

Galaxy 105–106
Deltic House
Kingfisher Way
Silverlink Business Park
Tyne and Wear
NE28 9NX
Tel: 0191 206 8000
Fax: 0191 206 8080
www.galaxy1056.co.uk
mail@galaxy1056.co.uk
Music and news. Owned by the Chrysalis
Group, it covers north-east England.
Frequency 105.6 and 106.4 MHz.

Gemini Radio FM/Classic Gold
Hawthorn House
Exeter Business Park
Exeter
Devon
EX1 3QS
Tel: 01392 444444
Tel: 01392 444433
www.koko.com
gemini@geminifmmusicradio.com
News, travel, weather, sport. Owned by
the GWR Group, it covers Exeter, mid,
east and south Devon and Torbay.
Frequency 97.0 and 103 FM.

GWR FM (West)
PO Box 2000
The Watershed
Bristol
Avon
BS99 7SN
Tel: 0117 984 3200
Fax: 0117 984 3202
www.gwrfm.musicradio.com
reception@gwrfm.musicradio.com
Music and news, travel, weather and
sport. Owned by the GWR Group.
Frequency 103.0 MHz (Bath).

GWR FM Wiltshire
PO Box 2000
Swindon
SN4 7EX

Tel: 01793 842600
Fax: 01793 842602
www.koko.com
reception@koko.com

Music and news, travel, weather and sport. Owned by the GWR Group. Frequency 102.2 MHz (west Wiltshire), 96.5 MHz (Marlborough).

Hallam FM/Magic AM

Radio House
900 Herries Road
Sheffield
S6 1RH
Tel: 0114 285 3333
Fax: 0114 285 3159
www.hallamfm.co.uk
programmes@hallamfm.co.uk

Music, news and features. Owned by Emap.
Frequency 97.4 MHz (Sheffield), 102.9 MHz (Barnsley), 103.4 MHz (Doncaster).

Heart FM 100.7/Galaxy 102.2

1 The Square
111 Broad Street
Birmingham
B15 1AS
Tel: 0121 6950000
Fax: 0121 6950055
www.heartfm.co.uk
mail@galaxy1022.co.uk
mail@heartfm.co.uk

Heart FM broadcasts a combination of music, regional news and information. Galaxy broadcasts dance and soul music, news and information. Covers the West Midlands and Warwickshire.

Heart 106.2 FM

Chrysalis Building
Bramley Road
London
W10 6SP
Tel: 020 7468 1062
Fax: 020 7470 1095
www.heart1062.co.uk

Music and news. Owned by the Chrysalis Group, it covers Greater London.

Heartland 97.5 FM

Lower Oakfield
Pitlochry
Perthshire
PH16 5HQ
Tel: 01796 474040
Fax: 01796 474007
www.heartlandfm.co.uk
mailbox@heartlandfm.co.uk

Music and news. Gaelic and mixed language output. Owned by the Heartland Radio Foundation. Covers the Pitlochry and Aberfeldy area.

**102.7 Hereward FM/Classic Gold
Digital 1132**
PO Box 225
Queensgate Centre
Peterborough
Cambridgeshire
PE1 1XJ
Tel: 01733 460460
Fax: 01733 281445
www.koko.com
Music, news, travel, weather and sport.
Owned by the GWR Group, it covers
Peterborough.

Hertbeat 106.7 FM
Knebworth Park
Hertfordshire
SG3 6HQ
Tel: 01438 810900
Fax: 01438 815100
www.hertbeat.com
info@hertbeat.com
Music and news for Hertfordshire area.

Home 107.9
The Old Stableblock
Brewery Drive
Lockwood Park
Huddersfield
HD1 3UR
Tel: 01484 321107
Fax: 01484 311107

www.home1079.com
info@home1079.com
Music, news and sport. Owned by Radio
Investments, covers Huddersfield.

Horizon FM 103.3
Broadcast Centre
Crownhill
14 Vincent Avenue
Milton Keynes
Buckinghamshire
MK8 0AB
Tel: 01908 269111
Fax: 01908 564893
www.koko.com
crew@fm103.musicradio.com
Music, news and sport. Owned by the
GWR group, it covers Milton Keynes.

Invicta FM/Capital Gold
PO Box 100
John Wilson Business Park
Whitstable
Kent
CT5 3YR
Tel: 01227 772004
Fax: 01227 774450
www.invictafm.com
info@invictaradio.co.uk
Music-based station with news bulletins,
sport, entertainment and celebrity
interviews. Owned by Capital Radio.
Frequency Invicta FM 103.1 MHz

(Maidstone, Medway), 102.8 MHz (Canterbury), 95.9 MHz (Thanet), 97.0 MHz (Dover), 96.1 MHz (Ashford). Capital Gold 1242 kHz (west Kent), 603 kHz (east Kent).

Island FM
12 Westerbrook
St Sampson
Guernsey
Channel Islands
GY2 4QQ
Tel: 01481 242000
Fax: 01481 249676
www.islandfm.guernsey.net
Music, news and sport.
Owned by Tindle Radio.
Frequency 104.7 MHz (Guernsey), 93.7 MHz (Alderney).

Isle of Wight Radio
Dodnor Park
Newport
Isle of Wight
PO30 5XE
Tel: 01983 822557
Fax: 01983 821690
www.iwradio.co.uk
mail@iwradio.co.uk
Music, news and sport.
Frequency 107 and 102 MHz.

Isles FM
PO Box 333
Stornaway
Isle of Lewis
HS1 2PU
Tel: 01851 703333
Fax: 01851 703322
www.isles.org.uk
admin@islesfm.org.uk
Music, news and sport for the Western Isles.
Frequency 103 MHz.

ITN News Direct 97.3 FM/ LBC 1152 AM
200 Gray's Inn Road
London
WC1X 8XZ
Tel: 020 7333 0030 (News Direct)
Tel: 020 7973 1152 (LBC)
Fax: 020 7312 8470 (News Direct)
Fax: 020 7312 8565 (LBC)
www.newsdirect.co.uk
www.lbc.co.uk
news@newsdirect.co.uk
ITN News Direct 97.3 FM – 24-hour rolling news station; LBC 1152 AM – news, views and information for London.

Jazz FM
World Trade Centre
Exchange Quay
Manchester

M5 3EJ
Tel: 0161 877 1004
Fax: 0161 877 1005
www.jazzfm.com
info@jazzfm.com
Jazz, news and reviews. Owned by the
Guardian Media Group, it covers the
North West.
Frequency 100.4 MHz.

Jazz FM 102.2
26 Castlereagh Street
London
W1H 5DL
Tel: 020 7706 4100
Fax: 020 7723 9742
www.jazzfm.com
info@jazzfm.com
Jazz, news and reviews. Owned by the
Guardian Media Group, it covers Greater
London.

Juice 107.6 FM
27 Fleet Street
Liverpool
L1 4AR
Tel: 0151 707 3107
Fax: 0151 707 3109
www.juicefm.com
mail@juiceliverpool.com
Music and news.

Kestrel 107.6 FM
2nd Floor
Paddington House
The Walks Shopping Centre
Basingstoke
RG21 7LJ
Tel: 01256 694000
Fax: 01256 694111
www.kestrelfm.co.uk
info@kestrelfm.demon.co.uk
Music, news and local information for
Basingstoke.

Key 103
Castle Quay
Castlefield
Manchester
M15 4PR
Tel: 0161 288 5000
Fax: 0161 288 5001
www.clickmanchester.com
Music, news and sport. Owned by Emap,
it covers Manchester.

Kingdom FM
Haig House
Haig Business Park
Markinch
Fife
KY7 6AQ
Tel: 01592 753753
Fax: 01592 757788

www.kingdomfm.co.uk
kingdomfm@aol.com
Music, news and sport. Covers Fife.
Frequency 95.2 and 96.1 MHz.

96.7 KL-FM
18 Blackfriars Street
Kings Lynn
Norfolk
PE30 1NN
Tel: 01553 772777
Fax: 01553 766453
www.ukrd.com
Music, news and local information.
Owned by the UKRD Group, it covers
Kings Lynn.

Lantern FM
2b Lauder Lane
Roundswell
Commercial Park
Barnstaple
EX31 3TA
Tel: 01271 340340
Fax: 01271 340345
www.koko.com
lanternfm@musicradio.com
Music, news and local information.
Owned by the GWR Group, it covers north
Devon.
Frequency 96.2 MHz.

LBC 97.3 FM
200 Gray's Inn Road
London
WC1X 8XZ
Tel: 020 7973 1152
Fax: 020 7312 8565
www.lbc.co.uk
news@lbc.co.uk
24-hour news, talk and phone-ins for
London and the surrounding area. Owned
by London News Radio.
Frequency 97.3 FM.

105.4 FM Leicester Sound
Granville House
Granville Road
Leicester
LE1 7RW
Tel: 0116 256 1300
Fax: 0116 256 1305
www. koko.com
leicestersound@musicradio.com
Music and news. Owned by the GWR
Group, it covers Leicester.

Lincs FM
Witham Park
Lincoln
LN5 7JN
Tel: 01522 549900
Fax: 01522 549911
www.lincfm.co.uk
enquiries@lincsfm.co.uk

Music and news. Owned by Lincs FM.
Covers the Lincolnshire, Newark area.
Frequency 102.2, 96.7 and 97.6 FM.

Lite FM
5 Church Street
Peterborough
PE1 1XB
Tel: 01733 898106
Fax: 01733 898107
www.litefm.co.uk
admin@litefm.co.uk
News and sport for Peterborough.
Frequency 106.8 MHz.

Lochbroom FM
Radio House
Mill Street
Ullapool
Ross-shire
IV26 2UN
Tel: 01854 613131
Fax: 01854 613132
www.lochbroomfm.co.uk
radio@lochbroomfm.co.uk
Music, news and sport covering the
north-west coast of Scotland.
Frequency 102.2 MHz.

London Greek Radio
Florentina Village
Vale Road
London

N4 1TD
Tel: 020 8800 8001
Fax: 020 8800 8005
www.lgr.co.uk
programming@lgr.co.uk
Music, news and information for Greek-
speaking listeners. Covers the Haringey
area.
Frequency 103.3 MHz.

Magic AM
900 Herries Road
Sheffield
S6 1RH
Tel: 0114 285 2121
Tel: 0114 220 1548 (studio)
Fax: 0114 285 3159
www.magicam.co.uk
programmes@magicam.co.uk
Music, news and sport. Owned by Emap.
Frequency 990 kHz, 1305 kHz and 1548
kHz.

Magic 828
PO Box 2000
51 Burley Road
Leeds
LS3 1LR
Tel: 0113 283 5500
Fax: 0113 283 5501
www.magic828.com
magic@magic828.com
Music, news and sport.
Covers Leeds, West Yorkshire.

Magic 999
PO Box 974
Preston
Lancashire
PR1 1XS
Tel: 01772 556301
Fax: 01772 201917
www.emap.co.uk
Music, news and sport for Preston
and Blackpool.
Frequency 97.4 MHz.

Magic 105.4
Mappin House
4 Winsley Street
London
W1W 8HF
Tel: 020 7955 1054
Fax: 020 7975 8165
www.emap.co.uk
Music, news and sport. Covers the
Greater London area.

Magic 1152
Longrigg
Swalwell
Newcastle upon Tyne
NE99 1BB
Tel: 0191 420 0971
Fax: 0191 488 9222
www.emap.co.uk
enquiries@metroandmagic.com

Music, news and sport.
Owned by Emap Radio. Covers Tyneside,
Wearside, Northumberland, Durham.

Magic 1152 Manchester
Castle Quay
Castlefield
Manchester
M15 4PR
Tel: 0161 288 5000
Fax: 0161 661 1152
www.emap.co.uk
Music, news and sport.
Owned by Emap Radio, it covers
Manchester.

Magic 1161
Commercial Road
Hull
HU1 2SG
Tel: 01482 325141
Fax: 01482 593067
www.magic1161.co.uk
magic1161.co.uk
Music, news and sport. Owned by Emap
Radio.

Magic 1170
Radio House
Yales Crescent
Thornaby
Stockton on Tees
TS17 6AA

Tel: 01642 888222
Fax: 01642 868288
www.magicam.co.uk
Music, news and sport.
Owned by Emap Radio. Covers Teesside.

Manx Radio
PO Box 1368
Broadcasting House
Douglas
Isle of Man
IM99 1SW
Tel: 01624 682600
Fax: 01624 682604
www.manxradio.com
postbox@manxradio.com
News and sport for the Isle of Man.
Frequency 97.2, 89.0, 103.7 MHz and 1368
kHz.

Mercia FM/Classic Gold 1359
Hertford Place
Coventry
West Midlands
CV1 3TT
Tel: 0247 686 8200
Fax: 0247 686 8202
www.merciafm.co.uk
reception@merciafm.musicradio.com
Music, news and sport. Owned by the
GWR group, it covers Coventry,
Warwickshire.
Frequency 97.0 (Mercia Classic Gold),
102.9 (Mercia FM).

Mercury FM
1 East Street
Tonbridge
Kent
TN9 1AR
Tel: 01732 369200
Fax: 01732 369201
www.koko.com
mercurymusic@musicradio.com
News, travel, weather, sport. Owned by
the GWR Group, it covers Tonbridge,
Tunbridge Wells and Sevenoaks.
Frequency 96.2 (south) or 101.6 MHz
(north).

Mercury 96.6 FM
Unit 5
Metro Centre
Dwight Road
Watford
WD18 9UP
Tel: 01923 205470
Fax: 01923 205471
www.mercuryfm.co.uk
information@mercuryfm.co.uk
News, travel, weather and sport.
Owned by the GWR Group, it covers St
Albans, Hemel Hempstead, Watford.

**Mercury FM 101.7/Classic Gold
Digital – Breeze 1521**
The Stanley Centre
Kelvin Way

Manor Royal
Crawley
West Sussex
RH10 2SE
Tel: 01293 519161
Fax: 01293 560927
www.mercuryfm.co.uk
studios@mercuryfm.co.uk

Music station carrying local and national news bulletins. Owned by the GWR Group, it covers the Harlow area. Frequency 101.7 MHz.

Mercury 107.9 FM

Berkley House
186 High Street
Rochester
Kent
ME1 1EY
Tel: 01634 841111
Fax: 01634 841122
www.mercuryfm.co.uk

News, travel, weather and sport. Owned by KM Radio, it covers the Medway towns.

Metro Radio/Magic 1152 AM

Longrigg
Swalwell
Newcastle upon Tyne
NE99 1BB
Tel: 0191 420 0971 (Metro)
Tel: 0191 496 0505 (Magic)
Fax: 0191 488 0933

www.clickmetroradio.com
enquiries@metroradio.co.uk

Music, news and sport. Owned by Emap Performance.
Frequency 97.1 MHz (Tyneside, Wearside), 103.2 MHz (Tyne Valley), 102.6 (Alnwick, Hexham).

Minster FM

PO Box 123
Dunnington
York
YO19 5ZX
Tel: 01904 488888
Fax: 01904 488811
www.minsterfm.co.uk
www.minsterfm.com

Music, local news and sport for the York area. Owned by Radio Investments. Frequency 104.7 and 102.3 MHz.

Moray Firth Radio

PO Box 271
Scorguie Place
Inverness
IV3 8SF
Tel: 01463 224433
Fax: 01463 243224
www.mfr.co.uk
gerry.robinson@mfr.co.uk

Music, news, entertainment and sport for Inverness. Owned by Scottish Radio Holdings.
Frequency 97.4, 96.6 MHza and 1107 kHz.

Northants 96/Classic Gold Digital 1557
19–21 St Edmund's Road
Northampton
NN1 5DY
Tel: 01604 795600
Fax: 01604 795601
www.northants96.com
reception@northants96.musicradio.com
Music and news. Part of the GWR Group, it covers the Northampton area.
Frequency 96.6 MHz and 1557 AM.

North Sound Radio
45 King's Gate
Aberdeen
Grampian
AB15 4EL
Tel: 01224 337000
Fax: 01224 400003
www.northsound.co.uk
northsound@srh.co.uk
Music, news and sport. Owned by Scottish Radio Holdings, it covers Aberdeen.
Frequency 96.9, 97.6, 103 MHz (One) and 1035 kHz (Two).

Ocean Radio
Radio House
Whittle Avenue
Segensworth West
Fareham

PO15 5SH
Tel: 01489 589911
Fax: 01489 589453
www.oceanradiofm.com
info@oceanradio.co.uk
Music, news and entertainment. Owned by Capital Radio. Covers Portsmouth, Soton and Winchester.
Frequency 96.7 and 97.5 MHz.

Orchard FM
Haygrove House
Shoreditch
Taunton
Somerset
TA3 7BT
Tel: 01823 338448
Fax: 01823 321611
www.orchardfm.co.uk
news@orchardfm.co.uk
Music, news and entertainment. Owned by the GWR Group, it covers Somerset.
Frequency 96.5, 97.1 and 102.6 MHz.

Pirate FM 102
Wilson Way
Redruth
Cornwall
TR15 3XX
Tel: 01209 314400
Fax: 01209 314345
www.piratefm102.co.uk
onair@piratefm102.co.uk

Music and news. Owned by the UKRD Group. Covers Cornwall, West Devon, Isles of Scilly.
Frequency 102.2 MHz (east Cornwall, west Devon), 102.8 (west Cornwall, Isle of Scilly).

Plymouth Sound 97 FM Radio

Earl's Acre
Alma Road
Plymouth
Devon
PL3 4HX
Tel: 01752 227272
Fax: 01752 275605
www.plymouthsound.com
mail@plymouthsound.com
News and sport. Owned by the GWR Group, it covers the Plymouth area. Frequency 1152 kHz (AM), 97.0 and 96.6 MHz (FM).

Power 103.2 FM

Radio House
Whittle Avenue
Segensworth West
Fareham
Hampshire
PO15 5SH
Tel: 01489 589911
Fax: 01489 589453
www.powerfm.com
info@powerfm.com
Music-based station with news bulletins, sport, entertainment and celebrity

interviews. Owned by Capital Radio, it covers Portsmouth, Southampton and Winchester.

The Pulse

Pennine House
Foster Square
Bradford
West Yorkshire
BD1 5NE
Tel: 01274 203040
Fax: 01274 203120
www.pulse.co.uk
general@pulse.co.uk
News, sport, entertainment and local news. Owned by the Wireless Group. Covers Bradford, Huddersfield and Halifax area.

Radio Borders

Tweedside Park
Tweedbank
Galashiels
Borders
TD1 3TD
Tel: 01896 759444
Fax: 01896 759494
www.radioborders.com
dannygallagher@radioborders.com
Music-based station with local and national news. Covers the Scottish Borders and north Northumberland. Frequency 96.8, 97.5, 103.1 and 103.4 MHz.

Radio Ceredigion
Yr Hen Ysgol Cymraeg
Heol Alecsandra
The Old Welsh School
Alexandra Road
Aberystwyth
Ceredigion
SY23 1LF
Tel: 01970 627999
Fax: 01970 627206
www.ceredigionradio.co.uk
admin@radioceredigion.f9.co.uk
News and local information. Covers
Ceredigion.
Frequency 103.3, 97.4 and 96.6 FM.

Radio City 96.7
8–10 Stanley Street
Liverpool
L1 6AF
Tel: 0151 472 6800
Fax: 0151 471 0330
www.yourliverpool.com
Music, news and sport.
Owned by Emap, it covers Merseyside.

Radio Maldwyn
The Studios
The Park
Newtown
Powys
SY16 2NZ

Tel: 01686 623555
Fax: 01686 623666
www.radiomaldwyn@uk.online.co.uk
radio.maldwyn@ukonline.co.uk
News and sport, owned by Murfin Music
International. Covers mid-Wales, the
Welsh Borders.
Frequency 750 AM.

102.8 Ram FM
35–36 Irongate
Derby
DE1 3GA
Tel: 01332 205599
Fax: 01332 851199
www.koko.com
ramfm@musicradio.com
News, travel, weather, sport. Owned by
the GWR Group, it covers Derby.

Real Radio
PO Box 6105
Cardiff
CF15 8YS
Tel: 029 2031 5100
Fax: 029 2039 6129
www.realradiofm.co.uk
info@realradiofm.co.uk
Music, news and sport. Covers Cardiff,
Newport, Swansea.
Frequency 105.4, 105.9 and 106.0 MHz.

Red Dragon FM, Capital Gold
Atlantic Wharf
Cardiff
CF10 4DJ
Tel: 029 2066 2066
Fax: 029 2066 2060
www.reddragonfm.co.uk
mail@reddragonfm.co.uk
Music-based station with news bulletins,
sport, entertainment and celebrity
interviews. Owned by Capital Radio,
it covers south-east Wales.
Frequency 103.2 MHz (Cardiff), 97.4 MHz
(Newport).

Rutland Radio
40 Melton Road
Oakham
Rutland
LE15 6AY
Tel: 01572 757868
Fax: 01572 757744
www.rutland-on-line.co.uk
enquiries@rutlandradio.co.uk
Covers Rutland and Stamford.
Frequency 107.2 and 97.4 FM.

Sabras Sound
63 Melton Road
Leicester
LE4 6PN
Tel: 0116 261 0666
Fax: 0116 266 7776

www.sabrasradio.com
enq@sabrasradio.com
Music, news and information service for
Asian communities. Covers Leicester,
Nottingham, Derby and the East
Midlands.
Frequency 1260 MHz.

Scot FM
Number 1
Albert Quay
Leith
Edinburgh
EH6 7DN
Tel: 0131 554 6677
Fax: 0131 625 8401
www.scot-fm.com
Speech and adult contemporary music.
Owned by the Guardian Media Group,
it covers Central Scotland area.
Frequency 100.3 and 101.1 MHz.

Severn Sound
Bridge Studios
Eastgate Centre
Gloucester
GL1 1SS
Tel: 01452 313200
Fax: 01452 313213
www.koko.com
reception@severnsound.musicradio.com
News, travel, weather, sport. Owned by
the GWR Group, it covers Gloucester and
Cheltenham.

Frequency 102.4, 103 MHz (Severn Sound), 774 kHz (Severn Sound), and 774 kHz (Classic Gold).

SGR FM 97.1/96.4
Alpha Business Park
6–12 Whitehouse Road
Ipswich
Suffolk
IP1 5LT
Tel: 01473 461000
Fax: 01473 241111 (newsdesk)
www.sgrfm.co.uk
editor@sgrfm.co.uk
Owned by the GWR Group, it covers Ipswich, Bury St Edmunds. Frequency 97.1 and 96.4 FM.

SGR Colchester
9 Whitwell Road
Colchester
CO2 7DE
Tel: 01206 575859
Fax: 01206 561199
www.koko.com
info@sgrfm.co.uk
News, travel, weather, sport. Owned by the GWR Group, it covers Colchester. Frequency 96.1 MHz.

Signal One/Big AM
Stoke Road
Shelton
Stoke on Trent
Staffordshire
ST4 2SR
Tel: 01782 441300
Fax: 01782 441301
www.signalone.co.uk
Music and news. Owned by the Wireless Group, it covers Stoke on Trent. Frequency 96.9 MHz.

Silk 106.9 FM
Radio House
Bridge Street
Macclesfield
Cheshire
SK11 6DJ
Tel: 01625 268000
Fax: 01625 269010
www.silkfm.com
mail@silkfm.com
Music and news. Owned by Radio Investments, it covers Macclesfield.

South City 107.8 FM
City Studios
Marsh Lane
Southampton
SO14 3ST
Tel: 02380 220020
Fax: 02380 220060
www.southcityfm.co.uk
info@southcityfm.co.uk
Music and news for Southampton area.

South Hams Radio
South Hams Business Park
Churchstow
TQ7 3QH
Tel: 01548 854595
Fax: 01548 857345
www.koko.net
southams@virgin.net
News, travel, weather, sport. Owned by
the GWR Group, it covers the South
Hampshire area.
Frequency 100.5–101.9 FM.

Southern FM
PO Box 2000
Brighton
East Sussex
BN41 2SS
Tel: 01273 430111
Fax: 01273 430098
www. southernfm.com
info@southernfm.com
Music, news, entertainment and
competitions. Owned by Capital Radio, it
covers Brighton, Newhaven, Eastbourne
and Hastings area.
Frequency 103.5 MHz (Brighton), 96.9
MHz (Newhaven), 102.4 MHz
(Eastbourne), 102.0 MHz (Hastings).

Spire FM
City Hall Studios
Malthouse Lane
Salisbury

Wiltshire
SP2 7QQ
Tel: 01722 416644
Fax: 01722 416688
www.spirefm.co.uk
admin@spirefm.co.uk
Music, news, current affairs, quizzes and
sport. Owned by Radio Investments, it
covers Salisbury.
Frequency 102 MHz.

Stray 97.2 FM
PO Box 972
Station Parade
Harrogate
HG1 5YF
Tel: 01423 522972
Fax: 01423 522922
www.972strayfm.co.uk
mail@972strayfm.co.uk
Music, local news and information.
Owned by Radio Investments, it covers
the Harrogate area.

Sun FM 103.4
PO Box 1034
Sunderland
Tyne and Wear
SR5 2YL
Tel: 0191 548 1034
Fax: 0191 548 7171
www.sun-fm.com
mail@sun-fm.com

Music, local news, sport and information.
Owned by Radio Investments, it covers
Sunderland, Washington, South Tyneside
and County Durham.

Sunrise FM

30 Chapel Street
Little Germany
Bradford
BD1 5DN
Tel: 01274 735043
Fax: 01274 728534
www.sunrisefm.com
sunrisefm@hotmail.com
Music, news and information for the
Asian community. Covers the Bradford
area.
Frequency 103.2 MHz.

Sunshine 855

South Shropshire
Communications Ltd
Sunshine House
Waterside
Ludlow
Shropshire
SY8 1PE
Tel: 01584 873795
Fax: 01584 875900
www.sunshine855.co.uk
sunshine855@ukonline.co.uk
Music, news and information for Ludlow
and South Shropshire.
Frequency 855 kHz.

Swan FM

PO Box 1170
High Wycombe
Buckinghamshire
HP13 6YT
Tel: 01494 446611
Fax: 01494 445400
www.elevenseventy.co.uk
info@elevenseventy.co.uk
Music and news for High Wycombe area.
Frequency 1170 kHz.

Swansea Sound/The Wave 964

Radio House
Victoria Road
Gowerton
Swansea
West Glamorgan
SA4 3AB
Tel: 01792 511170
Fax: 01792 511171
www.swanseasound.co.uk
sales@swanseasound.co.uk
Some Welsh language broadcasting,
news and sport. Owned by the Wireless
Group, it covers Swansea.
Frequency 96.4 MHz and 1170 kHz.

Tay FM/Radio Tay AM

Radio Tay Ltd
PO Box 123
Dundee
DD1 9UF

Tel: 01382 200800
Fax: 01382 423252
www.radiotay.co.uk
tayfm@radiotay.co.uk
tayam@radiotay.co.uk
Music and news. Owned by Scottish Radio Holdings, it covers Perth.
Frequency 96.4 and 102.8 FM; 1161 or 1584 MW.

Ten 17
Latton Bush Centre
Southern Way
Harlow
Essex
CM18 7BU
Tel: 01279 432415
Fax: 01279 445289
www.ten17.co.uk
studios@ten17.co.uk
News, travel, weather and sport. It covers the Harlow area.
Frequency 101.7 MHz.

107.8 FM Thames Radio
Brentham House
45c High Street
Hampton Wick
Kingston upon Thames
Surrey
KT1 4DG
Tel: 020 8288 1300
Fax: 020 8288 1312
www.thamesradio.com

Music and news. It covers south-west London and north Surrey.

Trax FM
PO Box 444
Doncaster
DN4 5GW
Tel: 01302 341166
Fax: 01302 326104
www.traxfm.co.uk
enquiries@traxfm.co.uk
Music and news. Owned by Lincs FM, it covers the Doncaster area.
Frequency 107.1 FM.

Trax FM
PO Box 444
Worksop
Notts
S80 1GP
Tel: 01909 500611
Fax: 01909 500445
www.traxfm.co.uk
enquiries@traxfm.co.uk
Music and news. Owned by Lincs FM, it covers the Bassetlaw area.
Frequency 107.9 FM.

96 Trent FM/Classic Gold GEM AM
29–31 Castlegate
Nottingham
NG1 7AP

Tel: 0115 952 7000

Fax: 0115 912 9302

www.koko.com

admin@trentfm.musicradio.com

News, travel, weather, sport. Owned by the GWR Group, it covers Nottingham and Mansfield area.
Frequency 96.2 MHz.

Vale FM

Longmead

Shaftesbury

Dorset

SP7 8QQ

Tel: 01747 855711

Fax: 01747 855722

www.valefm.co.uk

studio@valefm.co.uk

News, sport and entertainment. Owned by Radio Investments, it covers north Dorset, south Somerset, west Wiltshire.
Frequency 96.6 and 97.4 MHz.

Valleys Radio

PO Box 1116

Festival Park

Victoria

Ebbw Vale

NP23 8XW

Tel: 01495 301116

Fax: 01495 300710

www.valleysradio.co.uk

admin@valleysradio.co.uk

News, sport and entertainment. Owned by the Wireless Group, it covers the heads of the south Wales valleys.
Frequency 999 or 1116 MW.

Viking 96.9 FM/Magic 1161

Commercial Road

Hull

North Humberside

HU1 2SG

Tel: 01482 325141

Fax: 08454 587067

Fax: 01482 593161 (studio)

www.clickviking.com

stuart.baldwin@vikingfm.co.uk

Music and news. Owned by Emap, it covers Yorkshire and Lincolnshire.
Frequency 96.9 MHz.

Virgin Radio

1 Golden Square

London

W1F 9DJ

Tel: 020 7434 1215

Fax: 020 7434 1197

www.virginradio.co.uk

reception@virginradio.co.uk

Music, news, sport and entertainment. Owned by SMG, it covers London and the South-east.
Frequency 105.8 FM and 1215 AM nationwide.

Wessex FM
Radio House
Trinity Street
Dorchester
Dorset
DT1 1DJ
Tel: 01305 250333
Fax: 01305 250052
www.wessexfm.co.uk
admin@wessexfm.co.uk
Music, local news, information, reviews and features. Covers the Dorset area. Frequency 97.2 MHz and 96.0 MHz.

West Sound AM/West FM
Radio House
54 Holmston Road
Ayr
KA7 3BE
Tel: 01292 283662
Fax: 01292 283665 (news)
www.west-fm.co.uk
www.west-sound.co.uk
westfm@srh.co.uk
News, sport, traffic and travel. Covers Ayrshire, Arran and the Cumbraes. Frequency 1035 AM.

Wire FM
Warrington Business Park
Long Lane
Warrington
WA2 8TX
Tel: 01925 445545
Fax: 01925 657705
www.wirefm.com
mail@wirefm.com
News, sport and entertainment. Covers the Warrington area.

102.4 Wish FM
Orrell Lodge
Orrell Road
Wigan
WN5 8HJ
Tel: 01942 761024
Fax: 01942 777694
www.wishfm.net
general@wishfm.net
Music-based programming plus news and sport. Owned by the Wireless Group. Covers Wigan, St Helens, Skelmersdale.

Wyvern FM
5–6 Barbourne Terrace
Worcester
WR1 3JZ
Tel: 01905 612212
Fax: 01905 746637
www.koko.com
News, travel, weather, sport. Owned by the GWR Group, it covers Hereford, Worcester, Kidderminster. Frequency 96.7, 97.6 and 102.8 MHz.

XFM
30 Leicester Square
London
WC2H 7LA
Tel: 020 7766 6600
Fax: 020 7766 6601
www.xfm.co.uk
News, entertainment, sport. Covers the
London area.
Frequency 104.9 MHz.

Yorkshire Coast Radio
PO Box 962
Scarborough
North Yorkshire
YO12 5YX
Tel: 01723 500962
Fax: 01723 501050
www.yorkshirecoastradio.co.uk
News, travel and sport. Covers the
Scarborough area.
Frequency 96.2 MHz.

UK News Agencies

*News agencies supply news about their
particular region or specialism to news
organizations.*

AA Roadwatch
Buckingham House West
The Broadway

Stanmore
HA7 4EG
Tel: 020 8420 8602
Fax: 020 8420 8732
www.theaa.com
lynn.healey@theaa.com
Traffic and travel information provider to
commercial radio, television, new media
and online services.

AllScot News and Features Agency
PO Box 6
Haddington
East Lothian
EH41 3NQ
Tel: 01620 822578
Fax: 01620 825079
101324.2142@compuserve.com
Provides news agency services about
Scotland for UK and overseas media
outlets.

Anglia Press Agency
91 Hythe Hill
Colchester
Essex
CO1 2NU
Tel: 01787 249001
Fax: 01787 249001
News and picture agency covering the
Essex, Suffolk and Norfolk area.

BBC Parliament
160 Great Portland Street
London
W12 5TB
Tel: 020 7299 5000
Fax: 020 7299 5300
http://news.bbc.co.uk/1/hi/
programmes/bbc_parliament/
default.htm
viewer_tpc@flextech.co.uk
Provider of unedited live coverage of daily
proceedings in the House of Commons
and recorded coverage of the Lords,
Parliamentary committees and business
statements.

Bellis News Agency
Sea Breezes
14b Kenelm Road
Rhos-on-Sea
Colwyn Bay
North Wales
LL28 4ED
Tel: 01492 549503
Fax: 01492 543226
bellisd@aol.com
News and features for national and
regional newspapers, TV and radio.

**Bournemouth News and Picture
Service**
14 Lorne Park Road
Bournemouth

BH1 1JN
Tel: 01202 558833
Fax: 01202 553875
bnpsnews@aol.com
Covers the Hants, Dorset and Wiltshire
area.

Devon News Agency
4 Clifton Road
Exeter
Devon
EX1 2BR
Tel: 01392 276338
Fax: 01392 435248
Covers the Devon and Cornwall area.

Dragon News and Picture Agency
21 Walter Road
Swansea
SA1 5NQ
Tel: 01792 464800
Fax: 01792 475264
www.dragon-pictures.com
mail@dragon-pictures.com
Covers the south and west Wales area.

Dundee Press Agency
10 Victoria Road
Dundee
DD1 1JN
Tel: 01382 907700
Fax: 01382 907790
Covers all of Scotland.

Essex News Service

121 High Street
Witham
Essex
CM8 1BE
Tel: 01376 521222
Fax: 01376 521222
perfect@essexnews.freeserve.co.uk
Local news and features.

Ferrari Press Agency

14 Hurst Road
Sidcup
Kent
DA15 9AE
Tel: 020 8302 6622
Fax: 020 8302 6611
ferraripress@compuserve.com
Covers Kent, south London, Essex, Surrey
and Sussex.

Fleet News Agency

Fleet House
68a Stanfield Road
Bournemouth
Dorset
BH9 2NR
Tel: 01202 515151
Covers Bournemouth, Dorset and
surrounding area.

Fourth Estate Press Agency

12 North Campbell Avenue
Glasgow
G62 7AA
Tel: 0141 956 1540
Covers Glasgow and west Scotland.

FT Business News

50 Lisson Street
London
NW1 5DF
Tel: 020 7402 1011
Fax: 020 7723 6132
www.ft.com
Business and personal finance news.

Gloucestershire News Service

26 Westgate Street
Gloucester
GL1 2NG
Tel: 01452 522270
Fax: 01452 300581
glosnews@cwcom.net
Local news and sports coverage.

Hayter's Sports Agency

146–148 Clerkenwell Road
London
EC1R 5DG
Tel: 020 7837 7171
Fax: 020 7837 2420
www.hayters.co.uk
sport@hayters.com

Sports reporting, features, statistics and event support.

Hill's Welsh Press
58 Lower Cathedral Road
Cardiff
CF11 6LT
Tel: 029 2022 7606
Fax: 029 2022 4947
mail@hillswelshpress.co.uk
Covers south and west Wales.

Hopkinson News and Feature Service
22 Hallfield Road
Bradford
BD1 3RQ
Tel: 01274 725565
Fax: 01274 725565
Covers Yorkshire and Humberside.

Hull News and Pictures
Room 115
Hull Microfirms Centre
266–290 Wincolmlee
Hull
HU2 0PZ
Tel: 01482 210267
Fax: 01482 210267
hull@hullnews.karoo.co.uk
Covers East Yorkshire and north Lincs.

IRN – Independent Radio News
200 Gray's Inn Road
London
WC1X 8X2
Tel: 020 7430 4090
Tel: 020 7430 4814 (news desk)
Fax: 020 7430 4092
www.irn.co.uk
news@irn.co.uk
IRN is Britain's main radio news agency, supplying bulletins and services to over 95 per cent of the commercial radio stations. IRN is effectively a commissioning agency acting on behalf of its customers with its news provided by ITN.

Jarrolds Press Agency
68 High Street
Ipswich
Suffolk
IP1 3QJ
Tel: 01473 219193
Fax: 01473 218447
jarroldspress@cix.compulink.co.uk
Covers Suffolk and the surrounding area; also provides football coverage.

Jenkins Group
186 High Street
Rochester
Kent
ME1 1EY

Tel: 01634 830888
Fax: 01634 830930
Covers Kent for news features.

John Connor Press Associates
57a High Street
Lewes
East Sussex
BN7 1XE
Tel: 01273 486851
Fax: 01273 486852
www.jcpa.freeserve.co.uk
connorpress@cix.co.uk
Covers East and West Sussex.

Kett's News Service
53 Christchurch Road
Norwich
Norfolk
NR2 3NE
Tel: 01603 508055
Fax: 01603 508066
ketts@dircon.co.uk
Covers Norfolk and Suffolk.

Lakeland Press Agency
480 Marine Road East
Morecambe
Lancashire
LA4 6AF
Tel: 01524 413356
Fax: 01524 419699

Covers the Lake District and north
Lancashire.

Lucas Media
72 New Bond Street
London
W1S 1RR
Tel: 0870 707 0870
Fax: 0870 707 8080
www.lucasmedia.net
Go@LucasMedia.net
UK national and international news
information provider. Entertainment and
current affairs for radio.

Masons News Service
Chesterton Mill
French's Road
Cambridge
CB4 3NP
Tel: 01223 366996
Fax: 01223 361508
masons.news@dial.pipex.com
Covers eastern England.

Mercury Press Agency
The Cotton Exchange
Old Hall Street
Liverpool
L3 9LQ
Tel: 0151 236 6707
Fax: 0151 236 2180
www.mercurypress.co.uk

Covers north-west England and North Wales news.

National News Press Agency
4–5 Academy Buildings
Fanshaw Street
London
N1 6LQ
Tel: 020 7684 3000
Fax: 020 7684 3030
nnwords@hotmail.com

Court and general news and features in London and the South East.

National News and Press Photo Agency
109 Clifton Street
London
EC2A 4LD
Tel: 020 7684 3000
Fax: 020 7684 3030

North Scot Press Agency
18 Adelphi
Aberdeen
AB11 5BL
Tel: 01224 212141
Fax: 01224 212163

Covers Grampian and the North of Scotland.

North Wales Press Agency
157 High Street
Prestatyn
Denbighshire
LL19 9AY
Tel: 01745 852262
Fax: 01745 855534

North West News and Sports Agency
148 Meols Parade
Meols
Merseyside
CH47 6AN
Tel: 0151 632 5261
Fax: 0151 632 5484

Covers the Wirral and Birkenhead, mainly court reporting and sport.

Northants Press Agency
51–53 Shakespeare Road
Northampton
NN1 3QG
Tel: 01604 473030
Fax: 01604 602153

Covers Northants and surrounding counties.

Nottingham News Service
Jarrodale House
Gregory Boulevard
Nottingham
NG7 6LB

Tel: 0115 960 7772
Fax: 0115 960 3522
newsdesk@raymonds.demon.co.uk
Local news, sport and pictures.

Orbit News Service
1 Froghall Lane
Warrington
Cheshire
WA2 7JJ
Tel: 01925 631592
orbit.news.mcmail.com
Covers Cheshire and south Manchester.

Page One
11 West Avenue
West Bridgford
Nottingham
NG2 7NL
Tel: 0115 981 8880
Fax: 0115 981 3133
www.pageonemedia.com
news@pageonemedia.com
pictures@pageonemedia.com
Covers Central and East Midlands
including TV filming and editing.

Parliamentary and EU News Service
19 Douglas Street
London
SW1P 4PA
Tel: 020 7233 8283
Fax: 020 7821 9352

info@parliamentary-
monitoring.co.uk
News and diaries on Parliament and
the EU.

Press Agency (Gatwick)
1a Sunview Avenue
Peacehaven
Sussex
BN10 8PJ
Tel: 01273 583103
Fax: 01273 589112
Covers Gatwick Airport and area.

Press Gang News
137 Endlesham Road
London
SW12 8JN
Tel: 020 8673 4229
Fax: 020 8673 3205
www.pressgangnews.co.uk
mail@pressgangnews.co.uk
Covers London.

Press Team Scotland
22 St John's Street
Coatbridge
ML5 3EJ
Tel: 01236 440077
Fax: 01236 440066
pteam@globalnet.co.uk
Covers Lanarkshire and Glasgow.

Press Association Headquarters
PA News Centre
292 Vauxhall Bridge Road
London
SW1V 1AE
Tel: 020 7963 7000
Tel: 020 7963 7107 (newsdesk)
Fax: 020 7963 7192 (newsdesk)
www.pressassociation.press.net
newsdesk@pa.press.net

Press Association Belfast
10 Royal Avenue
Belfast
BT1 1DB
Tel: 028 9024 5008
Fax: 028 9043 9246
www.pressassociation.press.net
newsdesk@pa.press.net

Press Association Birmingham
Charles House
148–149 Great Charles Street
Birmingham
B3 3HT
Tel: 0121 212 3225
Fax: 0121 212 3350
www.pressassociation.press.net
newsdesk@pa.press.net

Press Association Bristol
Bristol Evening Post and Press
Building

Temple Way
Bristol
BS99 7HD
Tel: 0117 929 4673
Fax: 0117 930 4157
www.pressassociation.press.net
newsdesk@pa.press.net

Press Association Cardiff
11 Brynawelon Road
Cardiff
CF2 6QR3
Tel: 029 207 64211
Fax: 029 207 64213
www.pressassociation.press.net
newsdesk@pa.press.net

Press Association Dublin
41 Silchester Road
Glenageary
Dublin
Tel: 00 353 1 28 00936
Fax: 00 353 1 28 04221
www.pressassociation.press.net
newsdesk@pa.press.net

Press Association East Anglia
3 Edieham Cottages
Angle Lane
Shrepreth
Royston
SG8 6QJ
Tel: 01763 262638

Fax: 01763 262638
www.pressassociation.press.net
newsdesk@pa.press.net

Press Association Exeter
143 Sweetbriar Lane
Exeter
Devon
EX1 3AP
Tel: 01392 431166
Fax: 01392 431166
www.pressassociation.press.net
newsdesk@pa.press.net

Press Association Glasgow
124 Portman Street
Kinning Park
Glasgow
G41 1EJ
Tel: 0141 429 0037
Fax: 0141 429 1596
www.pressassociation.press.net
newsdesk@pa.press.net

Press Association Howden
The Bishop's Manor
Howden
East Yorkshire
DN14 7BL
Tel: 0870 1203200
www.pressassociation.press.net
newsdesk@pa.press.net

Press Association Leeds
PA News Centre
Central Park
New Lane
Leeds
LS11 5DZ
Tel: 0113 234 4411
Fax: 0113 244 0758
www.pressassociation.press.net
newsdesk@pa.press.net

Press Association Liverpool
PO Box 48
Old Hall Street
Liverpool
L69 3EB
Tel: 0151 472 2548
Fax: 0151 472 2411
www.pressassociation.press.net
newsdesk@pa.press.net

Press Association Manchester
Royal Exchange
Old Bank Street
Manchester
M2 7EP
Tel: 0161 832 4452
Fax: 0161 832 8467
www.pressassociation.press.net
newsdesk@pa.press.net

Raymonds Press Agency
Abbots Hill Chambers
Gower Street
Derby
DE1 1SD
Tel: 01332 340404
Fax: 01332 386036
newsdesk@raymonds.demon.co.uk
Large agency covering the Central and
East Midlands area.

Ross-Parry Agency
40 Back Town Street
Farsley
Leeds
LS28 5LD
Tel: 0113 236 1842
Fax: 0113 236 1539
Reporters and photographers covering
Yorks and Humberside.

Samuels News and Photo Service
71 Stafford Road
Uttoxeter
Staffordshire
ST14 8DW
Tel: 01889 566996
Fax: 01889 567181
samuelnews@supanet.com
News, features and PR.

Scarborough News/Ridings Press Agency
19 Hall Garth Lane
West Ayton
Scarborough
YO13 9JA
Tel: 01723 863395
Fax: 01723 865054
david@jjeffels.fsnet.co.uk
News and features.

Scase News Service
Congham
Kings Lynn
Norfolk
PE32 1DR
Tel: 01485 600650
Fax: 01485 600672
www.scase.co.uk
news@scase.co.uk
Covers East Anglia; specializes in news,
royal news and features.

scoop2001@aol.com.uk
Covers Cheshire and the North West,
North Midlands for national, regional and
local press, TV and radio.

Scottish News Agency
99 Ferry Road
Edinburgh
EH6 4ET
Tel: 0131 478 7711

Fax: 0131 478 7327

g.ogilvy@scottishnews.com

Scottish news and sports pictures.

Seven Day Press

132 West Nile Street

Glasgow

G1 2RQ

Tel: 0141 572 0060

Fax: 0141 572 0265

daypress@aol.com

Sports news and features providing
coverage of all senior Scottish football
games.

Shrewsbury Press Service

1a Victorian Arcade

Hills Lane

Shrewsbury

Salop

SY1 1PS

Tel: 01743 352710

Fax: 01743 247701

Covers the Shropshire area.

Somerset News Service

43–44 High Street

Taunton

Somerset

TA1 3PW

Tel: 01823 331789

Fax: 01823 332862

Covers Somerset and the South West.

South Bedfordshire News Agency

Bramingham Park Business Centre

Enterprise Way

Bramingham Park

Luton

LU3 4BU

Tel: 01582 572222

Fax: 01582 493486

news@southbedsnewsagency.co.uk

Covers Hertfordshire, Bedfordshire and
Buckinghamshire.

South Coast Press Agency

22 St Peter's Road

Bournemouth

Dorset

BH1 2LE

Tel: 01202 290199

Fax: 01202 554937

Covers Dorset and surrounding counties.

South West News Service

Media Centre

Abbeywood Office Park

Filton

Bristol

BS34 7JU

Tel: 0117 906 6500

Fax: 0117 906 6501

news@swns.com

Covers the West Country and South
Wales.

South Yorkshire Sport
6 Sharman Walk
Apperknowle
South Yorkshire
Sheffield
S18 4BJ
Tel: 01246 414767
Mobile: 07970 284848
Fax: 01246 414767
Nicksport1@aol.com
Written/broadcast coverage of sport in
the South Yorkshire area.

Space Press News Agency
Bridge House
Blackden Lane
Goostrey
Cheshire
CW4 8PZ
Tel: 01477 533403
Fax: 01477 535756
www.CountrylifeOnline.com

Sportsmedia Broadcasting
Number 47
Canalot Studios
222 Kensal Road
London
W10 5BN
Tel: 020 8962 9000
Fax: 020 8960 6999
www.sportsmedia.co.uk
info@sportsmedia.co.uk

UK national and international sports and
video production.

Stewart Bonney News Agency
17 St Peter's Wharf
Newcastle upon Tyne
NE6 1TZ
Tel: 0191 275 2600
Fax: 0191 275 2609
www.bonneysphotography.co.uk
Covers north-east England.

Strand News Service
226 The Strand
London
WC2R 1BA
Tel: 020 7353 1300
Fax: 020 7936 2689
james@strandnews.co.uk
Provider of general news coverage.

Teespress Agencies
15 Baker Street
Middlesbrough
Teesside
TS1 2LF
Tel: 01642 880733
Fax: 01642 880744
Covers Teesside, North Yorkshire and
South Durham area.

Torbay News Agency
20 Higher Union Lane
Torquay
Devon
TQ2 5QR
Tel: 01803 214555
Covers Torbay and south Devon area.

Trafficlink
29th Floor
Centre Point
London
W1CA 1RH
Tel: 020 7312 1300
Fax: 020 7312 1320
www.trafficlink.co.uk
enquiries@trafficlink.co.uk
UK national and international news and
travel news provider for UK radio
stations.

Unique Entertainment News
50 Lisson Street
London
NW1 5DF
Tel: 020 7453 1615
Fax: 020 7724 5373
www.unique.com
anna.burles@unique.com
Multi-media entertainment news content
provider for commercial radio, websites
and interactive TV.

Wales News Service
Westgate House
Womanby Street
Cardiff
CF10 2UD
Tel: 029 2066 6366
Fax: 029 2066 4181

**Warwickshire News and Picture
Agency**
41 Lansdowne Crescent
Leamington Spa
Warwickshire
CV32 4PR
Tel: 01926 424181
Fax: 01926 424760
Covers Warwickshire and the West
Midlands.

Wessex News and Features Agency
108 High Street
Hungerford
Berkshire
RG17 0NB
Tel: 01488 686810
Fax: 01488 684463
www.britishnews.co.uk
news@britishnews.co.uk
News, features, photos. Covers England
and Scotland.

West Riding News and Sports Service

Field House

Wellington Road

Dewsbury

West Yorkshire

WF13 1HF

Tel: 01924 437555

Fax: 01924 437564

Covers Huddersfield, Halifax and Dewsbury. Specializes in soccer and rugby league.

X-trax

5–13 Leeke Street

London

WC1X 9HY

Tel: 020 7923 5000

Fax: 020 7923 5001

www.x-trax.com

Weekly entertainment features to stations throughout the UK and Ireland.

International Agencies and Exchanges

International news agencies supply global, regional or specialist news to news organizations. Some broadcasters also sell their material to other news organizations. News exchanges are, in effect, like clubs, where the members exchange their material with each other.

ABC News Intercontinental

3 Queen Caroline Street

London

W6 9PE

Tel: 020 8222 5500

Fax: 020 8222 5020

www.abc.com

London office of the American news network. News programmes include *Good Morning America, World News Tonight, Primetime.*

ABU – Asia Pacific Broadcasting Union

www.abu.org.my

An association of the television and radio networks in the Asia Pacific union. Active in every area of broadcasting. Daily exchange of news via satellite. Negotiates sports rights. Organizes the exchange of radio and television programmes. Provides consultancies to members needing help with technical programmes or development of their services.

AFI Research

The Ground Floor

27 The Avenue

Newton Abbot

Devon

TQ12 2BZ

Tel: 01626 335040
Fax: 01626 335040
www.freelancedirectory.org
afi@supanet.com
International information research and
news agency covering intelligence,
security, armed forces, terrorism and
current affairs.

AFX News
103–105 Bunhill Row
London
EC1Y 8LZ
Tel: 020 7422 4941
Fax: 020 7422 4999
www.afxnews.com
Global financial news agency. Subsidiary
company of Agence France Press.

Agence France Press
78 Fleet Street
London
EC4Y 1NB
Tel: 020 7353 7461
Fax: 020 7353 8359
www.afp.com
london.bureau@afp.com
London office of international agency.

Andes Press Agency
26 Padbury Court
London
E2 7EH

Tel: 020 7613 5417
Fax: 020 7739 3159
photos@andespress.demon.co.uk
Covers global social, religious, political,
economic and environmental stories with
an emphasis on Latin America.

ANSA
Essex House
12–13 Essex Street
London
WC2R 3AA
Tel: 020 7240 5514
Fax: 020 7240 5518
www.ansa.it
Italian news agency.

**APTN – Associated Press
Television News**
The Interchange
Oval Road
Camden Lock
London
NW1 7DZ
Tel: 020 7482 7400
Fax: 020 7413 8311
www.aptn.com
aptninfo@ap.org
APTN is the international video arm of
Associated Press. It delivers an
international news service to over 500
of the world's broadcasters.

Associated Press
12 Norwich Street
London
EC4A 1BP
Tel: 020 7353 1515
Fax: 020 7353 8118
www.apweb.com
UK office of the American agency.
Also runs the AP-Dow Jones.

Australian Associated Press
12 Norwich Street
London
EC4A 1QJ
Tel: 020 7353 0153
Fax: 020 7583 3563
www.aap.comm.au
aaplondon@hotmail.com
Australia's only UK news agency.

BBC Monitoring
Caversham Park
Reading
Berkshire
RG4 8TZ
Tel: 01734 469289
Fax: 01734 463823
www.bbc.co.uk
BBC Monitoring reports on foreign
broadcasts from around the world.
(This information is sold.)

Bloomberg News
City Gate House
39–45 Finsbury Square
London
EC2A 1PQ
Tel: 020 7330 7500
Fax: 020 7392 6000
www.bloomberg.com
newsalert@bloomberg.net
Economic, financial and corporate news.

CBS News
68 Knightsbridge
London
SW1X 7LL
Tel: 020 7581 4801
Fax: 020 7581 4431
www.cbsnews.com
London office of the American news
network. News summaries and breaking
news.

CNN International
19–22 Rathbone Place
London
W1T 1HY
Tel: 020 7637 6700
Fax: 020 7637 6738
www.cnn.com
US and global news provider with nearly
700 affiliated TV stations around the
world. Online news and information
delivery.

Deutsche Presse Agentur

30 Old Queen Street

London

SW1H 9HB

Tel: 020 7233 2888

Fax: 020 7233 3534

London@dpa.com

German news agency, owned by German media.

Dow Jones Newswires

10 Fleet Place

Limeburner Lane

London

EC4M 7RB

Tel: 020 7842 9900

Fax: 020 7842 9361

www.dowjonesnews.com

info@dowjonesnews.com

Regional head office of real-time financial news service owned by Dow Jones and Co, publishers of the *Wall Street Journal*. Supplies global news affecting all financial markets. Produced in association with Associated Press.

EBU – European Broadcasting Union

European Broadcasting Union

17A Ancienne Route

CH 1218 Grand Saconnex

Switzerland

Tel: +41 22 717 2111

Fax: +41 22 747 4000

www.ebu.ch

ebu@ebu.ch

European Broadcasting Union is the largest professional association of national broadcasters in the world. Activities include operation of the Eurovision news exchanges and Euroradio networks, coordination of news and sports programming.

ENEX – European News Exchange

45, bd Pierre Frieden

L-1543 Luxembourg

Tel: + 352 42142 3101

Fax: + 352 42142 3768

www.enex.lu

ENEX is a newsgathering organization and video exchange where broadcasters share news and picture facilities.

FSN – Feature Story News

40–44 Newman Street

London

W1P 3PA

Tel: 020 7580 4160

Fax: 020 7436 9138

www.fsntv.com

London.bureau@featurestory.com

Independent broadcast agency. Provides on-air coverage for radio and TV networks worldwide.

Gemini News Service

9 White Lion Street
London
N1 9PD
Tel: 020 7278 1111
Fax: 020 7278 0345
alexw@panoslondon.org.uk

London-based international news and features agency. Supplies weekly news features to the global media, business, pressure groups and aid agencies.

Global Radio News

www.globalradionews.com

Radio news story exchange website. An exchange point for independent journalists and radio stations.

Islamic Republic News Agency (IRNA)

3rd Floor
390 High Road
Wembley
Middlesex
HA9 6AS
Tel: 020 8903 1630
Fax: 020 8900 0705
www.irna.com
payam@irna.co.uk

The Islamic Republic News Agency was established in 1934 by the Foreign Ministry of Iran. It provides news, opinion polls, research and general interest stories through telex lines.

Jiji Press

International Press Centre
76 Shoe Lane
London
EC4A 3JB
Tel: 020 7936 2847
Fax: 020 7583 8353
jijildn2@ma.kew.net

Japanese news agency.

Kuwait News Agency

150 Southampton Row
London
WC1B 5AL
Tel: 020 7278 5445
Fax: 020 7278 6232
www.kuna.net
Kuwait@btclick.com

Kyodo News

2nd Floor
34 Threadneedle Street
London
EC2R 8AY
Tel: 020 7330 8000
Fax: 020 7330 8012
www.kyodo.com

Japanese news wire service. Covers UK, Ireland, Portugal and Scandinavia.

NBC News Worldwide

4th Floor
3 Shortlands

Hammersmith
London
W6 8HX
Tel: 020 8600 6600
Fax: 020 8600 6601
www.nbc.com
london.newsdesk@nbc.com
London bureau of the US network.

The News Market
www.thenewsmarket.com
Brings together news broadcasters' news via a single platform that enables the exchange of broadcast-quality video over the internet.

New Zealand Press Association
12 Norwich Street
London
EC4A 1EJ
Tel: 020 7353 5430
Fax: 020 7483 3563
kippyb@hotmail.com
National news agency for New Zealand.

Panos
www.oneworld.org/panos
London-based source of news, views and opinions from developing countries.

Reuters
85 Fleet Street
London

EC4P 4AJ
Tel: 020 7250 1122
Fax: 020 7542 4970
Tel: 020 7542 3334 (newsdesk)
Tel: 020 7542 2431 (newsdesk)
Fax: 020 7278 9345 (newsdesk)
www.reuters.com
rtv@reuters.com
alertnet@rtrlondon.co.uk
Delivers news feeds, news flashes, live coverage and features via satellite to more than 200 broadcasters, networks and affiliates.

**Russian Information Agency –
Novosti**
3 Rosary Gardens
London
SW7 4NW
Tel: 020 7370 1162
Tel: 020 7370 3002
Fax: 020 7244 7875
www.rian.ru
ria@novosti.co.uk
Russian news and information service/ photograph library.

Saudi Press Agency
18 Cavendish Square
London
W1M 0AQ
Tel: 020 7495 0418
Tel: 020 7495 0419

Fax: 020 7495 5074

www.spa.gov

Spanish News Agency (EFE)

299 Oxford Street

London

W1C 2DZ

Tel: 020 7493 7313

Fax: 020 7493 7314

agenciaefe@btconnect.com

News agency for Spain and Latin America.

Tass/Itar

320 Regent Street

London

W1B 3BD

Tel: 020 7580 5543

Fax: 020 7580 5547

Russian news agency.

TV News Web

www.tvnewsweb.com

A marketplace for freelance camera crews to sell their news footage.

United Press International

www.upi.com

WRN (World Radio Network)

Wyvil Court

10 Wyvil Road

London

SW8 2TG

Tel: 020 7896 9000

Fax: 020 7896 9007

www.wrn.org

online@wrn.org

Operates a twenty-four-hour service with news, current affairs and feature programmes from twenty-eight of the world's public service broadcasters in English, German and multilingual.

Xinhua News Agency of China

8 Swiss Terrace

Belsize Road

London

NW6 4RR

Tel: 020 7586 8437

Fax: 020 7722 8512

xinhua@easynet.co.uk

Chinese, foreign and domestic news.

8 education and training

UK University Media and Journalism Courses

University of Wales, Aberystwyth
Aberystwyth
Ceredigion
SY23 2AX
Tel: 01970 622021
Fax: 01970 627410
www.aber.ac.uk/media
ug-admissions@aber.ac.uk

Anglia Polytechnic University
The Admissions Office
East Road
Cambridge
CB1 1PT
Tel: 01223 363271 ext: 2495
Fax: 01223 352973
www.apu@ac.uk
answers@apu.ac.uk
Contact centre. BA single/combined honours in communication studies; film studies; photographic and digital media.

MA in communication, culture and production.

University of Wales, Bangor
Department of Media and Communication
Main Arts Building
Bangor
Gwynedd
LL57 2DG
Tel: 01248 383216
Fax: 01248 383291
www.bangor.ac.uk
e.l.jones@bangor.ac.uk
Admissions office. Welsh medium BA (hons) in communications and media; communication and journalism; theatre and media studies. Postgraduate Welsh medium MA/diploma/certificate in journalism; media production.

Bath Spa University College
Newton Park
Newton St Loe
Bath
BA2 9BN

Tel: 01225 875875
Fax: 01225 875444
www.bathspa.ac.uk
enquiries@bathspa.ac.uk
Prospectus officer. BA/BSc combined honours three years full-time (part-time available) degree in media communication plus another subject.

The University of Birmingham
Department of Cultural Studies and Sociology
Edgbaston
Birmingham
B15 2TT
Tel: 0121 414 3307
Tel: 0121 414 6060
Fax: 0121 414 6061
www.bham.ac.uk
Y.L.Jacobs@bham.ac.uk

Admissions office. Single honours three years full-time BA in media, culture and society. Joint honours degree in media and cultural studies.

University of Central England in Birmingham
Birmingham Institute of Art and Design
Department of Media and Communication
UCE Birmingham
Perry Barr

Birmingham
B42 2SU
Tel: 0121 331 5719
Fax: 0121 331 6501
www.uce.ac.uk
media@uce.ac.uk
Faculty admissions officer. BA (hons) three years full-time, media and communication; culture and society; journalism; multimedia; media photography; public relations; radio production; TV and radio; media communication and culture. BSc (hons) in multimedia technology; television, technology and production. BTEC/HND/HNC two years full-time media and communication; media production; multimedia and networks technology. PgCert/PgDip/MA courses in broadcast journalism (PgDip is full-time only). PgDip/MA in international broadcast journalism (full-time only).

University of Bournemouth
The Bournemouth Media School
Talbot Campus
Fern Barrow
Poole
Dorset
BH12 5BB
Tel: 01202 524111
Fax: 01202 595530
www.media.bournemouth.ac.uk
Undergraduate courses:
bmsugrad@bournemouth.ac.uk

Postgraduate courses:
bmspgrad@bournemouth.ac.uk
dhogan@bournemouth.ac.uk
Registrar: Dan Hogan. BA in media production (TV and video); multimedia journalism. Postgraduate courses in TV and video production; radio production; multimedia journalism (accredited by the NCTJ, PTC and the BJTC).Bournemouth University franchises/validates programmes of study at Blackpool and the Fylde College, the Arts Institute at Bournemouth, Cannington College, Isle of Wight College and Weymouth College.

The Arts Institute at Bournemouth
Wallisdown
Poole
Dorset
BH12 5HH
Tel: 01202 533011
Fax: 01202 537729
www.arts-inst-bournemouth.ac.uk
general@arts-inst-bournemouth.ac.uk
Admissions. BA (hons) in film and TV; film and animation. National Diploma in sound and moving image; multimedia.

University of Bradford
Richmond Road
Bradford
West Yorkshire
BD7 1DP
Tel: 01274 235963
Fax: 01274 233727
www.brad.ac.uk
enquiries@bradford.ac.uk
p.e.dale@brad.ac.uk
Enquiries office: Paula Dale. BSc (hons) three/four years in electronic imaging and media communications; media technology and production; computer animation and special effects. BA (hons) languages with new media.

University of Brighton
Mithras House
Lewes Road
Brighton
East Sussex
BN2 4AT
Tel: 01273 600900
Fax: 01273 642825
www.brighton.ac.uk
admissions@brighton.ac.uk
Admissions. Four years full-time sandwich course/six years part-time BSc (hons) in digital media development; interactive computing. Three years part-time BA (hons) communications and digital media. Combined honours subjects available with media.

University of Bristol
Department of Drama: Theatre, Film and Television
Cantocks Close

Woodland Road
Bristol
BS8 1UP
Tel: 0117 928 7833 (department)
Tel: 0117 928 9000 (university)
Fax: 0117 928 7832
www.bristol.ac.uk
admissions@bristol.ac.uk
mark.sinfield@bristol.ac.uk
Admissions officer: Mark Sinfield. One year full-time MA's in cultural performance; television studies; film and TV production; archaeology and media; composition of music for TV and theatre.

UWE: University of the West of England, Bristol
Frenchay Campus
Coldharbour Lane
Bristol
BS16 1QY
Tel: 0117 344 3333
Fax: 0117 344 2810
www.uwe.ac.uk
admissions@uwe.ac.uk
Enquiry and admissions service. BA (hons) cultural and media sciences; science, society and the media; time-based media; film studies. Short courses available.

Brunel University
Faculty of Arts and Human Sciences
Dept of Human Sciences
Uxbridge

Middlesex
UB8 3PH
Tel: 01895 274000
Fax: 01895 232806
www.brunel.ac.uk
admissions@brunel.ac.uk
Admissions office. BSc four-year sandwich degree course in communication and media studies. One year full-time/two years part-time MA in media technology and communications.

Buckinghamshire Chilterns University College
Faculty of Applied Social Sciences and Humanities
Arts and Media Department
Queen Alexandra Road
High Wycombe
Buckinghamshire
HP11 2JZ
Tel: 01494 603050
Fax: 01494 603050
www.bcuc.ac.uk
margot.coaxall@bcuc.ac.uk
Admissions. BA (hons) media studies and film studies with English studies; video production; drama production; creative writing.

Canterbury Christ Church University College
Department of Media
North Holmes Road

Canterbury
Kent
CT1 1QU
Tel: 01227 782349
Fax: 01227 782914
www.cant.ac.uk
admissions@cant.ac.uk
nb1@canterbury.ac.uk
BA/BSc in media and cultural studies;
radio, film and TV studies. HND in digital
media (full-time two years). MA one year
full-time/two years part-time in media
production. MA in popular culture and the
media (part-time two years/evenings).
PgDip in journalism (full-time over thirty
weeks plus work placement in
journalism).

Cardiff University
School of Journalism, Media and
Cultural Studies
Cardiff University
King Edward VII Avenue
Cardiff
CF10 3NB
Tel: 02920 874041 (general enquiries)
Tel: 02920 874041
(undergraduate enquiries)
Tel: 02920 874786
(diploma enquiries)
Tel: 02920 876186 (MA enquiries)
Tel: 02920 874509
(research enquiries)
Fax: 02920 238832

www.journalism.cf.ac.uk
General enquiries:
JOMEC@cardiff.ac.uk
Undergraduate enquiries: JOMEC-
BA@cardiff.ac.uk
Diploma enquiries: JOMEC-
Diploma@cardiff.ac.uk
MA enquiries: JOMEC-
MA@cardiff.ac.uk
Research enquiries: JOMEC-
Research@cardiff.ac.uk
Admissions@cardiff.ac.uk
Three years full-time BA in journalism,
film and broadcasting (single or
combined honours degree). Nine months
full-time NCTJ-recognized postgraduate
diploma in newspaper journalism; BJTC-
accredited course in broadcast (bi-media)
journalism; PTC-recognized course in
magazine journalism; IPR-recognized
course in public and media relations. MA
in journalism; European journalism
studies.

Trinity College Carmarthen
Faculty of Creative, Performing Arts
and Cultural Arts
School of English and
Communication
Carmarthen
SA31 3EP
Tel: 01227 782349 (university)
Tel: 01267 676702 (film studies)
Tel: 01267 676709 (media studies)

Fax: 01227 782914
www.trinity-cm.ac.uk
s.finney@trinity-cm.ac.uk
m.ryan@trinity-cm.ac.uk
Director of Film Studies: Susan Finney;
Director of Media Studies: Michele Ryan.
BA (hons) three years full-time film
studies can be combined with advertising,
English studies or media. BA (hons) in
media studies.

University College, Chichester
Bishop Otter Campus
College Lane
Chichester
Sussex
PO19 6PE
Tel: 01243 816002
Fax: 01243 816080
www.ucc.ac.uk
mribbans@ucc.ac.uk
admissions@ucc.ac.uk
Admissions. BA (hons) media studies
single or combined degree.

City University
Northampton Square
London
EC14 0HB
Tel: 020 7040 8221
Fax: 020 7040 8594
www.city.ac.uk/journalism
s.ball@city.ac.uk

Journalism department office. Full-time
three years/four years sandwich course
single honours degree in journalism; joint
honours with contemporary history. Nine
months full-time NCTJ-recognized
postgraduate diplomas in newspaper
journalism; BJTC-recognized course in
broadcast (bi-media) journalism; PTC-
recognized course in magazine
journalism. MA in international
journalism.

Colchester Institute
Sheepen Road
Colchester
Essex
CO3 3LL
Tel: 01206 518777
Fax: 01206 763041
www.colch-inst.ac.uk
info@colch-inst.ac.uk
Admissions office. Media studies courses.

Coventry University
Communication, Culture and Media
School of Art and Design
Priory Street
Coventry
CV1 5FB
Tel: 024 7688 7439
Fax: 024 7688 7440
www.coventry.ac.uk
afuture.ad@coventry.ac.uk

Admissions. MA/PgDip in media arts. MA in design and digital media; communication, culture and media. BA (hons) full/part-time in communication, culture and media. Short courses in journalism.

De Montfort University
The Department of Media and
Cultural Production
The Gateway
Leicester
LE1 9BH
Tel: 0116 255 1551
Fax: 0116 255 0307
www.dmu.ac.uk
huadmiss@dmu.ac.uk
Admissions. BA (hons) media studies; film studies. One-year postgraduate diploma in newspaper journalism, NCTJ-accredited. MA in TV scriptwriting.

University of East Anglia
Admissions office
School of English and American
Studies
Norwich
NR4 7TJ
Tel: 01603 592283 (undergraduate admissions)
Tel: 01603 593820 (postgraduate admissions)
Fax: 01603 593799
www.uea.ac.uk

eas.admiss@uea.ac.uk (undergraduate)
l.faith@uea.ac.uk (postgraduate)
Admissions office. BA (hons) film studies can be combined with English; American studies or film and television studies. MA in film studies; film studies and archiving.

East London University
Longbridge Road
Dagenham
Essex
RM8 2AS
Tel: 020 8223 3000
Fax: 020 8223 2900
www.uel.ac.uk
admiss@uel.ac.uk
Admissions office. Undergraduate programmes include single/combined honours in cinematics; journalism and print media; media studies; media and advertising. MA in media studies; multi-media; global media.

Essex University
Wivenhoe Park
Colchester
Essex
CO4 3SQ
Tel: 01206 873333
Fax: 01206 873598
www.essex.ac.uk
admit@essex.ac.uk

Student recruitment office. BA in sociology; culture and media; film studies and literature.

University of Exeter
Northcote House
The Queen's Drive
Exeter
EX4 4QJ
Tel: 01392 661000
Fax: 01392 263108
www.exeter.ac.uk
admissions@exeter.ac.uk

Admissions office. BA in film studies. MPhil/PhD in film and visual culture. MA in English studies; creative writing. Short courses in screen writing.

Glamorgan University
Pontypridd
Mid Glamorgan
CF37 1DL
Tel: 01443 480480 (university)
Tel: 0800 716925 (student enquiries)
Fax: 01443 822055
www.glam.ac.uk
ajudge@glam.ac.uk
gedward@glam.ac.uk

Major/minor/joint options in media practice or cultural studies in combination with art practice; cultural studies; drama (theatre and media) or English studies. MA in scriptwriting

(theatre, film and television). Foundation degrees in multimedia and digital video.

Glasgow Caledonian University
Division of Media, Language and Leisure Management
70 Cowcaddens Road
Glasgow
G4 0BA
Tel: 0141 331 3259
Fax: 0141 331 3264
www.gcal.ac.uk
media.journalism@gcal.ac.uk

Administrative staff. BA (hons) in journalism and social sciences. Nine months full-time PgDip in journalism, accredited by the NCTJ; involves print training plus broadcast options.

Greenwich University
Wellington Street
Woolwich
London
SE18 6PF
Tel: 0800 005006
(student enquiry unit)
Tel: 020 8331 8590
(main switchboard)
Fax: 020 8331 8145
www.gre.ac.uk
courseinfo@gre.ac.uk

Enquiry unit. BA (hons) in media writing as a joint honours degree. BA (hons) media communication; media, culture and communication.

University of Hertfordshire

College Lane
Hatfield
Hertfordshire
AT10 9AB
Tel: 01707 284800
Fax: 01707 284870
www.herts.ac.uk
admissions@herts.ac.uk

University admissions service. BA (hons) three/four years full-time applied media arts (2D or 3D media); digital lens media. Linguistics, English literature, philosophy or history can be combined with communication through media. BSc (hons) media technology with digital broadcast; software systems for arts and media.

University of Huddersfield

Queensgate
Huddersfield
West Yorkshire
HD1 3DH
Tel: 01484 422288
Fax: 01484 472765
www.hud.ac.uk
admissions@hud.ac.uk

Assistant registrar (admissions). BA (hons) three/four years full-time single or joint honours in media (media and print

or media and radio); interactive media; multimedia; theatre studies and media. BA (hons) English language or literature with journalism.

University of Wales, Lampeter

Media Centre
College Street
Lampeter
Ceredigion
SA48 7ED
Tel: 01570 424790
Fax: 01570 424714
www.lamp.ac.uk
caron@lamp.ac.uk

Admissions officer. Single/joint BA in media studies and film studies. MA in screen studies involves academic study of audiovisual media with vocational training in film and video production.

University of Central Lancashire

The Department of Journalism
Preston
Lancashire
PR1 2HE
Tel: 01772 201201
Fax: 01772 894954
www.uclan.ac.uk
admissions@uclan.ac.uk
gcelliot@uclan.ac.uk

Admissions office. BA (hons) three years full-time combined or joint honours degrees in journalism. IPR-recognized undergraduate BA (hons) in public relations. Postgraduate diploma courses in broadcast journalism; newspaper journalism and online journalism (NCTJ- and BJTC-accredited courses).

Lancaster University
Culture, Media and Communication
Lancaster
LA1 4YL
Tel: 01524 65201
Fax: 01524 846243
www.lancs.ac.uk
g.myers@lancs.ac.uk
b.vernon@lancs.ac.uk
Admissions Tutor: Greg Myers; *Admissions Officer:* Beryl Vernon. BA single/combined honours in culture, media and communications.

University of Leeds
Institute of Communication Studies
Leeds
LS2 9JT
Tel: 0113 233 5800
Fax: 0113 233 5808
www.leeds.ac.uk
admissions@ics-server.novell.leeds.ac.uk
Admissions office. BA (hons) three years full-time communications; broadcasting; broadcast journalism; communications and new media. MA in international communications; communication studies.

MSc in communication studies. MA/PgDip in broadcast journalism and radio journalism (accredited by BJTC).

Leeds Metropolitan University
City Campus
Leeds
LS1 3HE
Tel: 0113 283 3113
Fax: 0113 283 3114
www.lmu.ac.uk
course-enquiries@lmu.ac.uk
Admissions team. BA (hons) media and popular culture. PgDip/MA film and moving image production. Cert HE film and TV production. FDA film and TV production. BA/Edexcel HNC/HND moving image production. PgDip/MA in screenwriting.

University of Leicester
Centre for Mass Communication Research
Leicester
LE1 7LT
Tel: 0116 252 3863
Fax: 0116 252 3874
www.le.ac.uk
mec4@le.ac.uk
Department Administrator: Margaret Crawford. MA in mass communications; globalization and communications. MSc in media and communications research. PhD/MPhil in mass communications.

University of Lincoln
Marketing and Recruitment services
Admissions Department
Brayford Pool
Lincoln
LN6 7TS
Tel: 01522 882000
Fax: 01522 886880
www.lincoln.ac.uk
enquiries@lincoln.ac.uk
Admissions department. Three years full-time BA/BSc single/joint honours degree in journalism.

University of Liverpool
Liverpool
L69 3BX
Tel: 0151 794 2000
Fax: 0151 708 6502
www.liv.ac.uk
ugrecruitment@liv.ac.uk
Admissions. BA (hons) communications media with popular music.

Liverpool John Moores University
JMU Tower
24 Norton Street
Liverpool
L3 8PY
Tel: 0151 231 5090 / 5091
Fax: 0151 231 5632
www.livjm.ac.uk
recruitment@livjm.ac.uk

Recruitment team. Three years full-time, four to six years part-time BA (hons) in journalism and BA (hons) in international journalism (vocational course which aims to prepare students for media work in countries outside the United Kingdom). MA/PgDip vocational courses in print journalism, factual television and video production.

London College of Fashion (London Institute)
20 John Princes Street
London
W1M 0BJ
Tel: 020 7514 7400
Fax: 020 7514 7484
www.lcf.linst.ac.uk
enquiries@lcf.ins.ac.uk
Communications office. BA (hons) three years full-time journalism; fashion promotion with journalism NUJ and PTC-accredited (PR and broadcast options).

The London College of Printing (London Institute)
School of Media
10 Back Hill
Clerkenwell
London
EC1R 5EN
Tel: 020 7514 6500
Tel: 020 7514 6800
Fax: 020 7514 6848

www.lcp.linst.ac.uk
c.cornes@lcp.linst.ac.uk
Admissions. Two-year full-time HND course in media practice. BA (hons) full-time courses in film and video; journalism and media and culture studies. One year full-time BJTC-recognized postgraduate diploma in broadcast journalism; NCTJ-accredited postgraduate diploma in periodical journalism. MA in journalism and a range of courses in sound, photography, production and multimedia.

University of London, Goldsmiths College
Department of Media and
Communications
Lewisham Way
New Cross
London
SE1V 6NW
Tel: 020 7717 2232
(student enquiries)
Tel: 020 7717 2235
Tel: 020 7717 2239
Fax: 020 7717 2240
Tel: 020 7919 7766
(undergraduate programmes)
Tel: 020 7919 7060
(postgraduate programmes)
www.goldsmiths.ac.uk
media-comms@gold.ac.uk
admissions@gold.ac.uk

Admissions Office. Three years full-time BA (hons) in media and communications; anthropology and communications; communications and cultural studies; communications studies and sociology. Practical MA in feature film; image and communication; journalism; radio (BJTC-accredited); television journalism; TV documentary; TV drama. MA theory-based programmes in media and communications; transnational communications and the global media; science, culture and technology; new media: critical theory and practice. Postgraduate research in media and communications.

London Metropolitan University
133 Whitechapel High Street
London
E1 7QA
Tel: 020 7320 1616
Fax: 020 7320 1163
www.londonmet.ac.uk
enquiries.city@londonmet.ac.uk
Course enquiries. BA (hons) film and broadcast production. MA in audio-visual production; digital moving image; communications management; psychoanalysis and culture.

London Metropolitan University
North Campus
166–220 Holloway Road
London
N7 8DB

Tel: 020 7423 0000

Tel: 020 7133 4203

(undergraduate admissions)

Tel: 020 7133 4200

(course enquiries)

www.londonmet.ac.uk

admissions@londonmet.ac.uk

Admissions unit. BA single/combined honours in digital media; communications media. MA in mass communications.

Loughborough University

Department of Social Sciences

Ashby Road

Loughborough

Leicestershire

LE11 3TU

Tel: 01509 223365 (student enquiries)

Tel: 01509 223368

Tel: 01509 223383

Fax: 01509 223944

www.lboro.ac.uk

admissions@lboro.ac.uk

Admissions office. BA in communications and media studies. MA in media and cultural analysis.

Luton University

Park Square

Luton

Bedfordshire

LU1 3JU

Tel: 01582 489286

Fax: 01582 489323

www.luton.ac.uk

admissions@luton.ac.uk

Admissions office. BA single/combined honours in journalism; media practices; media performance; media production. MA in media culture and technology.

Manchester Metropolitan University

All Saints Buildings

All Saints

Manchester

M15 6BH

Tel: 0161 247 2000

Fax: 0161 247 6391

www.mmu.ac.uk

admissions@mmu.ac.uk

Department of Communication Media

Chatham Building

Cavendish Street

Manchester

M15 6BR

Tel: 0161 247 1284

Fax: 0161 247 6393

Admissions office. BA/BSc (hons) in film and media studies; media technology; television production. MA in communication design.

Middlesex University

White Hart Lane

London

N17 8HR

Tel: 020 8411 5898
Fax: 020 8411 5649
www.mdx.ac.uk
admissions@mdx.ac.uk

Admissions enquiries. BA (hons) journalism. Other courses include BA (hons) in journalism and communication studies, also media and cultural studies.

Napier University
10 Colinton Road
Edinburgh
EH10 5DT
Tel: 0500 353570
Fax: 0131 455 2588
www.napier.ac.uk
info@napier.ac.uk

Information officer. BA (hons) journalism three/four years full-time degree course offering opportunities to undertake news and feature writing assignments and production projects for newspapers, magazines, radio and TV. The university plays an active part in the European Journalism Training Association which means students get opportunities to work on projects funded by the EU and to study for a semester overseas. MSc/PgDip full- or part-time one-year course in journalism.

NE Wales Institute of Higher Education
Plas Coch
Mold Road
Wrexham
LL11 2AW
Tel: 01978 290666
Tel: 01978 293045 (admissions)
Fax: 01978 290008
www.newi.ac.uk
enquiries@newi.ac.uk

Admissions office. BA single/combined honours programmes include media studies; multimedia design; communication studies; digital media. BSc in sound production management.

University College, Northampton
Park Campus
Boughton Green Road
NN2 7AL
Tel: 01604 735500
Tel: 0800 3582232 (student enquiries)
Fax: 01604 713029
www.northampton.ac.uk
admissions@northampton.ac.uk

Registry. Courses include BA (hons) in film and television studies; media and cultural studies; media and popular culture.

University of Northumbria at Newcastle
Ellison Place
Newcastle upon Tyne
NE1 8ST
Tel: 0191 227 4472
Fax: 0191 227 3009

www.unn.ac.uk

evelyn.murray@unn.ac.uk

Admissions. BA (hons) three years full-time in media, culture and society; media production; politics and media studies. MA in film studies.

The Nottingham Trent University

Centre for Broadcasting and Media

Burton Street

Nottingham

NG1 4BU

Tel: 0115 941 8418

Fax: 0115 848 6063

www.ntu.ac.uk

Cbj@ntu.ac.uk

admissions@ntu.ac.uk

Registry. BA (hons) three years full-time degree course in broadcast journalism, accredited as a bi-media course by the Broadcast Training Council. MA/PgDip courses in television, radio, newspaper, and online journalism. MA courses are one year full-time or two years part-time including a placement. Diploma course is nine months full-time or twenty-one months part-time.

Paisley University

Paisley

PA1 2BE

Scotland

Tel: 0141 848 3727

Fax: 0141 848 3623

www.paisley.ac.uk

alison.copland@paisley.ac.uk

Admissions office. BA (hons) in media: theory and production; media technology. PgDip in multimedia communications.

Plymouth University

Drake Circus

Plymouth

PL4 8AA

Tel: 01752 232 137

Fax: 01752 232 141

www.plymouth.ac.uk

admissions@plymouth.ac.uk

Admissions office. BA single/combined honours in media arts. MA in media arts.

University of Portsmouth

Winston Churchill Avenue

Portsmouth

PO1 2UP

Tel: 02392 848484

Fax: 02392 843082

www.port.ac.uk

admissions@port.ac.uk

Admissions. BA single/combined honours in media studies; European media studies; digital media.

Queen Margaret University College, Edinburgh

Clerwood Terrace

Edinburgh

EH12 8TS

Tel: 0131 317 3247
Fax: 0131 317 3248
www.qmuc.ac.uk
admissions@qmuc.ac.uk
Assistant registrar (admissions). BA (hons) three/four years full-time in media and cultural studies; media and information; communication studies. MA media and cultural studies. PgDip/MA in advanced screen practice.

Robert Gordon University
School of Information and Media
Faculty Management
Garthdee Road
Aberdeen
AB10 7QE
Tel: 01224 263900
Tel: 01224 262105 (admissions)
Fax: 01224 263939
www. rgu.ac.uk
admissions@rgu.ac.uk
BA (hons) three years full-time publishing with journalism. BSc (hons) four years full-time design for digital media.

Royal Holloway University of London
Media Arts Centre
Williams Building
Egham
Surrey
TW20 OEX
Tel: 01784 443734

Fax: 01784 443832
www.rhul.ac.uk
MediaArts@rhul.ac.uk
Admissions. BA/BSc (hons) in media arts; science and the media. MAs in gender and sexuality on the screen; documentary by practice; producing film and TV; feature film; screenwriting.

University of Salford
School of Media, Music and Performance
Adelphi Campus
Peru Street
Salford
M3 6EQ
Tel: 0161 295 6021
Fax: 0161 295 6023
www.salford.ac.uk
course-enquiries@salford.ac.uk
Admissions. BA/BSc (hons) three years full-time TV and radio; journalism; media technology; media and performance; media language and business. MA/PgDips in TV and radio scriptwriting; TV features and documentary production.

University of Sheffield
Department of Journalism Studies
171 Northumberland Road
Sheffield
S10 1DF
Tel: 0114 222 2500
Fax: 0114 266 8918

www.shef.ac.uk/journalism
journalism@sheffield.ac.uk
Recruitment and admissions office. Three years full-time BA (hons) degree in journalism studies accredited by the NCTJ focuses on practical and theoretical aspects of contemporary journalism within an international context. MA one-year and PgDip nine-month courses in print, broadcast (BJTC-accredited) and e-journalism, with the emphasis on news. Full-time one year MA course in political communication.

Sheffield Hallam University
Northern Media School
The Workstation
15 Paternoster Row
Sheffield
S1 2BX
Tel: 0114 2534648
Fax: 0114 2254606
www.shu.ac.uk
swragg@shu.ac.uk
spalet@shu.ac.uk
Admissions office. BA (hons) media studies; communication studies. MA/PgDip/PgCert in broadcast journalism; media studies; international broadcast journalism; screen arts and film studies.

South Bank University
103 Borough Road
London
SE1 0AA

Tel: 020 7815 7815
Fax: 020 7815 8273
www.sbu.ac.uk
owenjs@sbu.ac.uk
Admissions office. BA single and joint honours in writing for media; media studies; film studies; digital media arts.

Southampton Institute
Faculty of Media, Arts and Society
East Park Terrace
Southampton
SO17 1BJ
Tel: 023 8031 9000
Fax: 023 8022 2259
www.solent.ac.uk
fmas@solent.ac.uk
patricia.arlott@solent.ac.uk
Admissions. BA (hons) journalism; media writing; media with cultural studies; film studies. MA in media.

Staffordshire University
College Road
Stoke on Trent
ST4 2DE
Tel: 01782 292752
Fax: 01782 292740
www.staffs.ac.uk
admissions@staffs.ac.uk
j.c.herbert@staffs.ac.uk
Admissions: Dr John Herbert (School of Humanities). Three years full-time BA (hons) in broadcast journalism and

politics. BA in journalism (single and combined honours).One year MA in broadcast journalism (BJTC-accredited).

The University of Stirling
Department of Film and Media Studies
Stirling
FK9 4LA
Scotland
Tel: 01786 467520
Fax: 01786 466855
www.stir.ac.uk
stirling.media@stir.ac
Admissions office. Four years full-time BA (hons) in journalism studies. MSc/PgDip courses via distance learning include media management; public relations and media research.

University of Sunderland
School of Art, Design and Media
Student Recruitment
Edinburgh Building
Chester Road
Sunderland
SR1 3SD
Tel: 0191 515 2110
Fax: 0191 515 2132
www.sunderland.ac.uk
student-helpline@sunderland.ac.uk
The Help Desk. Three years full-time BA (hons) in film and media studies; journalism studies; photography, video

and digital imaging; communications; cultural and media studies; media production (TV and radio); media production (video and new media); public relations. One year full-time or two years part-time MA courses include media and cultural studies; media production (TV and video); electronic media and design.

University of Surrey, Roehampton
West Hill
London
SW15 3SN
Tel: 020 8392 3232
Fax: 020 8392 3470
www.roehampton.ac.uk
enquiries@roehampton.ac.uk
Admissions. BA in media and cultural studies; film studies. MPhil/PhD in film and TV studies.

Surrey Institute of Art and Design, University College
Faculty of Media and Arts
Falkner Road
Farnham
Surrey
GU9 7DS
Tel: 01252 722441
Fax: 01252 892616
www.surrart.ac.uk
registry@surrat.ac.uk
Registry services. Three years full-time BA (hons) in journalism with radio and print options (accredited by the

Periodicals Training Council, BJTCouncil and NUJ). New degrees in fashion journalism and time-based media management. Range of arts and media courses available including research studentships for PhD or MPhil research and a taught MA in popular journalism.

University of Sussex
Essex House
Falmer
Brighton
BN1 9RQ
Tel: 01273 678019
Fax: 01273 678545
www.sussex.ac.uk
a.m.oxley@sussex.ac.uk
Admissions co-ordinator. BA in digital media production; media studies; media studies with European language; media studies with English; media studies with music. MA in media studies; digital media.

Swansea Institute of Higher Education
Mount Pleasant Campus
Swansea
SA1 6ED
Tel: 01792 481285
Fax: 01792 205305
www.sihe.ac.uk
enquiry@sihe.ac.uk
Admissions. BA in media arts; photo journalism; professional media practice.

University of Teesside
Middlesbrough
TS1 3BA
Tel: 01642 218121
Fax: 01642 342067
www.tees.ac.uk
reg@tees.ac.uk
Admissions administrator. BA (hons) three years full-time degree in media studies as a combined or single honours subject. BSc in media production; media technology. HND courses.

Thames Valley University
St Mary's Road
London
W5 5RF
Tel: 020 8579 5000
Fax: 020 8566 1353
www.tvu.ac.uk
learning.advice@tvu.ac.uk
Admissions. BA (hons) in advertising; arts and multimedia event management; digital broadcasting media; media arts; new media journalism; new media publishing. PgDip/MA in radio.

Trinity and All Saints College
Brownberrie Lane
Horsforth
Leeds
LS18 5HD
Tel: 0113 283 7100
Fax: 0113 283 7200

www.tasc.ac.uk

admissions@tasc.ac.uk

Admissions. BA (hons) in media studies. NCTJ-accredited MA/PgDip in print journalism. MA/PgDip in broadcast journalism (TV and radio) and radio journalism (BJTC-accredited). MA in journalism studies.

Warrington Collegiate Institute

Padgate Campus

Warrington

Cheshire

WA2 0DB

Tel: 01925 494494

Fax: 01925 494289

www.warr.ac.uk

registry.he@warr.ac.uk

Academic secretary. BA single/combined honours media studies. NCTJ-accredited courses in multimedia journalism and multimedia web.

University of Westminster

115 New Cavendish Street

London

W1W 6UW

Tel: 020 7911 5000

Fax: 020 7911 5858

www.wmin.ac.uk

admissions@wmin.ac.uk

Central student admissions. BA/BSc single or combined honours in media studies (journalism); contemporary

media practice; media technology. MA in journalism studies. PgDip in broadcast journalism; periodical journalism. MA in public relations. BJTC-accredited postgraduate diploma in journalism with periodical and broadcast pathways.

University of Wolverhampton

Wulfruna Street

Wolverhampton

WV1 1SB

Tel: 01902 321000

Fax: 01902 323744

www.wlv.ac.uk

enquiries@wlv.ac.uk

Admissions office. BA/BSc single or combined honours in journalism and editorial design; digital media; media and communication design.

UK College Media and Journalism Courses

Barnsley College

Programme Enquiries

PO Box 266

Church Street

Barnsley

South Yorkshire

S70 2YW

Tel: 01226 216171 / 216172

Fax: 01226 216166

www.barnsley.ac.uk

programme.enquiries@barnsley.ac.uk

Central registry. Full-time three year degree courses in BA (hons) combined studies (journalism) and BA (hons) combined studies (media). Two years full-time HND in media (journalism.) BSc creative multimedia technologies. All courses are validated/awarded by the University of Leeds, the University of Sheffield and Leeds Metropolitan University.

Bell College of Technology

Almada Street

Hamilton

Lanarkshire

ML3 0JB

Tel: 01698 283100

Fax: 01698 457525

www.bell.ac.uk

enquiries@bell.ac.uk

Admissions. National Council for the Training of Journalists accredited two year Higher National Diploma course in journalism. BJTC-recognized postgraduate diploma in radio journalism.

Brighton College of Technology

Pelham Street

Brighton

BN1 4FA

Tel: 01273 667788

Fax: 01273 667703

www.bricoltech.ac.uk

info@bricoltech.ac.uk

NCTJ-accredited.

Cheltenham and Gloucester College of Higher Education

The Park

Cheltenham

Gloucestershire

GL50 2QF

Tel: 01242 532824

Fax: 01242 256759

www.chelt.ac.uk

Media studies courses.

Coleg Gwent

The Rhadyr

Usk

NP15 1XJ

Tel: 01495 333333

Fax: 01495 333526

www.coleggwent.ac.uk

info@coleggwent.ac.uk

NCTJ-accredited pre-entry academic year course in newspaper journalism. AVCE media, two years full-time. HND/HNC graphic design, a range of full- and part-time courses. Edexcel design (photography), HND photography and digital imaging; national diploma in graphic design; GNVQ in media, also A-level and part-time courses.

Cornwall College

Centre for Arts, Media and Social
Sciences
Redruth
Cornwall
TR15 3RD
Tel: 01209 611611
Fax: 01209 616168
www.cornwall.ac.uk
enquiries@cornwall.ac.uk

Two-year HND in newspaper and
magazine journalism. BJTC-accredited
postgraduate diploma in broadcast
journalism. NCTJ-accredited
postgraduate diplomas in newspaper and
magazine journalism.

Crawley College

College Road
Crawley
West Sussex
RH10 1NR
Tel: 01293 442312 (arts and
humanities department)
Fax: 01293 442399
www.crawley-college.ac.uk
information@crawley-college.ac.uk

BTEC National Diploma in media
production (two years full-time).City and
Guilds certificate in print and radio
journalism (one year). NCTJ pre-entry
certificate/level 4 NVQ in newspaper
journalism (one year).

Cumbria Institute of the Arts

Brampton Road
Carlisle
Cumbria
CA3 9AY
Tel: 01228 400300
Fax: 01228 514491
www.cumbriacad.ac.uk
info@cumbria.ac.uk

Media production; new journalism.

Darlington College of Technology

Cleveland Avenue
Darlington
County Durham
DL3 7BB
Tel: 01325 503050
Fax: 01325 503000
www.darlington.ac.uk
enquire@darlington.ac.uk

NCTJ-accredited pre-entry academic
year, pre-entry one calendar year, pre-
entry short courses and block release
courses. BTEC Media Studies National
Diploma and International Diploma in
Journalism.

Doncaster College

Waterdale
Doncaster
DN1 3EX
Tel: 01302 553553
Tel: 0800 358 7575

Fax: 01302 553559

www.don.ac.uk

he@don.ac.uk

BA full-time three years performance based arts with digital media.

East Surrey College
(incorporating Reigate School of Art and Design)

Gatton Point North

Claremont Road

Gatton Point

Redhill

Surrey

RH1 2JX

Tel: 01737 788444

www.esc.org.uk

studentservice@esc.org.uk

GNVQ intermediate in media. BTEC National Diploma in media. NCTJ one year full-time or two-term fast-track course in journalism. One-year foundation diploma in professional media and journalism. Other courses include TV and video production; journalism.

Edge Hill College of Higher Education

Ormskirk

Lancashire

L39 4QP

Tel: 01695 584274 (student enquiries)

Fax: 01695 584355

www.edgehill.co.uk

enquiries@edgehill.ac.uk

Enquiries unit. BA (hons) journalism degree course accredited by Lancaster University and the NCTJ. Courses in media and communications; new media; journalism; science journalism.

Falmouth College of Arts

Faculty of media and culture

Woodlane

Falmouth

Cornwall

TR11 4RH

Tel: 01326 211077

Fax: 01326 212261

www.falmouth.ac.uk

admissions@falmouth.ac.uk

Admissions officer. Full-time three-year BA (hons) degree courses in journalism and broadcast journalism; English with media studies; film studies; journalism studies. Nine months full-time postgraduate diplomas in broadcast journalism (accredited as a bi-media programme by the BJTC); professional writing; television. BBC, ITV and Skillset endorse the postgraduate diploma in television. The BBC-donated Jill Dando bursary is awarded annually to a broadcast journalist student.

Farnborough College of Technology

Boundary Road

Farnborough

Hampshire
GU14 6SB
Tel: 01252 407028
Fax: 01252 407041
www.farn-ct.ac.uk
admissions@farn-ct.ac.uk

Admissions office. Two years full-time HND courses in media technology (broadcast systems operation); media technology (production with business). Three years BSc in media technology production. Courses in TV and radio technology (production with business); TV technology and moving image studies; TV and radio production with performance.

Gloucestershire College of Arts and Technology

Brunswick Campus
Brunswick Road
Gloucester
GL1 1HU
Tel: 01452 532000
Fax: 01452 426601
info@gloscat.ac.uk

One year BTEC national diploma in media production. NCTJ-accredited pre-entry academic year course.

Harlow College

Velizy Avenue
Town Centre
Harlow
Essex
CM20 3LH
Tel: 01279 868000
Tel: 01279 868145 (admissions clerk)
Fax: 01279 868260
www.harlow-college.ac.uk
learninglink@harlow-college.ac.uk

Admissions clerk. Postgraduate courses in magazine and newspaper journalism (nineteen weeks; not NCTJ-accredited); NCTJ-accredited post A-level course in newspaper journalism; Middlesex University accredits BA (hons) in journalism.

Harrow College

Lowlands Road
Harrow
Middlesex
HA1 3AQ
Tel: 020 8909 6000
Fax: 020 8909 6050
www.harrow.ac.uk
enquiries@harrow.ac.uk

Admissions office. NCTJ-accredited pre-entry course in print journalism.

Highbury College, Portsmouth

School of Media and Journalism
Dovercourt Road
Cosham
Portsmouth
Hants
PO6 2SA
Tel: 023 9231 3287

Fax: 023 9237 8382

www. highbury.ac.uk

studentservices@highbury-ac.uk

Admissions team. BJTC-accredited broadcast journalism postgraduate diploma (twenty weeks fast track). PTC-accredited magazine journalism pre-entry (twenty weeks fast track). Full-time two years BTEC/HND in media journalism.

King Alfred's College of Higher Education

Sparkford Road

Winchester

Hampshire

SO22 4NR

Tel: 01962 841515

Fax: 01962 842280

www.ukac.ac.uk

contact@kingalfreds.co.uk

Media and film studies.

Lambeth College

Vauxhall Centre

Belmore Street

Wandsworth

London

SW8 2JY

Tel: 020 7501 5424

Fax: 020 7501 5490

www.lambethcollege.ac.uk

courses@lambethcollege.ac.uk

NCTJ-accredited pre-entry academic course. Eighteen-week postgraduate.

Leeds, Trinity and All Saints College

Brownberrie Lane

Horsforth

Leeds

LS18 5HD

Tel: 0113 283 7166

Fax: 0113 283 7321

www.tasc.ac.uk

d-dodd@tasc.ac.uk

Media, joint honours; digital media, single honours.

Liverpool Community College

Journalism School

The Arts Centre

9 Myrtle Street

Liverpool

L7 7JA

Tel: 0151 707 8528

Fax: 0151 707 8528

www.liv-coll.ac.uk

sandy.felton@liv-coll.ac.uk

NCTJ day release for working journalists; NCTJ one year pre-entry; NCTJ eighteen week postgraduate fast track.

NE Wales Institute of Higher Education

Plas Coch

Mold Road

Wrexham

LL11 2AW

Tel: 01978 290666

Tel: 01978 293045 (admissions)
Fax: 01978 290008
www.newi.ac.uk
enquiries@newi.ac.uk
BA (hons) media studies, with other subject; BA (hons) multimedia design; BA (hons) animation.

Plymouth College of Art and Design
Tavistock Place
Plymouth
PL4 8AT
Tel: 01752 203434
Fax: 01752 203444
www.pcad-web.org
enquiries@pcad.ac.uk
HND in moving image; photography and electronic imaging; animation and creative media; multimedia; one-year conversion BA (hons). Professional diploma in photography, film and television.

Ravensbourne College of Design and Communications
Walden Road
Chislehurst
Kent
BR7 5SN
Tel: 020 8289 4900
Fax: 020 8325 8320
www.rave.ac.uk
info@rave.ac.uk

BA (hons) in content creation for broadcasting and new media; foundation degree in broadcasting and digital technology; BSc (hons) in broadcasting technology; BA (hons) in broadcasting production. Foundation degree in computer visualization and animation; BA (hons) in design for moving image; BA (hons) in interaction design; MA interactive digital media. HNC in post production.

College of Ripon and York
Lord Mayor's Walk
York
YO31 7EX
Tel: 01904 716672
Fax: 01904 716931
www.ucrysj.ac.uk
BA (hons) in theatre, film and television.

Salisbury College
Southampton Road
Salisbury
Wiltshire
SP1 2LW
Tel: 01722 344344
Fax: 01722 344345
www.salcol.com
enquiries@salcol.com
HND in photography, film and TV and BA (hons) degree in film and TV. Foundation degree in creative digital arts.

Sheffield College
Norton Centre
Dyche Lane
Sheffield
S8 8BR
Tel: 0114 260 2600
Fax: 0114 260 2301
www.sheffcol.ac.uk
mail@sheffcol.ac.uk
NCTJ-accredited block release, pre-entry
academic year and January–December
courses. Eighteen-week fast-track
graduate course. Also photojournalism
and press photography.

South Thames College
Wandsworth High Street
London
SW18 2PP
Tel: 020 8918 7777
www.south-thames.ac.uk
studentservices@south-
thames.ac.uk
BTEC in journalism; television and video;
television and video production; in
documentary video; non-linear editing;
directing drama. HNC in journalism;
multimedia; TV and video; 16mm
filmmaking; BA (hons) joint degree in
multi-media and marketing.

South East Essex College
Carnarvon Road
Southend-on-Sea
Essex

SS2 6LS
Tel: 01702 220400
www.se-essex-college.ac.uk
learning@se-essex-college.ac.uk
Three-year BSc (hons) media production
and technology; multimedia technology.
Two-year BTEC/GNVQ broadcast media;
print media. Two-year advanced media
communications and productions. NCTJ
pre-entry one year news journalism
certificate.

Suffolk College
Ipswich
IP4 1LT
Tel: 01473 296606
Fax: 01473 296558
www.suffolk.ac.uk
info@suffolk.ac.uk
BA (hons) in media studies; DipHE media
studies.

Sutton Coldfield College
34 Lichfield Road
Sutton Coldfield
B74 2NW
Tel: 0121 355 5671
Fax: 0121 355 0799
www.sutcol.ac.uk
cedwards@sutcol.ac.uk
NCTJ-accredited pre-entry certificate.

Warwickshire College
Warwick New Road
Leamington Spa

Warwickshire
CV32 5JE
Tel: 01926 318000
Fax: 01926 318311
www.warkscol.ac.uk
enquiries@warkscol.ac.uk
NCTJ-accredited pre-entry (academic year).

West Herts College
Watford Campus
Hempstead Road
Watford
Hertfordshire
WD17 3EZ
Tel: 01923 812565
Fax: 01923 812540
www.westherts.ac.uk
BA (hons) media production management.

City of Wolverhampton College
Wulfrun Campus
Paget Road
Wolverhampton
WV6 0DU
Tel: 01902 836000
Fax: 01902 423070
www.wolverhamptoncollege.ac.uk
mail@wolverhamptoncollege.ac.uk
BA (hons) in journalism and editorial design accredited by Wolverhampton University. Day release/pre-entry. NCTJ, C&G and BTEC courses.

Other Media Training and Education

The organizations listed below offer or oversee shorter, private and vocational training that is not part of a college or university course.

BBC Training and Development Broadcast Training
Wood Norton
Evesham
Worcestershire
WR11 4YB
Tel: 01386 420216
Fax: 01386 420145
www.bbctraining.co.uk
training@bbc.co.uk
BBC Training and Development offers training services in all production, operations and engineering skills. Training can be tailored to clients' requirements and is provided at dedicated training centres (including Wood Norton) or at clients' premises. Places for freelances on some courses are subsidized by Skillset.

BBME Training, the Radio and Television School
7–9 The Broadway
Newbury
Berkshire
RG14 1AS

Tel: 01635 572819
Fax: 01635 38802
www.radiotvschool.co.uk
info@bbme.co.uk
Short courses in radio and TV presentation to the public and corporate sector.

BKSTS – British Kinematograph Sound and TV Society

Walpole Court
Ealing Studios
London
W5 5ED
Tel: 020 8540 5220
Fax: 020 8584 5230
www.bksts.com
movimage@bksts.demon.co.uk
The BKSTS publishes 'Education, Training and Working in Film, Television and Broadcasting'. It accredits courses and runs its own courses.

British Film Institute

21 Stephen Street
London
W1P 2LN
Tel: 020 7255 1444
Fax: 020 7436 0439
www.bfi.org.uk
helpdesk@bfi.org.uk
The BFI has an education department which also publishes useful career guides.

British Universities Film and Video Council

77 Wells Street
London
W1T 3QJ
Tel: 020 7393 1500
Fax: 020 7393 1555
www.bufvc.ac.uk
ask@bufvc.ac.uk
The Council promotes the production, study and use of moving images and related media in higher education. It runs an information service, has editing facilities and organizes conferences and courses. It offers regular one-day courses for professionals.

Broadcasting Journalism Training Council

39 Westbourne Gardens
London
W2 5NR
Tel: 020 7727 9522
Fax: 020 7727 9522
www.bjtc.org.uk
secretary@bjtc.org.uk
The BJTC promotes professional standards in training broadcast journalists. It is a charity whose subscribers come from all sides of the radio and TV industry, the NUJ and colleges offering broadcast journalism courses. It offers consultation to those hoping to become broadcast journalists

and developers of BJTC-recognized courses.

Communication Skills Europe
City Bank House
16–22 Baltic Street
London
EC1Y OVL
Tel: 020 7670 0505
Fax: 020 7670 0515
www.cseltd.com
Course programme for journalists and editors which aims to cover the key skills of writing, subbing, editorial management and online.

Cyfle
Gronant
Penrallt
Isaf
Caernarfon
Gwynedd
LL55 1NS
Tel: 01286 671000
Fax: 01286 678831
www.cyfle.co.uk
cyfle@cyfle.co.uk
Media training provider for the Welsh film and TV industry.

Editorial Centre
Hanover House
Marine Court
St Leonards-on-Sea
East Sussex
TN38 ODX
Tel: 01424 435991
Fax: 01424 445547
www.editorial-centre@hinge.mistral.co.uk
pam@editorial-centre.co.uk
A range of journalism courses including pre-entry NVQ, starting three times a year. Run by senior journalists and designers for the newspaper and magazine industry.

FT2 – Film and Television Freelance Training
Warwick House
9 Warwick Street
London
W1R 5RA
Tel: 020 7734 5141
Fax: 020 7287 9899
www.ft2.org.uk
info@ft2.org.uk
FT2 provides new entrant training in the junior construction, production and technical grades for the freelance sector of the film and television industry. It is funded by the Skillset Freelance Training Fund, European Social Fund and Channel 4.

Journalism Training Centre
Unit G
Mill Green Business Park
Mill Green Road

Mitcham
Surrey
CR4 4HT
Tel: 020 8640 3696
Fax: 020 8640 6266
www.journalism-training-centre.co.uk
enq@journalism-training-centre.co.uk

NTJC foundation skills certificate in journalism approved by the NUJ. Three fourteen-week courses are run each year.

National Council for the Training of Journalists

Latton Bush Centre
Southern Way
Harlow
Essex
CM18 7BL
Tel: 01279 430009
Fax: 01279 438008
www.nctj.com
info@nctj.com

The NCTJ is a charity which runs independent training schemes for print journalists. It accredits courses at universities and colleges.

National Film and Television School

Beaconsfield Studios
Buckinghamshire
HP9 1LG

Tel: 01494 671234
Fax: 01494 674042
www.nftsfilm-tv.ac.uk
admin@nftsfilm-tv.ac.uk

Short modular courses in television programme making and broadcast management.

National Union of Journalists

Headland House
308–312 Grays Inn Road
London
WC1X 8DP
Tel: 020 7278 7916
Fax: 020 7837 8143
www.nujtraining.org.uk

Mid-career training courses in editorial skills.

Network Media

46 My Lady's Mile
Holywood
County Down
BT18 9EN
Tel: 028 9042 7265
www.northdown.co.uk/networkmedia
networkmedia@nireland.com

Offers tailor-made media training courses.

Newspaper Society

Bloomsbury House
74–77 Great Russell Street
London

WC1B 3DA

Tel: 020 7636 7014

Fax: 020 7631 5119

www.newspapersoc.org.uk

ns@newspapersoc.org.uk

Consults on all aspects of newspaper training and publishes a leaflet, 'Training to be a Journalist'.

No Sweat Journalism Training

25b Lloyd Baker Street

London

WC1X 9AT

Tel: 020 7713 1000

Fax: 020 7713 8493

Mobile: 07710 692550

www.nosweattjt.co.uk

nosweat@lineone.net

Offers National Council for the Training of Journalists training in the centre of London.

Northern Ireland Film Commission

3rd Floor, Alfred House

21 Alfred Street

BT2 8ED

Tel: 028 9023 2444

Fax: 028 9023 9918

www.nifc.co.uk

info@nifc.co.uk

The NIFTC's industry training programme is central to supporting the growth of the broadcast, film, video and multimedia industry in Northern Ireland. Includes

career development placements, short courses and hands-on training.

PMA Training

PMA House

Free Church Passage

St Ives

Cambridgeshire

PE27 5AY

Tel: 01480 300653

Fax: 01480 496022

www.pma-group.com

training@pma-group.com

Supplies editorial training for the industry. PMA courses are based in Clerkenwell, Central London. Over 500 workshops per year.

PressWise Trust

38 Easton Business Centre

Felix Road

Bristol

BS5 0HE

Tel: 0117 941 5889

Fax: 0117 941 5848

www.presswise.org.uk

pw@presswise.org.uk

Non-profit making organization providing media training.

Scottish Daily Newspaper Society

48 Palmerston Place

Edinburgh

EH12 5DE

Tel: 0131 220 4353

Fax: 0131 220 4344

www.snpa.org.uk

info@sdns.org.uk

The Scottish training co-ordinator.

Scottish Newspaper Publishers Association

48 Palmerston Place

Edinburgh

EH12 5DE

Tel: 0131 220 4353

Fax: 0131 220 4344

www.snpa.org.uk

info@snpa.org.uk

Contact point for SVQ, the Scottish version of NVQs.

Skillset

103 Dean Street

London

W1V 5RA

Tel: 020 7534 5300

Fax: 020 7534 5333

www.skillset.org

info@skillset.org

The national training organization for broadcast, film, video and multimedia. Recognized by the government as a primary industry training provider. Operates at a strategic level to improve training and education policy and provision. Publishes a careers handbook, plus information on employment and labour market trends, professional standards and qualifications and much more. Skillset is managed and funded by the BBC, Channel 4, Channel 5, the Federation of Entertainment Unions (FEU), International Visual Communications Association (IVCA), ITVA and the Producers Alliance for Film And Television (PACT).

Skillset – Scottish Screen Training

249 West George Street

Glasgow

G2 4QE

Tel: 0141 302 1700

Fax: 0141 302 1711

www.scottishscreen.com

info@scottishscreen.com

Provides training and development for film, television and new media. Scottish Screen is the Scottish Assessment Centre for Skillset Professional Qualifications (SVQ), offering the opportunity to gain recognized professional qualifications.

Skillset South West

59 Prince Street

Bristol

BS1 4QH

Tel: 0117 925 4011

Fax: 0117 925 1711

info@skillsetsouthwest.com

Training Direct International
Matlock
Derbyshire
DE4 5AW
Tel: 01629 534826

Fax: 01629 534116
peterhiscocks@tvtraining.freeserve.co.uk
A non-profit NGO for the training and
education of all journalists.

9 career help

Media Recruitment Websites

BBC Jobs
BBC Recruitment
PO Box 7000
London
W1A 6GJ
Tel: 0870 333 1330
Tel: 020 7765 1192 (text phone)
www.bbc.co.uk/jobs
recruitment@bbc.co.uk
Vacancies within the BBC. Online application system and postal request service. Careers advice and information about work experience programmes.

FINGTV
www.fingtv.com
Makes and displays showreels which are then put into an online database for broadcasters to view.

Freelancers.net
www.freelancers.net
Maintains databases of freelancers, freelance jobs and projects.

Guardian Media
www.jobs.guardian.co.uk/media
Website with media and new media vacancies. Archive of jobs from the *Guardian*'s media section.

Journalism UK
www.journalismuk.co.uk
Useful links to websites with media vacancies.

Mandy.com
www.mandy.com
Film/TV production vacancies.

News Jobs UK
www.freestats.com
Journalism jobs, writing and editing jobs in print and new media.

The Media Network
www.tmn.co.uk
Recruitment consultancy for editorial jobs.

Agents

These are all agents who deal with presenters and reporters in news broadcasting.

Arlington Enterprises Ltd
1–3 Charlotte Street
London
W1T 1RD
Tel: 020 7580 0702
Fax: 020 7580 4994
www.arlingtonenterprises.co.uk
info@arlington-enterprises.co.uk

Avalon Management Group Ltd
4a Exmoor Street
London
W10 6BD
Tel: 020 7598 8000
Fax: 020 7598 7300
Directors: Richard Allen-Turner, Jon Thoday.

Blackburn Sachs Associates
88–90 Crawford Street
London
W1H 2BS
Tel: 020 7258 6158
Fax: 020 7258 6161
www.blackburnsachsassociates.com
presenters@blackburnsachsassociates.com
Agents: Anthony Blackburn, Rosetta Licchelli, John Sachs.

Capel and Land
29 Wardour Street
London
W1D 6PS
Tel: 0207 734 2414
Tel: 0207 724 0244
Fax: 0207 734 8101
anita@algrade.demon.co.uk
Managing Director: Anita Land.

Curtis Brown
Haymarket House
28–29 Haymarket
London
SW1Y 4SP
Tel: 020 7396 6600
Fax: 020 7396 0110
cb@curtisbrown.co.uk

Noel Gay Artists Ltd
19 Denmark Street
London
WC2H 8NA
Tel: 020 7836 3941
Fax: 020 7287 1816
www.noelgay.com
mail@noelgay.com
Chief Executive: Alex Armitage.

KBJ Management
5 Soho Square
London
W1V 5DE

Tel: 020 7434 6767
Fax: 020 7287 1191
www.kbjmgt.co.uk
general@kbjmgt.co.uk
Contact: Joanna Kaye.

Knight Ayton Management
114 St Martin's Lane
London
WC2N 4BE
Tel: 020 7836 5333
Fax: 020 7836 8333
www.knightayton.co.uk
info@knightayton.co.uk
Contact: Sue Ayton, Sue Knight.

Billy Marsh Associates Ltd
174–178 North Gower Street
London
NW1 2NB
Tel: 020 7388 6858
Fax: 020 7388 6848
bmarsh@bmarsh.demon.co.uk

The Roseman Organisation
Suite 9
The Power House
70 Chiswick High Road
London
W4 1SY
Tel: 020 8742 0552
Fax: 020 8742 0554
presenters@tragents.freeserve.co.uk
Managing Director: R. Roseman.

Speak-Easy Ltd
1 Dairy Yard
High Street
Market Harborough
Leicestershire
LE16 7NL
Tel: 01858 461961
Tel: 08700 135126
Fax: 01858 461994
www.speak-easy.co.uk
enquiries@speak-easy.co.uk
Managing Director: Kate Moon.

10 staying informed

Journalism Websites

Alternative Press
www.altpress.org
Alternative press index.

American Journalism Review
www.ajr.org
News, comment, advice, online training and extensive links to journalism sites around the world.

Amnesty International
www.amnesty.org
A worldwide campaigning movement that works to promote human rights as enshrined in the Universal Declaration of Human Rights and other international standards. Activities range from public demonstrations to letter writing, from human rights education to fundraising concerts, from individual appeals on a particular case to global campaigns on a particular issue.

British Journalism Review
www.bjr.org.uk
Website of the *British Journalism Review*.

British Politics Page
www.ukpolitics.org.uk
Politics information. Free website resource of UKPOL magazine.

Broadcast Monitoring
www.bmcnews.com
Broadcast Monitoring's site for cuttings, plus radio and TV clips.

Campaign for Press Freedom
www.cpbf.org.uk
An independent voice for the media forum which works to promote policies for a diverse, democratic and accountable media.

CCTA Government Information Service
www.opengov.co.uk
Information from the House of Commons and links to government departments.

Centre for Media Education

www.cme.org

US Centre for Media Education.

Columbia Journalism Review

www.cjr.org

Website of the *Columbia Journalism Review*.

Committee for the Protection of Journalists

www.cpj.org

Committee dedicated to the global defence of press freedom.

Communications White Paper

www.communicationswhitepaper.gov.uk

For the latest government plans for the media.

Dart Centre Europe

www.darteurope.org

info@darteurope.org

Advice, information and mutual support and referral for journalists who have experienced traumatic stress and to help them identify the effects of stress.

Environmental News Network

www.enn.com

Environmental News Network.

Europa – European Commission's online Press Room

www.europa.eu.int/comm/
press_room/index_en.htm

Press releases from EU institutions, calendar of upcoming events, official euro rates, latest statistics and other news services.

Federal News

www.fednews.com

US government information.

Future Events News Service

www.fensap.com

Forthcoming news events. Many more events contained in the FENS database available by subscribing.

Freedom Forum Organisation

www.freedomforum.org

Focuses on Newseum, first amendment freedoms and newsroom diversity.

Freelance Directory

www.freelancedirectory.org

The NUJ's freelance directory, the biggest such list available.

Gallup

www.gallup.com

Official site of the polling organization. Contains poll findings.

Guardian Media

www.media.guardian.co.uk

HoldTheFrontPage

www.holdthefrontpage.co.uk

Online news service for UK journalists.

Honk

www.honk.co.uk/fleetstreet

A forum for journalists.

Independent Media Organizations

www.uk.indymedia.org

The Institute for War and Peace Reporting

www.iwpr.net

London-based NGO contributing to international understanding of conflict issues and supporting regional independent journalism.

The International Centre for Journalists

www.icfj.org

Established to improve the quality of journalism where there is little or no tradition of independent journalism.

International Federation of Journalists

www.ifj.org

ifj@ifj.org

World's largest organization of journalists. Promotes international action to defend press freedom and social justice, through strong, free and independent trade unions of journalists. Links to other IFJ websites which include the European Federation of Journalists; Authors Rights for All; International Freelance.

International Freedom of Expression Exchange

www.ifex.org

Human rights group.

Journalism Organization

www.journalism.org

Committee of concerned journalists dedicated to clarifying the principles of the profession. Includes projects for excellence in journalism.

Journalism

www.journalism.co.uk

Job vacancies, training, advice for online journalists.

Journalism net

www.journalismnet.com

Online resource for journalists. The latest world news, live news feeds, news headlines, find jobs and people, training, business news.

Journalists Tool Box

www.journaliststoolbox.com

Online resources for reporters and editors. Features more than thirteen thousand websites.

Journalism and Women Symposium

www.jaws.org

Journalism and women symposium. Website for women journalists.

Journolist

www.journolist.com

Advice about how to use the internet as a journalist's tool.

MediaChannel

www.mediachannel.org

Non-profit, public interest site dedicated to global media issues. News, reports and commentary from international network of media-issues organizations.

The Media Channel

www.themediachannel.co.uk

Online site for *Media Week*, *Press Gazette*, AV interactive and media moves.

Media Insider

www.mediainsider.com

News for PRs.

Mediatel

www.mediatel.co.uk

Media news and information database.

Megastories

www.megastories.com

Global news site.

Newseum

www.newseum.org

Website of the Washington-based Newseum.

Neravt

www.neravt.com/left

Environmental and financial news.

News Desk UK

www.newsdesk-uk.com

Contacts and links for UK journalists. Transcripts of congressional hearings and speeches. White House, State Department, federal departmental briefings.

Newslink Organization

www.newslink.org

Links to news sites in the US and around the world.

Newsnow.co.uk

www.newsnow.co.uk

UK news and current affairs site.

News World

www.newsworld.co.uk

News world conference and information plus industry news.

Power Reporting

www.powerreporting.com

Search tool for journalists.

Poynter Organization

www.poynter.org

US website for journalists. News, comment, advice, links and online training.

Reporters sans Frontières

www.rsf.fr

Defends press freedom. Works around the world, investigates and protests, takes action and raises awareness.

Reporting the World

www.reportingtheworld.org

Current issues in reporting international news.

Rory Peck Trust

www.oneworld.org/rorypeck

Only charity in the world dedicated to promoting the work, safety and security of freelance media workers in news and current affairs broadcasting worldwide. The Rory Peck Trust subsidizes training in hostile environments for freelancers, advises them on insurance and provides financial support to the families of those killed or seriously injured during the course of their work.

TV Cameramen

www.tvcameramen.com

Articles, advice, equipment, reviews and links for cameramen. Personal links to cameramen around the world.

TV News

www.tvnews.org

Current affairs, links to useful websites.

UK Government Online

www.ukonline.gov.uk

The front door to UK government sites.

Women News

www.womennews.org

Independent news service covering issues of particular concern to women.

Useful Magazines and Books

Magazines

British Journalism Review

University of Luton Press

75 Castle Street

Luton

LU1 3AJ

Tel: 01582 743297

Fax: 01582 743298

ulp@luton.ac.uk

Editor: Geoffrey Goodman. An academic quarterly magazine published by the University of Luton Press.

British Journal of Photography

39 Earlham Street

London

WC2H 9LT

Tel: 020 7306 7000

Fax: 020 7306 7112

www.bjphoto.co.uk

bjp.editor@bjphoto.co.uk

Editor: Jon Tarrant. Published by Timothy Benn Publishing.

Communications Law

2 Addiscombe Road

Croydon

Surrey

CR9 5AF

Tel: 020 8686 9141

Fax: 020 8686 3155

Rajni_Boswell@tolley.co.uk

A journal of computer, media and telecommunications law.

Free Press

2nd Floor

23 Orford Road

London

E17 9NL

Tel: 020 8521 5932

Fax: 020 8521 5932

www.cpbf.org.uk

freepress@cpbf.org.uk

Editor: Granville Williams. Journal of the Campaign for Press and Broadcasting Freedom with analysis of monopoly media ownership and control and other issues. Published by CPBF.

Freelance Market News

7 Dale Street

Manchester

M1 1JB

Tel: 0161 228 2362

Fax: 0161 228 3533

www.writersbureau.com

fmn@writersbureau.com

Editor: Angela Cox. Newsletter with details of markets for the work of freelance writers.

Index on Censorship

33 Islington High Street

London

N1 9LH

Tel: 020 7278 2313

Fax: 020 7278 1878

www.indexoncensorship.org

contact@indexoncensorship.org

Editor: Judith Vidal-Hall. International magazine for free speech, with interviews, reportage and debates on the important issues of the day.

Informa Publishing Group

69–77 Paul Street

London

EC2A 4LQ

Tel: 020 7553 1000

Fax: 020 7553 1100

www.informa.com

Acquired the media-related newsletters, magazines, reports and directories previously produced by Financial Times Business.

Journalism Studies

PO Box 25

Abingdon

Oxfordshire

OX14 3UE

Tel: 01235 401000

Fax: 01235 401550

www.tandf.co.uk/journals

enquiries@tandf.co.uk

Quarterly, academic journal published in cooperation with the European Journalism Training Association. Published by Routledge.

The Journalist

Headland House

308–311 Gray's Inn Road

London

WC1X 8DP

Tel: 020 7278 7916

Fax: 020 7837 8143

www.nuj.org.uk

acorn.house@nuj.org.uk

Editor: Tim Gopsill. Published by the National Union of Journalists.

Journalist's Handbook

1/4 Galt House

31 Bank Street

Irvine

KA12 0LL

Tel: 01294 311322

Fax: 01294 311322

jh@carrickmedia.demon.co.uk

Quarterly journal with articles and a contacts list. Published by Carrick Media.

Media Lawyer

3 Broom Close

Broughton in Furness

Cumbria

LA20 6JG

Tel: 01229 716622

Fax: 01229 716621

medialawyer@compuserve.com

A newsletter for editors, reporters, media lawyers, trainers and all concerned with media law.

Press Gazette

19 Scarbrook Road

Croydon

Surrey

CR9 1LX

Tel: 020 8565 4200
Fax: 020 8565 4395
www.pressgazette.co.uk
pged@qpp.co.uk
A weekly paper for all journalists with
a concentration on newspapers and
magazines, plus coverage of television
and radio. Published by Quantum
Business Media.

Books

Benn's Media
Riverbank House
Angel Lane
Tonbridge
Kent
TN9 1SE
Tel: 01732 377591
Fax: 01732 367301
www.ubminfro.co.uk
bennsmedia@bminternational.com
Published by United Media Information
Services. Benn's has comprehensive
listings of the general media directories.
It comes in three volumes, covering
the UK, Europe and the rest of the
world.

Encyclopaedia of the World Press
310 Regent Street
London
W1B 3AX

Tel: 020 7636 6627
Fax: 020 7636 6982
www.fitzroydearborn.com/
pressenc.htm
press@fitzroydearborn.demon.co.uk
An illustrated history of the press in 180
countries, its sponsors include the
Newspaper Society, the NPA, the World
Association of Newspapers and the
Freedom Forum. Published by Fitzroy
Dearborn.

Freelance Directory
Headline House
308 Gray's Inn Road
London
WC1X 8DP
Tel: 020 7278 7916
Fax: 020 7837 8243
acornhouse@nuj.org.uk
Biennial directory of freelance reporters,
photographers, broadcasters, editors,
subs, cartoonists and illustrators.
Published by the National Union of
Journalists.

IPO Directory
PO Box 30
Weatherby
West Yorkshire
LS23 7YA
Tel: 01937 541010
Fax: 01937 541083
nds@coi.gov.uk

The official directory of the information and press officers in government departments and public corporations. Bi-annual directory published by COI Communications.

The Media Guide

Media Relations
Communications Group
Open University
Walton Hall
Milton Keynes
MK7 6AA
Tel: 01908 653343
Tel: 01908 653256
Fax: 01908 652247
www.open.ac.uk
press-office@open.ac.uk

A guide for the media from Open University academics.

Media Pocket Book

Farm Road
Henley on Thames
Oxon
RG9 1EJ
Tel: 01491 411000
Fax: 01491 418600
www.warc.com
info@ntc.co.uk

World advertising trends and statistics. Published by NTC Publications.

Pims Media Directories

Pims House
Mildmay Avenue
London
N1 4RS
Tel: 020 7354 7000
Fax: 020 7354 7053
directories@pims.co.uk

Directories cover UK and regional media, European media and the financial sector. Published by Pims UK.

PR Newswire Europe Directories

Communications House
210 Old Street
London
EC1V 9UN
Tel: 020 7490 8111
Fax: 020 7454 5162
directories@prnewswire.eu.com

Produces a range of media contacts directories, each title includes full contact information. Published by PR Newswire.

Ulrich's Periodicals Directory

Third Floor
Farringdon House
Wood Street
East Grinstead
West Sussex
RH19 1UZ
Tel: 01342 326972
Fax: 01342 310463

www.bowker.co.uk
customer.services@bowker.co.uk
A five-volume American guide to the world's periodicals.

Willings Press Guide
34 Germain Street
Chesham
Buckinghamshire
HP5 1ZT
Tel: 01494 797300
Fax: 01494 797224
willings@mediainfo.co.uk
Over 50,000 entries on newspapers and periodicals worldwide. Published by Hoolis Directories.

Online News Sources

Agence France Press
www.afp.com

Al Daily
www.aldaily.com

Alertnet
www.alertnet.org

Annanova
www.annanova.com

Associated Press
www.wire.ap.org

BBC News Online
news.bbc.co.uk

Bloomberg
www.bloomberg.com

Britain in the USA
www.britain-info.org

CNN
www.cnn.com

The Economist
www.economist.co.uk

Financial Times Online
www.ft.com

The Guardian
www.guardian.co.uk

The Independent
www.theindependent.co.uk

International Herald Tribune
www.iht.com/frontpage

ITN ON-line
www.itn.co.uk

London Evening Standard
www.thisislondon.co.uk

Lycos Ticker Tape
www.lycos.com/webguides/business

Media Channel
www.mediachannel.org

News Index
www.newsindex.com

Newsnow
www.newsnow.co.uk

News Trawler
www.newstrawler.com

News Wales
www.newswales.com

Newswatch
www.newswatch-uk.co.uk

The New York Times
www.thenewyorktimes.com

ThePaperBoy.com
www.thepaperboy.com

PR Newswire
www.prnewswire.co.uk

Reuters
www.reuters.com/news

The Scotsman
www.thescotsman.co.uk

Showbizwire
www.showbizwire.com

Sky News
www.sky.co.uk/news

Sourcewire UK
www.sourcewire.com

The Telegraph
www.news.telegraph.co.uk

Teletext
www.teletext.co.uk

This is Britain
www.thisisbritain.co.uk

The Times
www.timesonline.co.uk

United Press International
www.upi.com

Voice on Line
www.voice-online.co.uk

7AM.com
www.7am.com/worldwires

11 journalism awards

Amnesty International UK Media Awards

Tel: 020 7814 6278

www.amnesty.org

annabel.harris@amnesty.org.uk

Contact: Annabel Harris. For journalists who have contributed to the public's understanding and awareness of human rights issues.

Asian Women of Achievement

www.awaawards.com

Anne Bolt Memorial Awards

Tel: 020 7278 7916

www.nuj.org.uk

NUJ. Photo-journalists under twenty-five years old.

BAFTA

www.bafta.org

Contact: Donna Bell. The main news and television awards including categories for journalists in news, current affairs and documentaries. Organized by the British Academy of Film and Television and Arts. News and current affairs journalism; twenty-four-hour coverage; factual series or strand.

Bar Council Legal Journalists of the Year

Tel: 020 7222 2525

epritchard@derbytelegraph.co.uk

Contact: Ben Abbot. Recognizes print and broadcast journalists whose work contributes to a greater understanding of legal issues.

BANFF TV Festival

www.btvf.com

Awards for radio and television news, documentary, individuals, institutions and organizations.

Bayeux Calvados Awards

www.prixbayeux.org

Categories include those for war reporting or consequences for civilians.

Bell's Scottish Photographer of the Year

Tel: 0131 557 6767

Contact: Cameron/Debbie. Ten categories open to press and student photographers based in Scotland.

BEMAS Awards

www.wwwf.org.uk/bemas

Environmental news award.

BNFL North West Press Awards

Tel: 01925 834036

www.bnfl.com

Seven categories open to journalists in the North West.

Bradford and Bingley Personal Finance Media Awards

Tel: 01274 554712

Contact: Maria Sutcliffe. Open to personal finance journalists in national and regional newspapers, magazines, broadcast and new media.

British Guild of Travel Writers Awards

Tel: 020 7720 9009

www.bgtw.metronet.co.uk

Contact: Ann Garland. Various categories recognising excellence in travel journalism. Open to Guild members only.

British Press Awards

Tel: 020 8565 4463

www.britishpressawards.com

Contact: Nicky Lusignani. The Oscars of British journalism for national newspaper journalists in twenty-three categories.

British Sports Journalist and Sports Photographer of the Year

Tel: 020 7273 1589

www.sportengland.org

Contact: Sandra Phillips. Seven journalism and six photography awards (according to yearly sporting events).

Broadcast Awards

www.broadcastnow.co.uk

Business Journalist of the Year Awards

Tel: 0207 464 8486

Fax: 0207 464 8656

www.bjoya.org

enquiries@bjoya.org

Categories include television and radio, in particular investigative journalism.

BT Media Awards

Tel: 0845 726 2624

Tel: 028 9021 4237

www.btplc.com/Mediacentre/
BTMediaAwards/
BTmediaawards.htm

Seven regional awards in fourteen categories, including news, features, websites; open to journalists in the regional press, including freelances. National awards also.

Catherine Pakenham Award

www.telegraph.co.uk/arts

Annual award for young women journalists aged between 18 and 25.

Commission for Racial Equality, Race in the Media Awards

Tel: 01494 671332

www.cre.gov.uk/media/rima

Contact: Amanda Rayner. Recognizes informed coverage of race relations in the UK media.

Du Pont Awards

www.jrn.columbia.edu/events/dupont

News programmes broadcast in the US.

Ethnic Multicultural Media [EMMA] Awards

www.emma.uk.com

mail@emma.uk.com

Wide range of awards. 'Open to any person who has a distinctive ethnic background regardless of race, creed or colour who represents their professionally rich and diverse ethnic and multicultural ability in their accomplishments.'

Felix Dearden Memorial Prize

Tel: 020 7278 7916

www.nuj.co.uk

NUJ. Ethnic minority students taking industry-recognized training courses.

Foreign Press Association Media Awards

Tel: 020 7930 0445

www.foreign-press.org.uk

Categories include journalist of the year; television story of the year; foreign story of the year; environmental story of the year; young journalist of the year.

Freedom of Information Awards

Tel: 020 7831 7477

www.cfoi.org.uk

For journalists, newspapers, magazines or broadcast programmes that have mounted campaigns to expose unjustified official secrecy.

George Polk Awards

Long Island Awards
The Brooklyn Campus
1 University Plaza
Brooklyn
NY 11201–5372
Tel: 001 718 488 1115
www.liu.edu/cwis/bklyn/polk/apply.html

International investigative journalism awards.

Glenfiddich Food and Drink Awards
Tel: 020 7255 1100

To recognize excellence in writing, publishing and broadcasting on the subject of food and drink.

Grierson Awards
Tel: 01733 245841
Fax: 01733 240020
www.editor.net/griersontrust/contacts.htm
awards@multimediaaventures.com

For documentaries but also reporters.

Guardian Student Media Awards
Tel: 020 7239 9936
www.media.guardian.co.uk/studentmediaawards

For journalists on student publications. Ten categories; for editors, reporters and designers on newspapers, magazines and websites.

Halifax Laing Homes Press Awards
Tel: 01908 209090

Contact: Gail Corbett. For residential, property and financial journalism.

Harold Wincott Awards
Tel: 01277 221246

Five awards for journalists reporting on business and finance including Business Programme/Series of the Year (TV), Business Programme/Series of the Year (Radio) and Business Broadcaster of the Year (TV and Radio).

Index on Censorship Annual Awards
Tel: 020 7278 2313
www.indexonline.org/news

Contact: Aron Rollin. Honouring journalists worldwide who fight for freedom of expression, often at great personal risk.

The Indies: Independent Broadcast Production Awards
Tel: 020 8948 5542

Various categories for companies, programmes and individuals.

Industrial Society Work World Award
Tel: 020 7262 2401
www.indsoc.co.uk

The Work Foundation. Celebrating journalism about the world of work in ten categories.

International Building Press Journalism Awards
Tel: 020 7357 6081

Contact: Gerald Bowey. Ten categories for journalists reporting on the building industry.

International Consortium of Investigative Journalists
www.icij.org/about/criteria

A journalist or team involved in investigative work. Reports must cover two countries.

International Emmys

www.iemmys.tv

Categories include news coverage: fifteen minutes unedited; continuing coverage: five segments up to forty minutes.

IWMF Courage in Journalism

www.iwmf.org

Women journalists in war or political oppression.

James Cameron Memorial Awards

Tel: 020 7477 8783

Award bestowed on journalists whose work has been in the tradition of James Cameron.

KPMG Commercial Radio Awards

Tel: 020 7306 2603

Twelve categories, including news and presenters.

Laurence Stern Fellowship

Tel: 020 7477 8000

Contact: Bob Jones (City University, London). For young journalists with experience of working on important national stories for newspapers or television.

London Press Club Awards

Tel: 020 7402 2566

www.newspapersoc.org.uk

Contact: Dennis Griffiths. Scoop of the Year, Edgar Wallace award for outstanding writing and the Freedom Award.

Lorenzo Natali Prize

www.ifj.org/hrights/lorenzo/inpr.html

Contact: Bettina Peters, IFJ. Annual award for outstanding reporting on human rights, democracy and development. Awarded in each of Europe, Africa, the Arab World, Iran and Israel, Asia and the Pacific, Latin America and the Caribbean.

Martin Wills Trust Racing Writing Awards

Tel: 020 7220 7477

www.racenews.co.uk

Contact: Charles Ponsonby. For young horse racing journalists.

Mind Journalist of the Year

Tel: 020 8522 1743

www.mind.org

Contact: Sue Baker. Recognizing enlightening reporting of mental health issues.

Monte Carlo Television Festival

www.tvfestival.com

Awards for short news programmes; twenty-four-hour news programmes and current affairs programmes.

NTL Commercial Radio Awards

Tel: 020 7306 2603

www.crca.co.uk

info@crca.co.uk

Contact: Alison Winter or Sandip Sarai. Twelve categories including news and presenters.

Netmedia European Online Journalism Awards

Tel: 020 7307 8118

www.net-media.co.uk

Contact: Milverton Wallace. An initiative to accelerate development and promotion of good practice in online journalism.

Neutrogena Beauty Journalism Awards

Tel: 020 7465 7700

For print and broadcast journalists.

Nikon Press Photographer of the Year

Tel: 020 8541 4440

Contact: Elaine Swift. Awards in nine categories, including sport, features, fashion, news, arts and entertainment and royals.

North East Press Awards

Tel: 01429 274441

Contact: Bernice Salter. Awards for journalists working in the north east.

Northern Business Journalist

Tel: 0113 247 2510

Yorkshire Bank. Three categories: newspapers, magazines and broadcast.

One World International Media Awards

Tel: 020 7383 4248

Fax: 020 7874 7609

www.owbt.org

Organized by the One World Broadcasting Trust for journalists and organizations that have furthered the cause of international affairs.

Online Journalism Awards

Tel: 020 7344 1236

www.net-media.co.uk

Organized by Net Media to recognize achievements in web-based journalism.

Peabody Awards

www.peabody.uga.edu

Prestigious US-based international awards in TV, radio and online journalism.

Plain English Media Awards

Tel: 01663 744409

Contact: John Lister. Regional and national categories for newspapers, radio and TV.

Prix Europa

www.prix-europa.de

TV and radio awards for programmes bringing European nations closer together.

Regional Press Awards

Tel: 020 8565 4463

www.pressgazette.co.uk

The premier regional newspaper awards, for editors and journalists on daily and weekly titles. Organized by the *Press Gazette* for editors and journalists working for regional newspapers.

Rory Peck Trust Awards

Tel: 020 7262 5272

www.rorypecktrust.org

Honours the initiative, courage and skill of freelance camera operators in TV news and documentaries. The award is named after Rory Peck, a freelance cameraman killed while filming the Moscow revolt in 1993.

Royal Television Society Journalism Awards

Tel: 020 7691 2473

www.rts.org.uk

Contact: Jo Proud. Categories include Current Affairs: Home and International; News: Home and International; Journalist of the Year; Young Journalist of the Year; News Event; Technician of the Year; Specialist Journalism; Interviewer of the Year; Production Award.

Scottish Press Awards

Tel: 0141 333 1551

Contact: Tony Mehan. For journalists writing about Scottish issues and those working on national and regional publications in Scotland.

Sony Radio Awards

Tel: 020 7723 0106

www.radioawards.org

Includes categories for journalists in radio news and talk programmes covering stations, programmes and individuals.

Student Broadcast Journalist of the Year

Tel: 020 7727 9522

www.bjtc.org.uk/award.html

Travelex Travel Writers Awards

Tel: 020 7400 4000

Contact: Anthony Wagerman. For travel journalists in eight categories including newspapers, magazines, radio and television.

Voice of the Listener and Viewer Awards

Tel: 01474 352835

www.vlv.org.uk

Various categories covered in radio and television.

What the Papers Say Awards

Tel: 0161 832 7211

www.psa.ac.uk

Contact: Christine Ruth. Organized by London Weekend Television with seven categories for the best national newspaper journalists.

12 broadcasting festivals and conferences

The BANFF Television Festival

www.banff2003.com

Held in Canada. The Banff Rockie Awards categories include prizes for television programmes, animation, sports, history and social and political programming.

FIPA – Festival International de Programmes Audiovisuels

www.perso.wanadoo.com

Held in Biarritz, France; categories include current affairs and reportage, series and serials, creative documentaries, short programmes.

Guardian Edinburgh International Television Festival

www.geitf.co.uk

Annual festival with industry leaders in debate and discussion.

The Golden Prague International Television Festival

www.czech-tv.com

Prague, Czech Republic. International Television Festival.

The International Documentary Film Festival

www.documentary.org

Los Angeles, California. The IDA awards for documentary film.

International Media Events: 'Television World'

www.tvworld.bg

Albena, Bulgaria.

Le Nombre d'Or Festival

www.ibc.org

Held in Amsterdam, the Netherlands, by the International Broadcasting Convention.

Monte Carlo Film Festival

www.tvfestival.com

Awards include Golden Nymph awards for best television film; best script; best direction.

News World

www.newsworld.co.uk

Annual Newsworld conference with seminars and workshops looking at current issues. Website has industry news.

NewsXchange

www.newsxchange.org

Annual NewsXchange conference with seminars and workshops looking at current issues.

Prix Danube
International Television Festival of
Programmes for Children and Youth

www.stv.sk/prixdanube

Festival of programmes for children and youth television programmes in Bratislava, Slovak Republic.

Prix Italia: RAI

www.prixitalia.rai.it

Held in Palermo, Italy.

Rose d'Or de Montreux

www.rosedor/ch

Held in Montreux, Switzerland. A festival for entertainment television programming.

Shanghai Television Festival

www.stvf.com

Held in Shanghai, China.

Vienna TV Awards – IMZ

www.imz.at

Held in Vienna, Austria.

13 professional bodies and unions

Association for International Broadcasting
www.aib.org.uk
Professional trade association for radio and television. Publishes regular newsletters which are available online. Online listings of organizations and companies connected with international broadcasting.

Association of Professional Recording Services (APRS)
PO Box 22
Totnes
Devon
TQ9 7YZ
Tel: 01803 868600
Fax: 01803 868444
www.aprs.co.uk
info@aprs.co.uk
Manager: Francesca Smith.

Audio Visual Association
Herkomer House
156 High Street

Bushey
Watford
Hertfordshire
WD3 3HF
Tel: 020 8950 5959
Fax: 020 8950 7560
click@tvadesign.co.uk
Chairman: Mike Simpson.

BAFTA – London
195 Piccadilly
London
W1V 0LN
Tel: 020 7734 0022
Fax: 020 7734 1792
www.bafta.org
Chairman: Simon Relph.

BAFTA – Scotland
249 West George Street
Glasgow
G2 4QE
Tel: 0141 302 1770
Fax: 0141 302 1771

www.baftascotland.co.uk
info@baftascotland.co.uk
Director: Alison Forsyth.

BAFTA – Wales

Chapter Arts Centre
Market Road
Canton
Cardiff
CF5 1QE
Tel: 029 2022 3898
Fax: 029 2066 4189
www.bafta-cymru.org.uk
post@bafta-cymru.org.uk

BECTU: Broadcasting Entertainment Cinematograph and Theatre Union

111 Wardour Street
London
W1V 4AY
Tel: 020 7437 8506
Fax: 020 7437 8258
Tel: 0121 632 5372 (Midlands office)
Tel: 0845 601 5045 (North West office)
Tel: 0141 248 9558 (Scottish office)
Tel: 029 2066 6557 (Wales office)
www.bectu.org.uk
bectu@geo2.poptel.org.uk
BECTU is the trade union for workers across the entertainment and media industry.

British Council

Films and Television Department
11 Portland Place
London
W1B 1EJ
Tel: 020 7389 3065
Fax: 020 7389 3041
www.britfilms.com
julian.pye@britishcouncil.org
Contact: Julian Pye.

British Institute of Professional Photography (BIPP)

Fox Talbot House
2 Amwell End
Ware
Hertfordshire
SG12 9HN
Tel: 01920 464011
Fax: 01920 487056
www.bipp.com
bipp@compuserve.com
Executive Secretary: Alex Mair.

British Interactive Media Association

Briarlea House
Southend Road
Billericay
Essex
CM11 2PR
Tel: 01932 706810

www.bima.co.uk
info@bima.co.uk
Office Administrator: Janice Cable.

British Video Association
167 Great Portland Street
London
W1W 5PE
Tel: 020 7436 0041
Fax: 020 7436 0043
www.bva.org.uk
general@bva.org.uk

Broadcasting Standards Commission
7 The Sanctuary
London
SW1P 3JS
Tel: 020 7808 1000
Fax: 020 7233 0397
www.bsc.org.uk
bsc@bsc.org.uk

The Chartered Institute of Journalists
2 Dock Offices
Surrey Quays Road
London
SE16 2XU
Tel: 020 7252 1187
Fax: 020 7232 2302
www.ioj.co.uk
memberservices@ioj.co.uk

Cinema and Television Benevolent Fund (CTBF)
22 Golden Square
London
W1F 9AD
Tel: 020 7437 6567
Fax: 020 7437 7186
www.ctbf.co.uk
charity@ctbf.co.uk
Head of Events and Marketing: Sandra Bradley; *Head of Welfare:* Mark Roberts.

Commercial Radio Companies Association
77 Shaftesbury Avenue
London
W1D 5DU
Tel: 020 7306 2603
Fax: 020 7470 0062
www.crca.co.uk
info@crca.co.uk

Committee to Protect Journalists
www.cpj.org
To defend the rights of journalists around the world. News for and about journalists working in dangerous places around the world.

Community Media Association (CMA)
15 Paternoster Row
Sheffield
S1 2BX

Tel: 0114 279 5219
Fax: 0114 279 8976
www.commedia.org.uk
cma@commedia.org.uk
Administrator: Keeley Scott.

The Directors Guild of Great Britain

Acorn House
314–320 Gray's Inn Road
London
WC1X 8DP
Tel: 020 7278 4343
Fax: 020 7278 4742
www.dggb.co.uk
guild@dggb.co.uk
Chief Executive: Malcolm Moore. The
union for directors in all media including
film, television and theatre.

Directors and Producers Rights Society

Victoria Chambers
16–18 Strutton Ground
London
SW1P 2HP
Tel: 020 7227 4757
Fax: 020 7227 4755
info@dprs.org
Chief Executive: Suzan Dormer.

Equity

Guild House
Upper St Martin's Lane
London
WC2H 9EG
Tel: 020 7379 6000
Fax: 020 7379 7001
www.equity.org.uk
info@equity.org.uk

European Union of Science Journalists' Associations

www.esf.c-strasbourg.fr/eusja
Includes the Association of British
Science Writers.

Federation of Entertainment Unions

1 Highfield
Twyford
Winchester
Hampshire
SO21 1QR
Tel: 01962 713134
Fax: 01962 713288
harris@interalpha.co.uk
Secretary: Steve Harris.

Gaelic Broadcasting Committee (CCG)

4 Harbour View
Cromwell Street Quay
Stornoway
Isle of Lewis
Western Isles
HS1 2DF
Tel: 01851 705550

Fax: 01851 706432
www.ccg.org.uk
admin@ccg.org.uk

Guild of British Camera Technicians

c/o Panvision UK
Bristol Road
Metropolitan Centre
Greenford
Middlesex
UB6 8GD
Tel: 020 8813 1999
Fax: 020 8813 2111
www.gbct.org
admin@gbct.org

Guild of British Film Editors

Travair
Spurlands End Road
Great Kingshill
High Wycombe
Buckinghamshire
HP15 6HY
Tel: 01494 712313
Fax: 01494 712313
cox.gbfe@btinternet.com
Honorary Secretary: Alfred Cox.

Guild of Television Cameramen

April Cottage
The Chalks
Chew Magna
Bristol

BS40 8SN
Tel: 01822 614405
www.gtc.org.uk
membership@gtc.org.uk

Guild of Vision Mixers

147 Ship Lane
Farnborough
Hampshire
GU14 8BJ
Tel: 01252 514953
Fax: 01252 656756
www.guildofvisionmixers.org.uk
guild.vm@ntlworld.com
Chairman: Peter Turl.

International Artist Managers' Association

4 Addison Bridge Place
London
W14 8XP
Tel: 020 7610 4884
Fax: 020 7610 4994
www.iamaworld.com
info@iamaworld.com
Executive Director: Atholl Swainston-Harrison.

International Federation of Journalists

www.ifj.org
ifj@ifj.org

World's largest organization of journalists. Promotes international action to defend press freedom and social justice, through strong, free and independent trade unions of journalists. Links to other IFJ websites which include the European Federation of Journalists; Authors Rights for All; International Freelance.

International Visual Communication Association (IVCA)
19 Pepper Street
Glengall Bridge
Docklands
London
E14 9RP
Tel: 020 7512 0571
Fax: 020 7512 0591
www.ivca.org
info@ivca.org

Journalism Organization
www.journalism.org
Committee of concerned journalists dedicated to clarifying the principles of the profession. Includes projects for excellence in journalism.

National Association of Broadcasters
www.nab.org
Website of the national association of broadcasters, a trade association representing the interests of free radio

and television broadcasters. Extensive technical directories and details of NAB conventions.

National Union of Journalists (NUJ)
308–312 Gray's Inn Road
London
WC1X 8DP
Tel: 020 7278 7916
Fax: 020 7837 8143
www.nuj.org.uk
acorn.house@nuj.org.uk

New Producers Alliance
9 Bourlet Close
London
W1W 7BP
Tel: 020 7580 2480
Fax: 020 7580 2484
www.newproducer.co.uk
queries@npa.org.uk

PACT (Producers Alliance for Cinema and Television)
45 Mortimer Street
London
W1W 8HJ
Tel: 020 7331 6000
Fax: 020 7331 6700
www.pact.co.uk
davidalan@pact.co.uk
Information Manager: David Alan Mills.

PACT in Scotland
249 West George Street
Glasgow
G2 4QE
Tel: 0141 302 1720
Fax: 0141 302 1721
www.pactscot.co.uk

Performing Right Society (PRS)
29–33 Berners Street
London
W1T 3AB
Tel: 020 7306 4230
Fax: 020 7631 8957
www.mcps-prs-alliance.co.uk
press@mcps-prs-alliance.co.uk

Production Guild of Great Britain
Pinewood Studios
Pinewood Road
Iver Heath
Buckinghamshire
SLO ONH
Tel: 01753 651767
Fax: 01753 652803
www.productionguild.com
admin@productionguild.com
Administrator: Lynne Hames
(lynne@productionguild.com). *Chief
Executive Officer:* David Martin
(david@productionguild.com).

Production Managers Association
Ealing Studios
Ealing Green
London
W5 5EP
Tel: 020 8758 8699
Fax: 020 8758 8647
www.pma.org.uk
pma@pma.org.uk
Administrator: Caroline Flemming.

Radio Academy
5 Market Place
London
W1W 8AE
Tel: 020 7255 2010
Fax: 020 7255 2029
www.radioacademy.org
info@radioacademy.org
Director: John Bradford.

The Radio Authority
Holbrook House
14 Great Queen Street
Holborn
London
WC2B 5DG
Tel: 020 7430 2724
Fax: 020 7405 7062
www.radioauthority.org.uk
info@radioauthority.org.uk

Radio Communications Agency

Wyndham House
189 Marsh Wall
London
E14 9SX
Tel: 020 7211 0211
www.radio.gov.uk

Radio Television News Directors Association

www.rtnda.org

US radio and TV news association and foundation. Website of the world's largest and only professional organization exclusively serving the electronic news profession. News, comment, advice and workshops.

Royal Television Society

Holborn Hall
100 Gray's Inn Road
WC1X 8AL
Tel: 020 7430 1000
Fax: 020 7430 0924
www.rts.org.uk
info@rts.org.uk

Voice of the Listener and Viewer (VLV)

101 King's Drive
Gravesend

Kent
DA12 5BQ
Tel: 01474 352835
Fax: 01474 351112
www.vlv.org.uk
vlv:@btinternet.com
Chairman: Jocelyn Hay.

Women in Film and Television

6 Langley Street
London
WC2H 9JA
Tel: 020 7240 4875
Fax: 020 7379 1625
www.wftv.org.uk
info@wftv.org.uk
Executive Director: Jane Cussons.

Writers Guild of Great Britain

430 Edgware Road
London
W2 1EH
Tel: 020 7723 8074
Fax: 020 7706 2413
www.writersguild.org.uk
admin@writersguild.org.uk

19 journalists' safety

Safety Training

AKE
Mortimer House
Hereford
HR4 9TA
Tel: 01432 267111
Fax: 01432 350227
www.ake.co.uk
services@ake.co.uk

Hostile environments and first aid training courses designed specifically for journalists working in hostile regions.

Bruhn Newtech
1 Allenby Road
Winterbourne Gunner
Salisbury
Wiltshire
SP4 6HZ
Tel: 01980 611776
Fax: 01980 611330
www.bruhnnewtech.co.uk
info@bruhnnewtech.co.uk

Contact: Dave Butler. Specializes in the development of knowledge and maintenance of life-saving management information systems for operations in hazardous environments. Provides chemical, biological and radiation training.

First Action
1 Fox Crescent
Chelmsford
Essex
CM1 2BN
Tel: 01245 421782
Contact: Lenny May. First aid training, advanced life support, medical cover; supplier of qualified paramedics and first aiders.

Pilgrims
Pilgrims House
PO Box 769
Woking
Surrey
GU21 5EU
Tel: 01932 339180

www.pilgrimsgroup.com

info@pilgrimsgroup.com

Offers operational services and specialist training worldwide; advice and assistance to governments, business organizations and individuals on personal protection, sensitive information and valued assets. Hostile environments and first aid training, public order and all-terrain driving.

Rubicon

70 Upper Richmond Road

London

SW15 2RP

Tel: 0208 8874 0055

Fax: 0208 8874 5522

www.rubicon-international.com

info@rubicon-international.com

Crisis management, kidnap and ransom, detention specialists. Surveillance and counter surveillance.

Safety Equipment

Explosive Device Specialist

Mobile: 07844 313248

Contact: Roger Davies MBE, QGM.

Explosive Grenade Simulation

Tel: 01380 813251

Contact: Dave Leaming/Richard Greene

NP Aerospace

Tel: 02476 702 802

Contact: Tony Jones. Body armour and safety equipment.

Pretorian

Tel: 0208 923 9075

Contact: Martin Beale. Body armour specialists.

SCARFF Fire Safety UK

steve@scarff-fire.co.uk

Any equipment for safety supplies, including body armour, biological chemical radiation suits, cold and hot weather expedition clothing and kit. Radiation monitoring kits – riot packs, hot and cold expedition kits.

Dave Skeet

Tel: 01883 331030

Vehicle: special builds/high speed driving/ high specification modifications.

Medical Health/ Medical Evacuation and Stress Counselling

BA Travel Clinic

www.britishairways.com

health.services@britishairways.com

Offers advice about all travel health needs.

Dart Centre Europe

Tel: 020 8440 5550

Mobile: 07711 888682

www.darteurope.org

info@darteurope.org

Contact: Sue Brayne. Aims to help journalists find the support they need from recommended counsellors and therapists.

PEC – Personal Effectiveness Centre

108 Coombe Lane

London

SW20 0AY

Tel: 020 8879 0135

Fax: 020 8879 4290

www.pecltd.co.uk

pec@pecltd.co.uk

Counselling service includes stress management training, trauma and psychological services.

Gordon Turnbull (Ticehurst Clinic)

Tel: 0580 200391 ext 2216

Counselling and stress management.

Security Advice and Close Protection

Alan Harridine (in association with Ian Watt covert camera builds)

Mobile: 07974 924393

Security advice and training.

Chiron Resources Ltd

Mobile: 07880 602426

Contact: Chris Cobb Smith. Security consultancy and training.

Caroline Neale

Mobile: 07890 920609

Female close protection specialist.

Karen Peak

Mobile: 07810 553755

Female close protection specialist.

Rubicon

70 Upper Richmond Road

London

SW15 2RP

Tel: 0208 8874 0055

www.rubicon-international.com

info@rubiconinternational.com

Contact: John Davidson. Offers project management and logistic coordination. Intelligence and investigation. Security training.

Useful Safety Websites

Foreign Office Website

www.fco.gov.uk

The British government department responsible for overseas relations and foreign affairs, through its headquarters in London and embassies, High Commissions and consulates throughout the world.

Zero Risk International

www.zerorisk-international.com
information@zerorisk-international.com

One-stop shop for all UK and overseas risk analysis, supported by the News Industry Security Group (BBC/CNN/ABC/Reuters/CBS/APTN/SKY/CBS/ITN). Vital safety information when planning a story or assignment includes latest country risk assessments, country profiles, logistical support, latest newswire information, debriefing, health alerts.

15 camera crews

195 Television
Arjang
Main Road
Lacey Green
Princes Risborough
Buckinghamshire
HP27 0QU
Tel: 01844 344178
Fax: 01844 274724
Mobile: 07860 864608
195tv@ukgateway.net
Lighting Cameraman: John Poynter.

A1 Camera Crews (Scotland)
193 Silvertonhill Avenue
Hamilton
South Lanarkshire
ML3 7PG
Tel: 01698 427893
Fax: 01698 427893
ian193@connectfree.co.uk
Managing Director: Ian Boddie.

Acorn Film and Video Ltd
13 Fitzwilliam Street
Belfast

BT9 6AW
Tel: 028 9024 0977
Fax: 028 9022 2309
Manager: Roger Fitzpatrick;
Contact: Sarah Reid.

Actioncam
49 Woodfield Lane
Ashtead
Surrey
KT21 2BT
Tel: 01372 278919
Fax: 01372 279983
www.actioncamtv.com
actioncam@btinternet.com
Director/Lighting Cameraman:
Glenn Wilkinson.

Awfully Nice Video Company Ltd
30 Long Lane
Ickenham
UB10 8TA
Tel: 07000 345678
Fax: 07000 345679
Mobile: 07831 515678

www.awfullynicevideo.co.uk
nicevideo@aol.com
Bookings: Debbie Crook; *Sound Recordist:* Keith Darbyshire; *Lighting Cameraman:* Graham Maunder.

Blue Fin Television Ltd
34 Fitzwilliam Road
London
SW4 0DN
Tel: 020 7622 0870
Fax: 020 7720 7875
Mobile: 07973 502349
www.bluefintv.com
antleake@bluefin-tv.demon.co.uk
Managing Director: Anthony Leake.

Blue Planet Television
Unit 9
Regis Road
London
NW5 3EW
Tel: 020 7267 4537
Fax: 020 7428 0252
www.blueplanet-tv.com
info@blueplanet.tv.com
Facilities Manager: Dominic Kipling.

Broadcast Television Facilities
Acuba House
Lymm Road
Little Bollington
Altrincham

Cheshire
WA14 4SY
Tel: 0161 926 9808
Fax: 0161 929 9000
info@broadcast-tv.co.uk
Director: Robert Foster.

Cine Wessex Ltd
13 Winnall Valley Road
Winchester
Hampshire
SO23 0LD
Tel: 01962 844900
Fax: 01962 840004
www.cinewessex.co.uk
joe@cinewessex.co.uk
Facilities Director: Joe Conlan;
Contact: Kelly Dyer.

The Creation Company Ltd
Unit 1
The Sandycombe Centre
Sandycombe Road
Richmond
Surrey
TW9 2EP
Tel: 020 8332 0888
Fax: 020 8332 1123
www.creationcompany.tv
production@creationcompany.tv
Director: Scott Drummond; *Production Manager:* Louise Glen; *Managing Director:* Steve Montgomery.

Creative Camera Partnership
Slades Farm
Bushcombe Lane
Cleeve Hill
Cheltenham
Gloucestershire
GL52 3PN
Tel: 01242 676003
Fax: 01242 676003
Mobile: 07860 598323
Director of Photography: Rickie Gauld.

Crewed Up Ltd
4th Floor
The Bonded Warehouse
c/o Granada TV
Quay Street
Manchester
M60 9EA
Tel: 0161 827 2971
Fax: 0161 827 2972
Mobile: 07802 283459
www.crewedup.co.uk
crews@crewedup.co.uk
Crew Manager: Jessica Leech;
Director: Mike Turnbull.

The Cruet Company Ltd
11 Ferrier Street
London
SW18 1SN
Tel: 020 8874 2121
Fax: 020 8874 9850

www.cruet.com
hire@cruet.com
Director: Bill Morrey.

Dales Broadcast Ltd
Nettle Hill
Brinklow Road
Coventry
West Midlands
CV7 9JL
Tel: 024 7662 1763
Fax: 024 7660 2732
Mobile: 07803 584925
www.dales-ltd.com
sales@dales-ltd.com
Managing Director: Julian Boden;
Marketing Director: Kate Boden.

David Baillie Camera Crews
Windy Hall
Alston
Cumbria
CA9 3NJ
Tel: 01434 381067
Mobile: 07802 406334
www.wildcats.demon.co.uk
wildcatfilms@btinternet.com
Director/Lighting Cameraman:
David Baillie.

Debrouillard Ltd
74 Ashland Road
Sheffield
S7 1RJ
Tel: 0114 220 0667
Fax: 0114 220 0668
jonathan.y@blueyonder.co.uk
Director: Jonathan Young.

Decent Exposure TV Ltd
The Gardens
Watchet Lane
Little Kingshill
Buckinghamshire
HP16 0DR
Tel: 01494 862667
Fax: 01494 864583
www.decentexposure.tv
office@decentexposure.tv
Company Secretary: Michelle
O'Donoghue; *Production Co-ordinator:*
Carmen Radmore.

The Digital Garage Company Ltd
13 Devonshire Mews
Chiswick
London
W4 2HA
Tel: 07000 785821
Fax: 07000 785822
Mobile: 07788 145577
www.digitalgarage.co.uk
mail@digitalgarage.co.uk

Equipment Manager: Martin Norris;
Crew Manager: Janie Willsmore.

Electra Film and Television
Wharf House
Brentwaters Business Park
The Ham
Brentford
Middlesex
TW8 8HQ
Tel: 020 8232 8899
Fax: 020 8232 8877
www.electra-tv.com
mail@electra-tv.com

The Electronic Camera Company
5 Portland Square
London
E1W 2QR
Tel: 020 7734 5021
Fax: 020 7480 6253
www.electronic-camera.com
johntarby@elecamco.demon.co.uk
Director of Photography: John Tarby.

Equal Time
57 Glasney Place
Penryn
Cornwall
TR10 8LL
Tel: 01326 373611
rm_mimms@compuserve.com
Director: Martin Mimms.

Extreme Facilities
15–17 Este Road
London
SW11 2TL
Tel: 020 7801 9111
Fax: 020 7801 9222
www.extremefacilities.com
Contact: Andrew Schaale.

First Sight Communications Ltd
10 Novello Croft
Old Farm Park
Milton Keynes
MK7 8QT
Tel: 07050 276484
Fax: 07050 133389
crewhire@firstsightcomms.co.uk
Lighting Cameraman: Andy Smith;
Contact: Roy Ford.

GAS (Guild Answering Service)
Panavision
Bristol Road
Metropolitan Centre
Greenford
Middlesex
UB6 8GD
Tel: 020 8813 1999
Fax: 020 8813 2111
www.gbct.org
gas@gbct.org

Garton Film and Video
Tranby Croft
Tranby Lane
Anlaby
Hull
East Riding of Yorkshire
HU10 7EF
Tel: 01482 651317
Fax: 01482 651317
Mobile: 07721 007100
garton@produxion.com
Proprietor/Cameraman:
Howard Garton.

Gloucestershire Film Unit
Bownham View Cottage
138 Thrupp Lane
Stroud
Gloucestershire
GL5 2EQ
Tel: 01453 882593
Fax: 01453 883482
emajdraeb:@hotmail.com
Proprietor: James Beard.

Goldmoor Television Ltd
20 Burners Lane South
Kiln Farm
Milton Keynes
MK11 3HB
Tel: 01908 370516
Fax: 01908 643119

www.goldmoor.co.uk
crewhire@goldmoor.co.uk
Managing Director: Peter Rimmington.

Hammerhead Television Facilities (Edinburgh)
9 Merchiston Mews
Edinburgh
EH10 4PE
Tel: 0131 229 5000
Fax: 0131 429 4211
www.hammerheadtv.com
scotland@hammerhead-tv.co.uk
Production Sound Mixer: Chris Orvis.

Hammerhead Television Facilities (London)
42 Webbs Road
London
SW11 6SF
Tel: 020 7924 3977
Fax: 020 7924 2154
www.hammerheadtv.com
hhlondon@aol.com
Facilities Manager: Will Wilkinson.

Hammerhead Television Facilities (North)
Unit 22
Waters Edge Business Park
Modwen Road
Manchester
M5 3EZ

Tel: 0161 872 6200
Fax: 0161 872 6300
www.hammerheadtv.com
manchester@hammerhead-tv.co.uk
Contact: Matt Turnbull, Gordon Hayman.

Heavy Pencil
41 Shakespeare Road
Hanwell
London
W7 1LT
Tel: 020 8579 3008
Fax: 020 8579 3009
Mobile: 07776 184481
www.heavypencil.net
sb@heavypencil.net
Director: Simon Bishop; *Rentals Manager:* Mike Howell.

Hoi Polloi Film and Video
50–52 Close
Newcastle upon Tyne
NE1 3RF
Tel: 0191 233 0050
Fax: 0191 233 0052
www.filmcrew.co.uk
info@filmcrew.co.uk
Production Co-ordinator: Dawn Briggs.

M and K Jones
15 Star Lane
Lymm
Cheshire

WA13 9LE
Tel: 01925 753893
Fax: 01925 753893
www.fisticufffilms.co.uk
martin@fisticuff.freeserve.co.uk
Sound Recordist: Karen Jones;
Cameraman: Martin Jones.

Guy Littlemore
1 The Old Inn
Kingsweston Road
Bristol
BS11 0UW
Tel: 01179 626811
Fax: 01179 626856
www.camera-crews.co.uk
guy@camera-crews.co.uk

Logan Baird Camera Crews
Crafthole
Torpoint
Plymouth
Devon
PL11 3DD
Tel: 01503 230739
Fax: 01503 230739
logan.baird@virgin.net
Cameraman: Logan Baird.

John Lubran
19 Mill View Close
Howey
Llandrindod Wells

Powys
LD1 5RA
Tel: 01597 860575
Fax: 01597 860655
Mobile: 07721 429181
www.movingvision.co.uk
john@lubran.demon.co.uk

Luk Luk Productions
67 Stone Close
Seahouses
Northumberland
NE68 7YW
Tel: 01665 721195
Fax: 01665 721195
Mobile: 07980 164047
lukluk@talk21.com
Producer/Cameraman: Jimmy France.

Mac Film and Video Services
37 The Chase
Penns Park
Sutton Coldfield
West Midlands
B76 1JS
Tel: 0121 384 2093
Fax: 0121 350 7500
mfv@globalnet.co.uk
DOP/Lighting Cameraman: Robin
MacDonald.

MBP
Saucelands Barn
Coolham
Horsham
West Sussex
RH13 8QG
Tel: 01403 741620
Fax: 01403 741647
info@mbptv.com
Director of Productions: Phillip Jennings.

MD Camera Services
21 Claygate Road
London
W13 9XG
Tel: 020 8567 4482
Fax: 020 8840 2138
Mobile: 07831 101 654
martindoyle@virgin.net
Contact: Martin Doyle.

Mighty Fine Production Facilities
28 Willows Avenue
Morden
Surrey
SM4 5SG
Tel: 020 8286 2867
Fax: 020 8286 2826
Mobile: 07050 054482
mightyfine@blueyonder.co.uk
Contact: Mark Jackson.

Millbank Studios
4 Millbank
Westminster
London
SW1P 3JA
Tel: 020 7233 2020
Fax: 020 7233 3158
www.millbank-studios.co.uk
facilities@millbankstudios.co.uk
Production Manager: Nicola Goulding;
Managing Director: Richard Rose; *Head
of Operations:* Pippa Walker.

News Crews
The Gables
The Green
Pulham Market
Norfolk
IP21 4SY
Tel: 01379 608071
Fax: 01379 608071
Mobile: 0860 223943
www.newscrews.co.uk
news@newscrews.co.uk
Contact: Lesley Venables.

Orchid Video Crewing
11 Sommerville Road
St Andrews
Bristol
BS7 9AD
Tel: 0117 924 5687
Fax: 0117 924 7323

Mobile: 07831 301295
naomi@orchid-ltd.demon.co.uk
Contact: Naomi Knott.

The Plant Room
25 Butterfield
Woodburn Green
High Wycombe
Buckinghamshire
HP10 0PX
Tel: 01628 810246
Fax: 01628 810246
Mobile: 07973 435763
www.tvplant.com
info@tvplant.com

Pollen Productions
10 Bromley Avenue
Urmston
Manchester
M41 6HZ
Tel: 0161 613 8031
Fax: 0161 613 8031
Mobile: 07899 915494
www.pollenprod.demon.co.uk
mail@pollenprod.demon.co.uk
Contact: Tom Jeffs.

Positive Film and Television
Positive Film and Video
31 Oval Road
London
NW1 7EA
Tel: 020 7323 6956

Fax: 020 7323 6957
equiptment@positive.co.uk
Camera Facilities: Zelida Gordan;
Post Production: Tim Jones.

Prima Vista
Unit 1a
The Workshops
Askew Crescent
London
W12 9DP
Tel: 020 8743 4663
Fax: 020 8740 5859
ross@primavista.co.uk

Prime Television International
Unit 7
Latimer Road
London
W10 6RQ
Tel: 020 8969 6122
Fax: 020 8969 6144
www.primetv.com
info@primetv.com
Hire Manager: Chris Earls;
Operations Manager: Mark Jackson.

Procam Television Ltd
7 Brooks Court
Cringle Street
London
SW8 5BX
Tel: 020 7622 9888

Fax: 020 7498 1580
www.procamtv.com
info@procamtv.com
Director: Cal Barton; *Operations Manager:* John Brennan.

PTO Location Television Crews
10 Land's Business Park
Tilburstow Hill Road
South Godstone
Surrey
RH9 8LJ
Tel: 01342 893399
Fax: 01342 892925
www.ptocrews.com
info@ptocrews.com
Contact: Carol, Sallie-Ann.

Quadrillion Video Productions
The Old Barn
Kings Lane
Cookham Dean
Maidenhead
Berkshire
SL6 9AY
Tel: 01628 487522
Fax: 01628 487523
www.quadrillion.net
enq@quadrillion.net
Managing Director: Roland Armstrong.

Redapple Television Facilities
214 Epsom Road
Guildford
Surrey
GU1 2RA
Tel: 01483 455044
Fax: 01483 455022
Mobile: 07802 246076
redappletv@msn.com
Contact: Nigel Reynolds.

Redwood Television
The Old Stables
The Street
Walberton
Arundel
West Sussex
BN18 0PQ
Tel: 07831 604338
Fax: 07967 075521
chris@redwoodtv.co.uk
Lighting Cameraman: Chris Evans.

Shooting Partners Ltd
9 Mount Mews
High Street
Hampton
Middlesex
TW12 2SH
Tel: 020 8941 1000
Fax: 020 8941 0077
Mobile: 01459 114572
www.shooting-partners.co.uk

Production Co-ordinator: Jenny Bigrave;
Facilities Manager: Darrin Dart; *Displays and Projection:* Mark Holdway.

Smashing Glass Television
39 Doncrest Road
Donwell Village
Washington
Tyne and Wear
NE37 1ED
Tel: 0191 431 1279
Fax: 0191 431 1279
Mobile: 07802 815555
sglass1003@aol.com
Lighting Cameraman: Simon Glass.

Stryder
Falcon Croft
Water Street
Somerton
Oxfordshire
OX25 6NE
Tel: 01869 345699
Fax: 01869 346699
Mobile: 07831 171556
www.stryder.tv
steve.ryder@stryder.tv
Proprietor: Steve Ryder; *Contact:*
Clare Ryder.

Television News
9 Chesterton Hill
French's Road

Cambridgeshire
CB4 3NP
Tel: 01223 366220
Fax: 01223 361508
dave@masons-news.co.uk
Partner: Melvyn Sibson.

Torque Media
The Old Post Office
Main Street
Rockingham
Leicestershire
LE16 8TG
Tel: 01536 771768
Fax: 01536 772220
www.torquemedia.com
admin@torquemedia.com
Contact: David Harmon.

Track Two Ltd
17 Fallowfield
Ancells Farm
Fleet
Hampshire
GU13 8UU
Tel: 01252 812022
Fax: 01252 810486
www.track2.co.uk
crews@track2.co.uk
Assignments Manager: Caroline Troy.

Tri Cam
9 Woodcroft Avenue
Bridge of Don
Aberdeen
AB22 8WY
Tel: 01224 705250
Fax: 01224 705250
tricam@enterprise.net
Lighting Cameraman: George Leslie.

Vector Broadcast Camera Crews
19 Belchamps Road
Wickford
Essex
SS11 8LH
Tel: 01268 733908
Mobile: 07860 444634
www.vectorbroadcastnews.co.uk
info@vectorbroadcastnews.co.uk
Director: Steve Verdon.

Video Europe
The London Broadcast Centre
11–13 Point Pleasant
London
SW18 1NN
Tel: 020 8433 8000

Fax: 020 8433 8001
www.videoeurope.co.uk
crewing@videoeurope.co.uk

VMI Crews
Unit 1
Granville Industrial Estate
146–148 Granville Road
London
NW2 2LD
Tel: 020 8922 9488
Fax: 020 8922 9489
www.vmi.co.uk
vmi@vmi.co.uk
Crew Co-ordinator: Tony Lewis.

Widescreen
The Garth
Barnet Lane
Elstree
Hertfordshire
WD6 3HJ
Tel: 020 8953 5190
Fax: 020 8236 0553
www.widescreenuk.com
info@widescreen.uk.com
Manager: Shirley Taylor.

16 useful information

International Contacts and Bodies

Association for International Broadcasting

www.aib.org.uk

Professional trade association for radio and television. Publishes regular newsletters which are available online. Online listings of organizations and companies connected with international broadcasting; international broadcasting publications; shows; international radio and television broadcasts.

BESO – British Executive Services Overseas

www.beso.org

BOND – British Overseas NGOs for Development

Tel: 020 7837 8344
www.bond.org.uk

Book Aid International

www.bookaid.org

British Council

Tel: 020 7930 8466
Tel: 020 7389 4268 (press)
www.britcoun.org

Commonwealth Broadcasting Association

Tel: 020 7765 5144
www.oneworld.org/cba

Commonwealth Institute

Tel: 020 7603 4535
www.commonwealth.org.uk

Commonwealth Journalists Association

Tel: 020 7486 3844
www.commonwealthjournalists.org

Commonwealth Press Union

Tel: 020 7583 7733
www.cpu.org.uk

Commonwealth Secretariat

Tel: 020 7839 3411
www.thecommonwealth.org

Crown Agents
Tel: 020 8643 3311
www.crownagents.com

**Department for International
Development**
Tel: 020 7917 7000
Tel: 020 7917 0532 (press/
information)
Tel: 0845 300 4100 (public enquiries)
Tel: 020 7917 0632 (aid policy
department)
www.dfid.gov.uk

Foreign and Commonwealth Office
Tel: 020 7270 1500
Tel: 020 7270 3100 (press)
Tel: 020 7270 6052 (information
department)
www.fco.gov.uk

International Care and Relief
www.icrcharity.com

**IFNP – International Federation of
Newspaper Publishers**
Tel: +33 1 4742 8500 .

**International Committee
of the Red Cross**
Geneva Headquarters
Tel: +41 22 734 6001
www.icrc.org

International Labour Organization
Tel: 020 7233 5925
www.ilo.org

International Maritime Organization
Tel: 020 7735 7611
www.imo.org

International Monetary Fund
www.imf.org

International Whaling Commission
Tel: 01223 233971
www.iwcoffice.org

**IPPF – International Planned
Parenthood Federation**
www.ippf.org

Inter Press Service
www.ips.org

NATO
Tel: +32 2 7074111
www.nato.int

**OECD – Organization for Economic
Co-operation and Development**
Tel: +33 1 4524 8200 (Paris HQ)
www.oecd.org

One World
Tel: 01494 481629
www.oneworld.net

Overseas Development Institute
Tel: 020 7922 0300
www.odi.org.uk

United Nations
Tel: 020 7630 1981 (UK Information
Centre)
Tel: +1 212 963 4475 (Headquarters,
New York)
www.un.org

World Bank
Tel: 020 7930 8511
Tel: +1 202 4771234
www.worldbank.org

World Health Organization
Tel: +41 22 791 2111 (Geneva
Headquarters)
www.who.int

Government Press Offices

Prime Minister's Office
10 Downing Street
London

SW1A 2AA
Tel: 020 7270 3000
Tel: 020 7930 4433 (press office)
www.number-10.gov.uk

Cabinet Office
70 Whitehall
London
SW1A 2AS
Tel: 020 7270 6000 (press)
Tel: 020 7270 1080 (media
monitoring)
www.cabinet-office.gov.uk

Department for Culture, Media and Sport
2-4 Cockspur Street
London
SW1Y 5DH
Tel: 020 7211 6000 (public enquiries)
Tel: 020 7211 6273 (press)
Tel: 020 7211 6263 (media
information)
www.culture.gov.uk

Ministry of Defence
Horseguards Avenue
London
SW1A 2HB
Tel: 020 7218 9000
Tel: 020 7218 6645 (public enquiries)
Tel: 020 7218 2906 (press)

Tel: 020 7218 2206 (D-Notice
Committee)
www.mod.uk
Tel: 020 7218 3256 (Army press)
www.army.mod.uk
Tel: 020 7218 3258
www.royal-navy.mod.uk
Tel: 020 7218 3254
www.raf.mod.uk
Tel: 01722 433208 (C-in-C Land)
Tel: 01932 87650 (C-in-C Fleet)
Tel: 01494 461461 (Headquarters
Strike Command)
Tel: 020 7218 7873 (Chief of General
Staff)

Department for Education and Skills
Sanctuary Buldings
Great Smith Street
London
SW1P 3BT
Tel: 020 7925 6789 (press office)
Tel: 0870 001 2345 (publicity)
www.dfes.gov.uk

**Department of Environment,
Food and Rural Affairs**
17 Smith Square
London
SW1P 3JR
Tel: 020 7270 3000
Tel: 020 7238 5608 (press)
Tel: 0845 933 5577 (helpline)

Tel: 0845 050 4141 (foot-and-mouth
helpline)
www.defra.gov.uk

Foreign and Commonwealth Office
King Charles Street
London
SW1A 2AH
Tel: 020 7270 1500
Tel: 020 7270 3100 (press office)
Tel: 020 7270 6052 (information
department)
www.fco.gov.uk

Department of Health
79 Whitehall
London
SW1A 2NS
Tel: 020 7210 3000
Tel: 020 7210 4850 (public enquiries)
Tel: 020 7210 5221 (press)
www.doh.gov.uk

Home Office
50 Queen Anne's Gate
London
SW1H 9AT
Tel: 020 7273 4000
Tel: 020 7273 4545 (press)
www.homeoffice.gov.uk

Department for International
Development
94 Victoria Street
London
SW1E 5JL
Tel: 020 7917 7000
Tel: 020 7917 0950 (press)
Tel: 0845 300 4100 (public enquiries)
www.dfid.gov.uk

Law Offices Department
9 Buckingham Gate
London
SW1P 6JP
Tel: 020 7271 2440

Lord Chancellor's Department
Selbourne House
54–60 Victoria Street
London
SW1E 6QW
Tel: 020 7210 8500
Tel: 020 7210 8512 (press)
www.lcd.gov.uk

Privy Council
68 Whitehall
London
SW1A 2AT
Tel: 020 7210 1030
Tel: 020 7270 0487 (press)
www.privycouncil.gov.uk

Department of Trade and Industry
1 Victoria Street
London
SW1H 0ET
Tel: 020 7215 5000
Tel: 020 7215 2345 (press)
Tel: 020 7215 5057 (publicity)
www.dti.gov.uk

Department for Transport, Local
Government and the Regions
Eland House
Bressenden Place
London
SW1E 5DU
Tel: 020 7944 3000
Tel: 020 7944 3041 (press)
Tel: 020 7944 3066 (press: transport)
Tel: 020 7944 3044 (press: local
government)
www.dft.gov.uk

HM Treasury
1 Horse Guards Road
London
SW1A 2HQ
Tel: 020 7270 5000
Tel: 020 7270 4558 (public enquiries)
Tel: 020 7270 5238 (press)
www.hm-treasury.gov.uk

Department for Work and Pensions
79 Whitehall
London
SW1A 2NS
Tel: 020 7238 3000
Tel: 020 7712 2171 (enquiries)
Tel: 020 7238 0800 (press)
www.dss.gov.uk

Whitehall Departments and the National Parliaments

Northern Ireland Office
11 Millbank
London
SW1P 4PN
Tel: 020 7210 3000
Tel: 020 7210 6473 (press)
www.nio.gov.uk

Northern Ireland Assembly
Parliament Buildings
Belfast
BT4 3XX
Tel: 028 9052 1333
Tel: 028 9052 1137
www.ni-assembly.gov.uk

Northern Ireland Office
Parliament Buildings
Belfast
BT4 3ST
Tel: 028 9052 0000
Tel: 028 9052 8228
www.nio.gov.uk

Northern Ireland Executive
Castle Building
Belfast
BT4 3SR
Tel: 028 9052 0000
Tel: 028 9052 3355
www.nics.gov.uk

Scotland Office
Dover House
Whitehall
London
SW1A 2AU
Tel: 020 7270 6754
Tel: 020 7270 6828 (press)
www.scottishsecretary.gov.uk

Scottish Parliament
Edinburgh
EH99 1SP
Tel: 0131 348 5000
Tel: 0845 278 1999 (enquiries)
Tel: 0131 348 5605 (press)
www.scottish.parliament.uk

Scottish Executive
St Andrew's House
Regent Road
Edinburgh
EH1 3DG
Tel: 0131 556 8400
Tel: 0131 244 2019 (press)
Tel: 0845 774 1741 (enquiries)
www.scotland.gov.uk

Scottish Executive Communications Unit
St Andrew's House
Edinburgh
EH1 3DG
Tel: 0131 244 2764
Fax: 0131 244 1721
www.scotland.gov.uk
Government information service.

Wales Office
Gwydyr House
Whitehall
London
SW1A 2ER
Tel: 020 7270 3000
Tel: 020 7270 0565
Tel: 020 7270 0583
www.walesoffice.gov.uk

National Assembly for Wales
Cardiff Bay
Cardiff
CF99 1NA
Tel: 029 2082 5111
Tel: 029 2089 8200 (enquiries)
Tel: 029 2089 8124 (press)
www.wales.gov.uk
www.cymru.gov.uk

Index